The Young Couple's Guide to
Growing Rich
TOGETHER

JILL GIANOLA, CFP®

McGraw-Hill

New York Chicago San Francisco Lisbon London Madrid
Mexico City Milan New Delhi San Juan Seoul
Singapore Sydney Toronto

Copyright © 2004 by The McGraw-Hill Companies, Inc. All rights reserved.
Printed in the United States of America. Except as permitted under the United
States Copyright Act of 1976, no part of this publication may be reproduced or
distributed in any form or by any means, or stored in a data base or retrieval
system, without the prior written permission of the publisher.

1 2 3 4 5 6 7 8 9 0   AGM/AGM   9 0 9 8 7 6 5 4

ISBN 0-07-141355-3

This publication is designed to provide accurate and authoritative information in regard to the subject matter covered. It is sold with the understanding that
the publisher is not engaged in rendering legal, accounting, or other professional
service.

*—From a Declaration of Principles jointly adopted by a Committee
of the American Bar Association and a Committee of Publishers.*

McGraw-Hill books are available at special quantity discounts to use as
premiums and sales promotions, or for use in corporate training programs. For
more information, please write to the Director of Special Sales, McGraw-Hill
Professional, Two Penn Plaza, New York, NY 10011-2298. Or contact your
local bookstore.

This book is printed on recycled, acid-free paper containing a
minimum of 50% recycled, de-inked fiber.

Library of Congress Cataloging-in-Publication Data

Gianola, Jill.
   The young couple's guide to growing rich together / by Jill Gianola—1st ed.
      p.   cm.
   ISBN 0-07-141355-3 (pkk.)
   1. Couples—Finance, Personal.   2. Financial security.   I. Title.
HG179G477   2003
332.024'01—dc21   2003013244

To my parents, Ann and Gerald Isaacson. Thank you for your love, your encouragement, and your example.

CONTENTS

ACKNOWLEDGMENTS

M any people helped with this book. My daughter, Magda, and my son, Daniel, read several chapters, and their insights and thoughtful comments made the book much better. Thanks to Annie Meser, whose comments on a draft of the book were right on target.

I am so lucky to work with Stephanie Elmerick and Sarah Garland, the other two members of the Gianola Financial Planning team. They read drafts, served as sounding boards, and kept the office humming. Sarah carved out book time for me and Stephanie did research and fact-checked. My special thanks to you both. Any remaining errors are, of course, my own.

John Ryan, Kathleen Hanley, and Norma Berry generously lent their expertise. Edie Milligan and Angie Hollerich shared their own writing experiences with me.

I have learned so much from Bert Whitehead and my fellow Cambridge Advisors. They are an incredible group of smart, caring people. I am grateful to David Stone and Karin McKerahan, who took time from their own busy practices to review chapters.

Eight years ago, I had the good fortune to meet Jo Anne Paynter, Kathleen Rehl, and Elizabeth Caldwell, as we were all starting our financial planning practices. Many of the ideas we have shared over the years are reflected in this book.

My fellow members of the National Association of Personal Financial Advisors (NAPFA) have generously shared their best ideas. NAPFA members showed me I could set up a financial planning practice to work with middle-income clients.

It was just over a year ago that Kelli Christiansen, my wonderful editor at McGraw-Hill, contacted me about writing a personal finance book for couples. Thank you, Kelli, for your idea, for giving me the opportunity, and for making the process such a pleasure.

Finally, thank you, Dan. You encouraged me with exactly the right words and in exactly the right doses.

INTRODUCTION

One afternoon, almost 25 years ago, I was listening to a financial advisor on the radio explaining the benefits of a relatively new savings plan called an Individual Retirement Account or IRA. I was in my mid-20s, married three years, with a new baby. I remember thinking the advisor was probably aiming her comments at people in their 50s and 60s—wasn't I much too young to think about retirement? I decided to call the radio station and ask the advisor. Her reply surprised me: "You're *not* too young to begin saving for retirement," she said, "and contributing to an IRA is a great way to start. In fact, the younger the better." Of course, she was right.

Young couples today are a lot savvier about money than I was back then. Terms like 401(k), IRA, and diversification that sounded like so much jargon when I was recently married are probably quite familiar to you. You need to be smarter about your money because you have more responsibility for your financial futures than your parents or grandparents did. The Social Security system is shaky, company pensions are rare, and jobs come and go. Your success at reaching your goals and becoming financially independent depends largely on you.

Thankfully, there's more help available to guide you through your financial decisions. In addition to television stations devoted to financial news, there are plenty of good books, magazines, and Web sites. I have listed some of my favorites at the end of each chapter. And you have many more choices—Roth IRAs, 529 plans, and SIMPLE IRAs didn't even exist 20 years ago.

The expansion of the Internet has made it easy to look up the price of a stock or the interest rate on a credit card. The hard part is figuring out how to make smart money decisions and how you and your partner can fit all the pieces of your financial life together. That's what this book is about.

During your life, you'll face lots of choices, and many of them will involve money. Do you pay off your credit cards before contributing to your 401(k) plan? Do you save for college before saving for retirement? Should you go back to school to try to jump-start your career?

In my financial planning practice, I work with young couples who are trying to figure out the answers to questions just like those. In addition to tips and charts and advice on preparing your own financial plan, this book also tells the story of a young couple—Mike and Cathy. They're not a real couple, but the choices they face are real and their concerns might sound very familiar to those you and your partner have.

Twelve chapters in this book include "meetings" with Mike and Cathy. I answer their questions and help them figure out strategies that are right for them, just as I do with my own clients. I have also included chapters on what to do before you get married, special issues for unmarried couples, and how to find and work with a financial planner. The last chapter is a step-by-step guide for staying on track. After all, circumstances change, your goals might shift, and everyone needs a gentle nudge from time to time to get back on course.

I wrote this book as a do-it-yourself guide. Even if you decide to consult a financial planner—as Mike and Cathy did—you and your partner are ultimately in charge of your own money. Don't be afraid to aim high, and don't worry if you make some mistakes along the way—we all do. And don't be swayed by people who tell you personal finance is way too complicated to tackle on your own. As long as you're willing to learn some of the basics, you can get a huge head start. Many couples who are closing in on retirement tell me, wistfully, "We wish we had known then what we know now" and "We wish we had started when we were younger."

So don't obsess about money, but don't neglect it either. By making some smart choices early on, you and your partner can successfully manage your finances together. You've already taken the first steps on that path.

CHAPTER 1

Meet Mike and Cathy

M ike is 29 and works as a programmer at an accounting software firm. He makes $45,000 a year and has good benefits. He's been at the firm for three years and hopes to be promoted to project manager within the next two years.

Cathy is 27 and is halfway through the MBA program at a local university. She plans to complete the degree in another year. She is a self-employed human resources consultant working with small businesses. Cathy is on target to earn $15,000 this year, after expenses, and she works at home.

Mike and Cathy have been married for almost two years and are renting a townhouse. They are a bit overwhelmed with all of the financial decisions facing them in the next several years. Although Cathy learned some basic investment theory in one of her MBA courses and Mike occasionally picks up a personal finance magazine, they don't feel like they have the time or knowledge to put together a financial plan.

Cathy suggested they consider working with a financial planner to help get them on track. They spoke to friends and contacted professional organizations. (For more on finding and working with a financial planner, see Chapter 15.)

Mike and Cathy scheduled a get-acquainted meeting with me late one afternoon. After they arrived and we had introduced ourselves, we all sat down around a table in my office.

"Thank you for contacting me. I am delighted to meet you," I said. "I have reviewed the preliminary questionnaire you filled out. To get started, would you mind telling me why you think you might want to hire a financial planner?"

"Okay if I jump in first?" asked Mike, looking at Cathy. She nodded and Mike continued, "There were several reasons. Cathy and I were talking the other night, and we decided we both have a lot on our plates and we have pretty ambitious goals. We're not dumb, but we don't even know how to get started putting together a plan. I'll give you an example—we hear a lot about how people aren't saving enough for retirement, but how much is enough?"

"We want to get it right from the beginning," added Cathy. "I'm afraid we'll make some decisions now that will make it hard for us to live the life we want later on. Some of our friends have already bought pretty big houses or expensive cars and we're not sure how they manage. Are we doing something wrong? We'd like to buy a house soon, and I want to expand my consulting business when I finish my MBA. Eventually, we'd like to start a family."

"That's right," agreed Mike. "I don't have a good feeling for how all the pieces fit together. For example, do we pay off Cathy's student loans before we buy a house? I have been contributing to my 401(k), but I don't know if that's a good idea when we're so young. Maybe we should hold off for a while and concentrate on buying the house and paying down some debt first."

"Plus, I'm self-employed," said Cathy, "so I don't even have a retirement plan. Taxes are another big issue with us. It would be really nice to save some money there. I would also like to get a better handle on how we spend our money. We earn a decent amount, but at the end of the month there's nothing left over. I think we spend too much."

"Wait a minute," said Mike. "We had fun on our vacation. And who bought all those gifts for her family last year?"

"Okay, okay, truce," said Cathy, "but I would still like to get a professional's opinion on our spending habits."

"There's something else I'd like to talk about," said Mike. "Cathy, remember I told you an insurance agent gave a seminar at work? Well, it turned out he was selling a bunch of insurance policies. I don't know if we need all that stuff."

"You've obviously both given a lot of thought to what works and what doesn't in your financial situation," I said. "That's a giant first step. Those of us who are further along in our lives—okay, older— wish we had paid more attention to our finances when we were your age. I know I made some financial bloopers along the way. Of course, even with the best intentions, you'll make a few mistakes and regret some money decisions. But if we set out some specific guidelines and you learn more about making smart financial choices, you're more likely to reach your goals—and feel more confident along the way."

"That's it," said Mike. "We need a plan."

"I agree," I said, "as long as we're clear on what a financial plan is. Let's face it, a fancy leatherette binder chock full of colorful graphs and pages of text is not going to change your lives. You may look at it a few times, and then it will migrate to a closet or bookshelf. In a few months, the numbers will be outdated and in a year or two your situation will have changed enough that many of the recommendations will be stale.

"Sure, we'll be crunching numbers and looking at spreadsheets, but those are just the visible pieces of the financial planning process. The real value will be in figuring out where you are now and where you want to go, developing specific recommendations for getting on track and acquiring tools and information you can use on your own.

"Advisors are fond of saying financial planning is not a product but a process. Even if I answer all of your questions and you implement all my recommendations, within a few months or a year you'll have new choices and new decisions, and I want you to be confident and smart about how you figure out what's best for you. How does that sound?"

"I think I get it," said Mike. "We're not looking for someone to take over our finances; we need to get on course and get some money knowledge. After that, we might need a nudge from time to time, but basically we'll be able to take it from there."

"So that's why we're here," said Cathy. "We want to fix what's wrong, start doing the things we should be doing, and learn enough to be smart on our own. Are we expecting too much, or too little?"

"Just right," I said. "Frankly, I'm worried when couples expect to dump their finances in my lap. It's your money and your lives, so you two need to be in charge. An advisor can guide and teach you, but whether you are successful or not will depend much more on what you do than what your advisor does."

"I think we can handle that," said Cathy.

CHAPTER 2

Getting Started

I f you've ever planned a trip on the Web, you know the first question you have to answer—What's your starting point? It's the same with financial planning. You need to know where you are now before you can make plans about the future. A good way to determine your starting point is to put together a personal balance sheet or net worth statement. I know that may sound like accounting jargon, but it's not hard to prepare one, and you can learn a lot about your money—and yourselves.

Mike and Cathy are about to take that first step. They have gathered their financial paperwork, and we're just about to sort through it. Please join us.

"Welcome," I said. "I'm happy to see you both. Have a seat and make yourselves comfortable."

"We're glad to be here," said Mike. "We were talking about this meeting on the way over to your office, and we're really looking forward to getting a handle on our finances."

"Great," I said. " Thank you for sending me all the information I requested. You rounded up everything on my list, so you must have a good filing system at home."

Mike and Cathy looked at each other and grinned.

"I wouldn't call it a system," said Cathy. "In fact, it took us a long time to find everything. I had put some stuff in file folders, but most of our papers are in stacks on a table in the spare bedroom. We could use some help getting organized."

"I have just the thing for you two," I said, pulling out a package. "It's called a Homefile® kit, and it's a set of cardboard tabs that can help you sort and file your financial paperwork. At the bottom of each tab are some guidelines for archiving or discarding financial papers."

"What a concept," said Mike, smiling at Cathy. "Do you mean we don't need to keep every investment statement and every credit card bill we ever got?"

"I know, I know," said Cathy. "I'm a packrat. But I never knew what to throw away and what to keep. I promise I'll start shredding this weekend."

"You're in good company, Cathy. Most of us have a tendency to hang on to papers too long," I said.

"I have something else I want to show you before we get down to business. Here's a three-ring binder with tabs for each financial planning topic we'll cover: net worth, cash flow, insurance, taxes, estate planning, retirement and college planning, and investments. I tucked some reference materials behind a few of the tabs. You'll notice there's also a tab at the front marked Recommendations. Each time we meet, I'll keep a running list on the computer of specific recommendations I make, plus some follow-up assignments."

"Homework?" asked Mike.

"I prefer to think of it as the implementation of your plan," I said, "but homework is a good word. At the end of each meeting I'll print out one copy of the recommendations for your notebook and one for my files. I'll also give you a copy of any spreadsheets or charts I generate during the meeting."

"Great," said Cathy. "I was wondering how I was going to remember everything we talk about. I'd rather listen than take notes."

"Please bring the binder to each meeting," I said, "and we'll add additional pages each time we meet. Do you have any questions or concerns at this point?"

"We know we'll be meeting with you several times," said Mike, "but this is our first experience working with a planner. Can you talk a little about how the process will work?"

"Absolutely," I said. "And I'm glad you used the word 'process.' Financial planning is not a one-time event—it's a work in progress, whether you do it with an advisor or on your own."

"To answer your question, Mike," I continued, "each time we meet we'll discuss one of the topics listed on the tabs in your binder. I'll go over some of the basic concepts, explain my recommendations, and answer your questions. I'm happy to go into as much detail as you like on any subject, and I'll try to be clear and not use a lot of jargon."

"So this will be a real learning experience for us," said Cathy, "but without those pesky exams. I'm ready to get going."

"It might seem logical to start by figuring out where you want to go and what changes you would like to make in your financial picture," I said. "After all, it's called financial planning so you must be planning for something. However, I'd like to postpone our look into the future until our next meeting. I'm going to ask some personal questions during that session, and I think we should get to know each other a little first. A better place to start is by figuring out where you are now. The easiest way to do that is to put together a balance sheet or personal net worth statement. This is simply a snapshot of your financial condition at a particular point in time."

Your Personal Balance Sheet

"I work for an accounting software firm," said Mike, "but I write computer code, not accounting rules. Remind me what a balance sheet looks like."

"Hold on," said Cathy. "I'll take this question. A balance sheet shows assets, liabilities, and net worth. The net worth of a company is just the difference between the assets and the liabilities."

"That's right," I said, "and it works the same way for individuals or couples. You add up all your assets—everything you own—and then add up all your liabilities—everything you owe. Subtract your liabilities from your assets and what's left is your net worth.

"It's as if you held a giant garage sale and sold everything you own—your car, TV, computer, clothes, furniture, dishes, and your house, if you own one. Next you cashed in all your bank accounts, investments, and retirement plans. Imagine you piled up all the cash you collected on the kitchen table. Well, you've sold the table, so you'll have to stack the cash on the floor.

"Next, imagine you take the money and pay off all your debts—your student loans, credit card balances, mortgages, bank loans, car loans, and personal loans. When you have paid everything off, the money that's left is your net worth or wealth. "

"I have a feeling we wouldn't have much left after paying off all our loans," said Mike. "This may be a depressing exercise."

"Not at all," I said. "You two haven't been out of school long and, Cathy, you're only working part-time while you're finishing your degree. You haven't had much time to build up wealth. In fact, young couples with hefty student loans may have a negative net worth for a while.

"Your balance sheet is just a line in the sand—in this case, the mark of where you were when we started working together. It's the direction you take from here that's important. As the years pass, your financial situation will have some ups and downs, but your net worth—your wealth—should be steadily increasing."

"It seems like it's good to have a healthy balance sheet, but does it really matter?" asked Cathy. "We're not a company with investors."

"Eventually, you'll probably want to stop working," I said. "At that time, you'll live off your wealth, instead of your paycheck. Your balance sheet tracks your wealth. Think of it as the big-picture view of your finances. If you don't accumulate enough wealth during your working years, you'll either have to cut back on your lifestyle when you retire or keep working until you save some more."

"So our wealth is our retirement nest egg?" asked Mike.

"Your retirement investments will be a big part of your wealth, but you also count your equity in your house, your possessions, and your savings in your balance sheet," I said.

"OK, now I'm curious," said Cathy. "I wonder how much wealth we have."

Collecting the Information

If you are following along with Mike and Cathy, your next step is to collect all your financial paperwork. Here's a checklist of what you'll need to gather. After you've pulled together all your documents, divide them into the categories shown in the right-hand column. It's a long list, so don't worry if some of the items don't apply to your situation.

Most recent bank statements	☐	Asset: Cash
Most recent 401(k), 403(b), or deferred compensation statements	☐	Asset: Investments
Most recent statements from IRAs	☐	Asset: Investments
Most recent statements from any company or public pension plans	☐	Asset: Investments
Most recent nonretirement investment statements (mutual funds, stocks, bonds, money market accounts)	☐	Asset: Cash or Investments
List of savings bonds (value, serial number, date purchased)	☐	Asset: Investments
Most recent statements of life insurance policies showing cash value (Note: term insurance does not have cash value.)	☐	Asset: Investments
Car(s) information: year, model, current market value	☐	Asset: Use Asset
Current market value of home and vacation home	☐	Asset: Use Asset
Current market value of rental real estate	☐	Asset: Investments
Fair market value of any other assets such as jewelry, original art, collections	☐	Asset: Use Asset
Fair market value of any other assets (things you own)	☐	Asset: Use Asset
Payoff value of your home mortgage	☐	Liability: Long-Term Debt
Outstanding amount of car loan(s)	☐	Liability: Long-Term or Short-Term Debt
Outstanding amount of student loan(s)	☐	Liability: Long-Term or Short-Term Debt
Amounts owed and interest rates on credit cards	☐	Liability: Long-Term or Short-Term Debt
Information on any other debt (bank loans, personal loans) including amounts owed and interest rates.	☐	Liability: Long-Term or Short-Term Debt

Income tax returns for the past two years	☐	
Car, homeowner's, renter's, umbrella insurance policies	☐	
Life insurance policies	☐	
Other:	☐	

Adding up the Assets

"Let's start by sorting the information you gathered into five categories," I said. "We'll use three asset categories—cash, investments, and use assets—and two liability categories—short-term debt and long-term debt. Let's start with cash. What goes in that category?"

"I assume you don't just mean cash in our pocket," said Cathy, "because I think I have about a dollar and 20 cents. Maybe you mean our checking and savings accounts?"

"Yes," I said, "that's exactly right. The full name of the category is "Cash and Cash Equivalents," so anything that could be readily converted into a known amount of cash belongs here. You could convert the balances in your checking and savings accounts to dollar bills by going to the bank and requesting a withdrawal. If you emptied out your accounts, you would know exactly how much you would get—assuming you had balanced your checkbook and kept your last savings statement. A money market account at a mutual fund company is also a cash equivalent."

"I have a few shares of stocks," said Cathy. "I could sell those at any time for cash, so don't they belong in the cash category?"

"Without getting too technical, your stocks are marketable—meaning they can be sold easily—but we classify them as investments instead of cash because you don't know how much you would get for them until you actually sell them. However, I would list savings bonds under Cash and Cash Equivalents because you can sell them anytime and their value is stable."

"I have five $100 EE savings bonds that I got when I graduated from college," said Cathy, "so I guess you can put $500 down for those."

"Actually, savings bonds work a little differently than some other bonds," I said. "EE Savings Bonds are purchased for one-half their face value—$50 for each of your bonds—and every six months, interest is added to the value of the bonds. I plugged in the serial number and issue date for your bonds on *www.savingsbonds.gov* to find the current value. They're worth just about $300 now. We'll talk more about savings bonds when we discuss investments."

"Do we have enough cash?" asked Mike.

"That's a great question, but let's tackle that subject when we have our cash flow meeting," I said. "The amount of emergency cash you hold is closely tied to how much you spend.

"In the meantime, let's take a look at your bank accounts. Cathy, I see you have a credit union account."

"Yes, that's a holdover from my first job out of college. Should I close it?"

"I would keep it open," I said. "Credit unions often pay a higher rate of interest than commercial banks, and they offer competitive car loans and mortgages. I'd use that account for the money you set aside from your business for quarterly taxes.

"And Mike, you have a savings account as well," I said.

"I got a bonus at work," said Mike, "and I plunked part of it in that account. I thought it might be the start of our house fund."

"Good idea," I said. "You may want to put that account in both your names, and you and Cathy can start making regular contributions to it. Again, we'll talk more about that in our cash flow meeting.

"Now to the second category of assets—Use Assets. The name suggests the kind of assets that belong here—vehicles, jewelry, and your personal possessions. Some planners add a Real Estate category, but I'll put your house—when you buy one—under Use Assets to keep it simple.

"Let's start with cars. Your Honda Civic, Cathy, is worth about $4000, and your Jeep, Mike, is worth about $12,000. I looked up the values on the Web."

"I still owe about $3000 on my Jeep," said Mike, "so shouldn't we list the value as $9000?"

"We could do it that way, but we generally separate the asset from its liability so we'll put the full value of the Jeep on the asset side and the loan balance on the liability side," I said. "The bottom line's the same either way, but this method makes it a little easier to see what you own and what you owe.

"Cathy, it looks like you're wearing a few Use Assets," I said.

"Oh, you mean my wedding and engagement rings," said Cathy. "I also have a pearl necklace my parents gave me. I think the value of all my jewelry is about $4000."

"By the way, I recommend you list your jewelry on a separate rider on your renter's insurance policy," I said. "In fact, I'll add that as a homework item."

"What about our other stuff?" asked Mike. "Cathy has a computer she uses for work, plus we have some furniture, a TV, and a DVD player. Not to mention all of Cathy's clothes. You should see her closet."

"It's an optical illusion," said Cathy. "I just have a very small closet."

"When we list personal possessions on the balance sheet," I said, "we use their fair market value or the amount you would get if you sold them through ads in the newspaper or at a garage sale."

"We wouldn't get much for our stuff," said Cathy. "What value do you suggest?"

"It's not worth spending a lot of time trying to get an exact number," I said. "Let's just assume you'd get $3000 if you sold all your stuff. We could separate out the computer you use for work, Cathy, as a business asset under Investments, but for simplicity let's just lump it in with your other personal possessions. So your Use Assets, including the cars, are worth $23,000. We're down to the last asset category—Investments."

"My 401(k) plan balance changes with every statement, so what value do I put on the sheet?" asked Mike.

"A balance sheet represents your assets and liabilities as of a certain date," I said. "We picked December 31st of last year, so we'll use the value of your 401(k) on that date. We'll do the same for your 403(b) plan, Cathy. I assume that was money you contributed while you were at your old job."

"That's right," said Cathy. "I worked in the human resources department of a hospital for a couple of years out of college. I just left the money there because I wasn't sure what to do with it."

"I have some ideas about what to do with that investment," I said, "but we'll talk about that in another meeting. The last asset we need to add is your brokerage account, Cathy."

"That's my play money account," said Cathy smiling. "My parents gave me $2000 a couple of years ago, and I picked out a few stocks. I haven't exactly made a fortune, but I'm hanging on."

"Cathy was going for the gold," said Mike, "but it looks like she ended up with tin. It's a good thing we weren't counting on that money."

"I didn't lose it all, and I consider it a learning experience," said Cathy.

"We'll talk about the pros and cons of owning individual stocks in our investments meeting," I said. " I think we've finished adding up your assets. Let's take a look. You have $3350 in Cash or Cash Equivalents, $23,000 in Use Assets, and $21,700 in Investments for a total of $48,050." (See Figure 2-1.)

December 31, 2002

ASSETS		Mike	Cathy	Joint	Total
Cash and Equivalents					
	Checking accounts - First National Bank	$1,250	$750		$2,000
	Savings account - Credit Union		$600		$600
	Savings account - Main Street Bank	$450			$450
	EE Savings Bonds		$300		$300
Total Cash and Equivalents		$1,700	$1,650	$0	$3,350
Use Assets					
	Honda Civic		$4,000		$4,000
	Jeep Cherokee	$12,000			$12,000
	Jewelry		$4,000		$4,000
	Personal Possessions			$3,000	$3,000
Total Use Assets		$12,000	$8,000	$3,000	$23,000
Investments					
	Mike's 401(k) plan	$14,300			$14,300
	Cathy's 403(b) plan		$6,200		$6,200

Cathy's brokerage account	$14,300	$1,200		$1,200
Total Investments	$28,000	$7,400		$21,700
TOTAL ASSETS		$17,050	$3,000	$48,050
LIABILITIES				
Short-Term				
Mike's VISA card balance	$1,800			$1,800
Cathy's quarterly tax bill		$2,200		$2,200
Total Short-Term Liabilities	$1,800	$2,200	$0	$4,000
Long-Term				
Loan on Jeep Cherokee	$3,000			$3,000
Cathy's MasterCard balance		$2,800		$2,800
Cathy's student loans		$6,000		$6,000
Total Long-Term Liabilities	$3,000	$8,800	$0	$11,800
TOTAL LIABILITIES	$4,800	$11,000	$0	$15,800
NET WORTH	**$23,200**	**$6,050**	**$3,000**	**$32,250**

FIGURE 2-1 Mike and Cathy Stanford Balance Sheet

Adding up the Liabilities

"We divide liabilities, what you owe, into two groups: Short-Term Liabilities—due to be paid in a year or less—and Long-Term Liabilities," I said. "Cathy will need to pay $2200 in estimated taxes in a couple of months, so that's definitely a Short-Term Liability. How about your Visa bill, Mike?"

"I'm paying that off before the end of the year," said Mike.

"I seem to remember you said the same thing last year," said Cathy smiling. "But then you went in with your friends on season baseball tickets. And the year before that it was a CD player for the Jeep."

"Let's take Mike at his word and list his Visa debt as a short-term liability," I said. "No pressure, Mike."

"Your other debts are the Jeep loan, Cathy's student loans, and Cathy's MasterCard balance. Both the Jeep loan and the student loans are long-term obligations. How about your credit card debt, Cathy?"

"I put my start-up business expenses on that card," said Cathy, "and I'm paying it off from my business income. I plan to have it paid off in a year or two. I guess that makes it a Long-Term Liability."

"Let's go ahead and classify it as long-term debt. If you pay it off earlier, great. So you have $4000 in Short-Term Liabilities and $11,800 in Long-Term Liabilities for a total of $15,800," I said.

Putting It All Together

"It's time for the big moment," I said, "what is your net worth? Mike, you have the calculator. Subtract your liabilities ($15,800) from your assets ($48,050). The difference is your net worth. What's the answer?"

"It's $32,250," said Mike. "So that's what we're worth."

"Financially speaking," I said, "that's correct."

"I noticed you divided everything into Mike's, Cathy's, and Joint," said Cathy. "Mike's net worth is much higher than mine. That doesn't make me look too good."

"You're building your human capital by continuing your education, Cathy," I said. "The balance sheet doesn't tell the whole story—it's just a tool for analyzing your financial picture as of a particular date. Let's take a closer look.

"First, your net worth is positive, and it's equal to about half your annual income. Congratulations—that's just about where you should be at your age. About 10 years from now, when you're in your mid-to-late 30s, your net worth should be two to three times your gross annual income.

"Next, let's see how liquid you are. Liquidity refers to your ability to pay your debts. If we divide your Cash and Cash Equivalents of $3350 by your Short-Term Liabilities of $4000, we get a liquidity ratio of about .84. That means you have enough cash in the bank or assets readily convertible to cash to pay 84 percent of your near-term debt. I'd shoot for a ratio of at least 1.00 to make sure you have enough cash to pay off all your Short-Term Liabilities. We'll talk later about beefing up an emergency fund, but in the meantime, you may have to delay paying some of your credit card debt, Mike, so Cathy can make her quarterly estimated tax payment.

"One of my big clients is due to pay me before I have to make that tax payment," said Cathy, "so we should be all right."

"It sounds like you'll be fine," I said, "but it's still nice to have the money in the bank so you don't have to worry if your client's check gets delayed.

"Let's look at one more ratio before we print out your balance sheet and put it in your binder. It's your debt ratio—an indicator of how solvent, or financially stable, you are. To calculate your debt ratio, divide your total liabilities by your total assets."

"I can do that," said Mike. "Let's see—$15,800 divided by $48,050 is equal to about .33. Is that good?"

"It's very good," I said. "It means your assets would have to decline significantly, or your debt would have to take a big jump up before your net worth would slip into negative territory. If that were to happen, you would technically be bankrupt or insolvent, but a couple with a negative net worth doesn't have to declare bankruptcy if their income will continue to cover their debt payments. Take the case of a young physician who graduates with a stack of student loans but earns a good income. She might be insolvent on paper but in no danger of sliding into bankruptcy.

"In general, if your assets are at least twice your liabilities—a debt ratio of .5 or lower—you should be in pretty good shape. However, when you buy a house, your mortgage will push that ratio up, so we should recalculate it then."

"I feel better knowing where we stand now," said Mike. "It's kind of nice being able to put a number on our net worth—although it would be better if there were a few more digits on that number."

"And there will be," I said. "You two are off to a good start."

Goal-Setting Homework

"What's next?" asked Cathy.

"At our next meeting we're going to shift gears and talk about your goals and dreams," I said. "We won't be using any calculators, and I won't be plugging numbers into spreadsheets. Your homework assignment is to write down 10 personal goals and five financial goals you wish to accomplish over the next five years. The personal goals can relate to your careers, physical health, relationships with family and friends, social activities, how you spend your free time—just about any part of your life. Don't be bound by any thoughts about what you should be wishing for; this is your life, so feel free to dream. There's only one rule—I'd like you each to do this exercise on your own. Please don't share your lists until we meet. Any questions?"

"We're going to use an entire meeting talking about our goals?" asked Mike. "That seems like a lot of time. When do we get to investments?"

"Trust me on this one," I said. "I think you'll like the results. Spend some time over the next couple of weeks daydreaming about what you really want to do, where you want to be, and how you want to lead your life. You may surprise yourself. Are you willing to give it a try, Cathy?"

"It sounds like fun. I can already think of some things for my list. And, no peeking," said Cathy as Mike started to lean over her notes. "Get your own list."

"Great," I said. "Let's get out our calendars and schedule the next meeting."

Putting Together Your Own Balance Sheet

If you have already gathered up all your financial documents, it's time to add it all up and figure out your own net worth. Just as Mike and Cathy did, you'll need to sort through your paperwork, dividing it into five categories:

- Cash or Cash Equivalents
- Use Assets
- Investments
- Short-Term Debt (due in less than one year)
- Long-Term Debt

You can use shoeboxes or sticky notes or whatever sorting method works best for you.

Next, add up the assets or liabilities in each category. You can copy the worksheets printed at the end of this chapter, or you can set up your own spreadsheet on the computer. Separate the assets and liabilities by who owns it—you, your partner, or both of you together. And, if there is a liability associated with an asset, like a loan on a car, put the full value in the asset category and the value of the debt in the liability category, as we did with Mike's Jeep.

"Cash and Cash Equivalents" means anything with a stable and predictable value that can be readily converted into cash. Checking accounts, savings accounts, money market accounts, savings bonds, and certificates of deposit (CDs) all fall into this category. If you own an insurance policy that has an investment component, the cash value of the policy (the amount available for withdrawing or borrowing) usually counts as a cash equivalent. If the cash value of the policy is invested in stock mutual funds, list that amount in the Investments section instead.

"Use Assets" are tangible things that don't count as investments. Your house, cars, furniture, stereo equipment, clothes, and jewelry all fit this category. Except for your house or certain collectibles, most of your use assets will tend to lose value over time.

"Investments" are pension plans, IRAs, mutual funds, stocks, and bonds. If you own rental real estate, the value of the property belongs in this section and the mortgage in the liabilities section. I am reluctant to list collectibles in the Investments section unless you operate a business buying and selling them or they have a stable, well-established market value. I'm afraid those Beanie Babies collected over the years will turn out to be use assets and not part of retirement nest eggs.

If you own your own business, the value should be listed as an Investment. If you own a service business, like Cathy's human resource consulting business, list the fair market value of your computers, furniture, and other assets under the Investments section.

"Short-Term Liabilities" are debts that will be paid off within the next 12 months. Short-term credit card debt, same-as-cash arrangements, and estimated tax payments are included in this category.

"Long-Term Liabilities" are debts that will take longer than one year to pay off. Home mortgages and lines of credit, auto loans, and

How to Value Your Use Assets

Home:

- Look in the local paper for values of similar homes that have been sold recently.
- Visit *www.realtor.com* or other Web sites that show recent sales by area.

Car:

- Look up the value on *www.kbb.com* (Kelly's Blue Book Web site) or *www.edmunds.com*.
- If you are leasing a car, enter a "0" on this line.

Personal items:

- For rare or valuable assets, use appraised value or insured value or look on ebay.com for similar items.
- For general household items, estimate how much you could get if you sold them all at a giant garage sale. I usually estimate $5000 for possessions in an average 3-to-5-room apartment or house and $10,000 for a 6-to-12 room home. Remember—this is not the replacement value they are insured for.

student loans belong in this category, as well as credit card debt that won't be paid off in a year or less.

Finally, to calculate your net worth, add up all the asset categories, then separately add up the liability categories, and subtract the total liabilities from the total assets. Compare your net worth to your gross annual income. As Mike and Cathy learned, if you are in your 20s, your net worth may be less than your annual income. If you are in your 30s, a good benchmark for your net worth is one to three times your annual income and if you're in your 40s, aim for three to seven times your annual income.

Now that you have figured out your net worth, use it as a tool for measuring your big-picture financial progress. Each year, set aside some time to update your personal balance sheet. Compare it to the previous version to detect improvement or deterioration in any of the categories. Recalculate your liquidity and debt ratios and compare your net worth to your annual income.

ASSETS					
Category	**Description**	**Name 1**	**Name 2**	**Joint**	**TOTAL**
Cash and Equivalents					
Subtotal					
Use Assets					
Subtotal					
Investments					
Subtotal					
Total Assets					

Set up another sheet for Liabilities (debts):

LIABILITIES					
Category	**Description**	**Name 1**	**Name 2**	**Joint**	**TOTAL**
Short-Term					
Subtotal					

LIABILITIES					
Category	**Description**	**Name 1**	**Name 2**	**Joint**	**TOTAL**
Long-Term					
Subtotal					
Total Liabilities					

	Name 1	**Name 2**	**Joint**	**TOTAL**
Total Assets				
Minus				
Total Liabilities				
Equals				
Net Worth				

What Cathy and Mike Learned

- Their personal balance sheet is a snapshot of their net worth as of a particular date.
- Net worth is calculated by subtracting their liabilities (what they owe) from their assets (what they own).
- Their net worth is about half of their total annual income—about right for a couple in their 20s.

Recommendations for Cathy and Mike

1. Make sure your jewelry is listed on a separate rider on your renter's policy. (Cathy)

2. Don't close any bank accounts you currently hold. We'll discuss opening a joint account for the house fund at a later meeting.

3. Bring your lists of goals to our next meeting.

Your Homework

1. Set up your own three-ring binder with tabs for each financial planning topic.

2. Prepare your own balance sheet and make a note to update it annually.

Resources

1. For more information about benchmarking your net worth see the Financial Lifecycle™ section of *Facing Financial Dysfunction: Why Smart People Do Stupid Things With Money!* By Bert Whitehead, M.B.A., J.D. Haverford, PA: Infinity Publishing.com, 2002.

2. You can calculate and track your net worth on personal finance programs such as Quicken® and Money®.

CHAPTER 3

Planning for Now and Later

If we were playing a word association game and I said "financial planning," what words would pop into your head? You might think of "savings" or "investments" or "taxes." But there's an important part of financial planning that has nothing to do with banks or mutual funds prospectuses or IRS rules. It's setting your goals—figuring out why you are saving and investing and paying off debt.

The fact is that many of us spend more time planning our next party or ski trip than we do thinking about our future. And it's not just about the money. It's really about what's important to you and how you want to live your life. Financial planning is a very personal process. The choices you make—where you live, the work you do, even which car you drive—may be very different from the ones your neighbor, best friend, or parents make.

And it's not just about planning for some future date when you cash your last paycheck and glide into retirement. It's about what you do in the meantime, too. Although I believe that occasionally lucky events can drop into your lap, I also agree with the idea people often make their own luck. If you have a pretty clear idea of where you'd like to go, you'll recognize opportunities that can speed you along towards your goals, and you'll be more likely to take advantage of them. I don't mean you have to be a control freak—just someone who exercises a little more power over your choices. Life is unpredictable, but it doesn't have to be quite so haphazard.

The starting point is to figure out a time frame for your goals. I don't question the value of looking way out into the future, and Cathy, Mike, and I will be doing that during their retirement meeting. But it's easier to set specific action items for a shorter, more manageable period of time. A five-year horizon should be long enough to achieve some significant goals, but short enough to stay on track.

Are you ready to go through a goal-setting exercise? Whether you just became a couple or you've been together for years, I encourage you to give it a try. I think you'll find it can be a revealing and fun experience. Although Mike and Cathy are going to do goal setting with my help, you certainly don't need a financial planner—or anyone else—to have a great session together. Just follow a few guidelines and make it your own experience. Here are some tips:

1. Set aside a specific time and place for your goal-setting session. Pick a time when you'll be relaxed and unhurried, and choose a comfortable place. A Saturday evening at home with the TV off and a nice bottle of wine and a plate of cheese may work just fine. Or you might try Sunday morning at the kitchen table over bagels and coffee. I guess you can set goals without food, but why would you want to? Mark it on your calendar and shut out other activities.

2. Do the homework I assigned to Mike and Cathy at the end of the last chapter. Just remember to make up your lists individually— no collaborating—and put them in writing. You may really get into this and start thinking of dozens of personal and financial goals you would like to accomplish over the next five years—I know I did. No problem—just pick out the 10 most important personal and five most important financial objectives and move them to the top of the lists.

3. On your prearranged date, after you have poured the wine or the orange juice and coffee, start by sharing with each other some stories about how money was handled when you were growing up. Listen attentively to your partner and resist any temptation to jump in with advice or judgmental comments. The purpose of the storytelling is not to fix the past but to gain some understanding of your partner's attitudes toward money.

4. Next, share your lists with your partner. Again, no criticism is allowed. Some may seem like pie-in-the-sky dreams, but it's better to aim high at this point rather than set timid, incremental goals. Reality checks will come later.

5. Talk about the items on your lists. Look for common threads and ways you can achieve your goals as a couple. Creativity and understanding go a long way in this part of the exercise. For example, you may be dismayed to learn that your partner's goal of devoting more time to keeping the house clean will probably conflict with your plan to take a programming course in the evenings to boost you career. The solution might be to hire a cleaning service twice a month, even if it means fewer dinners out.

Maybe your partner has always dreamed of traveling to London but you think it's too far away and too expensive. If you agree to scour your budget, you may find a way to save $75 a month in a vacation fund. In two-and-a-half years, you will have saved about $2400 (if you earn 5 percent interest). London may still not be your first choice, but sharing your partner's dream can be a lot of fun. And I hear the food there is getting much better.

6. Fill out a Timeline Worksheet. The purpose of this chart is to summarize your goals and lay out immediate and future steps you'll need to take to reach them. Your action items should be specific and measurable. If your goal is to sort and file the stacks of papers that have accumulated on the dining room table, it's unlikely to happen unless you identify a time each week to work on your goal. I have put together a sample below.

7. Visualize your future. The final step in your goal-setting exercise is to visualize what your ideal future will look like five years from today. It's the capstone of the whole exercise and can be a lot of fun, as Mike and Cathy are about to learn.

Sharing Money Backgrounds

"Before we get started on the lists of goals you prepared, I'd like to ask you each a question: How was money handled when you were growing up?"

"I'll jump in," said Mike. "We weren't rich by any means—in fact, I don't even know how much my Dad makes—but we always seemed to have money when we wanted something like new clothes or a vacation. My parents didn't talk much about money to us kids, but I remember some arguments they had. Dad made the money and Mom paid the bills, but there must have been some tight months because I recall some loud voices and doors slamming a few times. My brothers and I just stayed out of the way."

Goal	Due Date	Immediate Actions	Future Actions
Keep house cleaner (bathrooms cleaned weekly, living areas vacuumed and dusted weekly, refrigerator cleaned out monthly)	One month from today	- Call cleaning services for quotes on twice-a-month cleaning. - Ask friends for recommendations. - Look at budget to see if feasible. - Divide up jobs for "off weeks."	- Interview and hire cleaning service. - Evaluate cost/benefit after 3 months.
Take one-week vacation to London	Two-and-a-half years from today	- Look at budget to see where to cut $75 a month. - Research appropriate type of savings account or mutual fund. - Set up account and automatic monthly contributions.	- Research Web sites and guide books for best deals. - Plan trip together. - Monitor performance of account.
Contribute $1,000 each into Roth IRAs	9 months from now	- Research most cost-effective way to set up a Roth IRA. - Choose no-load mutual funds with low minimum balance requirements. - Set up account and automatic monthly contributions.	- Check performance of funds annually. - Consider increasing monthly contributions.

"Did you get an allowance?" I asked.

"When I started elementary school, my parents told me they'd give me an allowance every week," said Mike. "I can't remember how much it was—maybe $5 a week by the time I was in high school—but they'd forget or not have the cash on hand so it was hit or miss. I didn't really mind because if I wanted to go to the movies or get a new pair of jeans, I could usually get the money from one of them—most often from Dad. Mom was more of a tightwad. I'm not saying they would spring for everything. When I began working at a local bakery during high school, I started paying for a lot of my expenses on my own."

"How about college?" I asked. "Who paid for that?"

"I was lucky," said Mike. "I went to a state university near my home, so I commuted the first two years. I also got some scholarship money, so the costs were pretty low. My parents helped out, my grandparents chipped in from time to time, and I took out a few student loans. Now that I think about it, I'm pretty sure my parents borrowed some money, too. Anyway, I ended up with about $8000 in student loans and I finished paying them off last year—with a lot of help from my grandparents."

"Great," I said. "Thanks, Mike. Cathy, what about you? How was money handled when you were growing up?"

"Mike and I had never really talked much about this," said Cathy, "and I hadn't realized how different our backgrounds are. Some things are the same, of course. I also grew up in a middle-class family. But both my parents worked and although my mom was the one who sat down each month to pay bills, I got the impression my parents consulted each other on big spending decisions.

"I remember we had family conferences to plan our vacations. My parents were pretty open with us about how much money they could afford to spend, and we children would throw out ideas about where we wanted to go. Then the older kids would go off and research the cost and bring back some estimates. It wasn't high-level budgeting—believe me—and Mom and Dad would tweak our numbers, but it was always a fun project."

"Did you get a regular allowance?" I asked.

"I did," said Cathy. "There were certain things I was supposed to pay for out of my allowance. When I was a sophomore in high school, my parents and I sat down and figured out a clothes budget. I got one-quarter of the budget each three months, and I was responsible for paying for my clothes out of that money. If there was anything left over, I got to keep it. If I ran out of money, too bad."

"Did that system work well?" I asked.

"It took a while to get used to it," said Cathy. "It seemed like such a big chunk of money but it didn't last long. During the first six months, I spent the whole budget and then remembered I needed a new ski jacket. I ended up asking for it for Christmas—even though I had planned on getting new speakers for my stereo. Oh well. Live and learn. By the time I was in college, my parents were giving me my tuition and living expenses money in one big chunk each semester. It was up to me to manage it. I worked during the summers and paid for my books and incidental expenses on my own."

"So your parents paid for college?" I asked.

"Most of it," said Cathy. "Like Mike, I went to a state school, but I lived away from home all four years. I only had a small loan when I graduated and I paid that off in a couple of years. However, my parents are not shelling out any money for graduate school—that's on my nickel. I've taken out loans for my MBA bills. If I had kept working at the hospital, I might have received some tuition assistance, but I was so anxious to start my own business that I jumped ship. I'm not sure that was so smart, but too late now."

Sharing Lists of Goals

"That was terrific," I said. "Thank you so much for telling your stories. Now it's time to share your lists. Cathy, would you like to go first?"

"Sure," said Cathy. "I'll start. Here are my 10 personal goals, in no particular order.

1. Exercise at least a half hour each day.

2. Have lunch with my girlfriends at least once a month.

3. Clean out my closet and donate stuff to Goodwill.

4. Set aside a monthly date with Mike to have dinner at a nice restaurant and go to a play or concert.

5. Finish my MBA by this time next year.

6. Read two non-business-related books every month.

7. Look into volunteering opportunities.

8. Send out Christmas cards this year.

9. Sit down with Mike to divide up the household chores more equitably.

10. Have our first child within the next three years.

"Good list," I said. "Okay, Cathy, go ahead with your five financial goals."

"I mixed my business and financial goals together," said Cathy. "Here they are:

1. Earn $60,000 a year after expenses in three years.

2. Buy a $250,000 house within two years, with Mike, of course.

3. Pay off my student loans in four years.

4. Start keeping track of personal expenses on Quicken.

5. Put away 10 percent of my income for long-term goals, like retirement."

"Wow," I said. "Those are really focused goals. Nice job. You even included some due dates. Mike, you're up next."

"Well, as usual, Cathy gets the gold star," said Mike. "Here are my personal goals:

1. Join a recreational basketball league.

2. Get a home theater system and hook it up myself.

3. Take a course in the new version of the programming language I use at work.

4. Get promoted to manager within two years or start looking around for a new job.

5. Look into getting a Master's degree at a local university after Cathy finishes her MBA.

6. Keep my car clean.

7. Start a family.

8. Take a great vacation with Cathy every year.

9. Get a dog.

10. Join a health club.

"I can already see Cathy squinching up her nose at the dog thing, but sorry—cats just aren't my thing. Ready for my list of financial goals?

1. Earn $80,000 a year within five years.
2. Buy a convertible.
3. Buy a house.
4. Enter my ATM withdrawals in my checkbook.
5. Learn more about the investment choices in my 401(k) plan."

"You both get gold stars," I said. "Those are great lists. Wouldn't it be terrific if five years from now you could look back and mark 'done' next to all of those goals?"

"Except for the dog," said Cathy, smiling.

"There are a few things you two will have to sort out," I said, "but there are several areas of agreement. Buying a house and starting a family were on both lists. Physical fitness seems to be a priority with both. You each want some time with your friends—either having lunch or playing sports—but you want time together as well.

"Every one of your financial goals is a topic for a future meeting. What did you two think of the lists?"

"I thought it was interesting that Mike had several big expensive things on his lists," said Cathy, "like new cars and vacations and stereo stuff. I don't know how we're going to do that if we buy a house and start a family."

"Don't forget," said Mike, "I'm also going to double my salary, and you said you're going to be making a lot more money in five years, too."

"And here's where the reality check comes into play," I said. "Setting your sights high is fine. Many people undervalue themselves, and their salaries stay low—almost like a self-fulfilling prophecy. But your goals should be realistic, so let's take a look at what will need to happen for you to make your earnings targets.

"Mike, a $35,000 jump in your salary over the next five years translates into a 12-percent annual pay raise. Obviously you're counting on promotions or even job changes to accomplish that—cost of living increases won't get you there. What level of managers in your current company are paid about $70,000 today? That's equivalent to about $81,000 in five years, taking inflation into account."

"My immediate supervisor makes about $55,000 and the head of the software development department makes about $70,000," said Mike. "I'd have to get two big promotions to get there. The department head has been at the company for almost 20 years, but he worked his way up from the bottom. I think if I got an advanced degree, I could get to the department head level a lot sooner. I'd have more flexibility with an MBA or a degree in marketing because I could move into sales. The guys who go out on the road and pitch software packages to big companies make a ton of money."

"So, if I'm hearing you correctly," I said, "it's going to take more education, hard work, and flexibility about where you work and what you do to get to your goal. Did I get that right?"

"That's exactly right," said Mike, "although I'll admit I never sat down and thought about it that way. I put down the advanced degree on my goal list because the company offers some education benefits and a bunch of us at work have been talking about it. It really does fit into my other goals."

"That's why we do this exercise," I said. "But don't stop here. Take some time over the next couple of weeks to map out a timeline with specific milestones like 'Get information on local graduate schools by September 1.'"

"I can do that," said Mike. "It will be like putting together a road map for the next five years."

"Exactly," I said. "How about your goal of making $60,000, after expenses, in your business, Cathy? What does your road map look like?"

"I'm not sure," said Cathy. "I just figured I should be able to quadruple my current income once I finished with my MBA and could spend full time on the business."

"That may be feasible," I said. "Because you are self-employed, Cathy, your timeline should look more like a business plan. I suggest setting up a spreadsheet showing projected number of clients, average revenue per client, and average direct time spent with each client so you can estimate how much you'll bring in over the next five years.

"For example, let's assume you'll need to bill $100,000 in order to clear $60,000 after expenses. There are 2080 hours in an average work year. I imagine about half of your working hours will be spent on marketing, continuing education, administration, and other activities that don't earn any money but are necessary parts of running a business. That leaves 1040 hours a year for working with clients. If we divide $100,000 by 1040 hours, we get $96. That should be pretty close to your billing rate. How many hours does a typical client's project take, Cathy?"

"I don't really have a typical project," said Cathy. "Some of my work involves big projects like writing an employee manual from scratch. Those can take 80 to 100 hours to write. Other times, clients hire me for specific projects like a review of a department's job classifications. Those usually take about 10 hours. I bill $40 an hour for my work now, so it looks like I'll need to kick up my rate to make my goal."

"You might consider changing the way you charge clients for your work. Instead of billing on an hourly basis, you could charge a flat fee based on the project. You could probably develop a price list for your typical services or projects. As you get more experience, you'll be able to complete the tasks in less time, but still provide a good value to your client. If you charged on an hourly basis, your bill would go down every time you got more efficient."

"That makes sense," said Cathy. "I can't wait to get going on my five-year plan. We've only touched on small business planning in my MBA coursework so far, so I'm going to get a head start."

"We haven't talked about an item you both had on your lists—starting a family. You'll need to take that into account as you develop your timelines and milestones. Mike, you intend to get extra training and enroll in graduate school and, Cathy, you have some ambitious plans for your business. Plus you both want to spend some fun time with each other. It's going to take some careful planning, and some compromises and flexibility along the way to hit all your goals."

"Do you think we're just way off base?" asked Mike.

"No," I said. "I didn't mean to sound like a wet blanket. On the contrary. I'm encouraging you to work out ways to reach your goals. Now that you have specific, written targets, you should revisit them from time to time to make sure you're on course. Tweak and adjust your action items and help each other out."

Visualizing Your Future

"The last item for today is a visualization experience,"[1] I said. "I want each of you to imagine yourself five years from today. Mike, you're 34 years old and Cathy, you're 32. You have had a great five years and you like the way you look and the way you feel. You enjoy what you're doing and you feel good about what you have accomplished over the past five years. Things have really gone your way. In fact, you're having a terrific day—the best so far. Sit back and imagine what you're doing at the best moment on that terrific day. Take a few minutes and close your eyes if you like."

I waited for a few minutes.

"Now, I'd like you to describe your perfect moment," I said. "Who wants to go first?"

"I'm ready to go," said Cathy.

"Great," I said. "Cathy, please describe where you are, what day it is, and what you're doing."

"It's a Friday afternoon and I'm in my home office in the wing we built off our new home. I'm leaning back in my chair, sipping a cup of mint tea, and I'm daydreaming and relaxing. I just got off the phone with a big client who called to tell me how pleased she was with the job I just completed and to ask about my availability for another big job. I'm smiling because I can just make out the sounds of a children's song, so I know the babysitter must be playing music for my baby. I'm feeling very content because I love my work, I can spend more time with my child than most working mothers do, and I have a great babysitter. Mike and I are really busy but we're happy. I know Mike will be home in a couple of hours and we're planning a quiet evening at home. The weekend's free, so we can just hang out and enjoy each other and our house. I bought some flats of flowers and I'll be planting them in the backyard. That will be my quiet time."

"Before you drift off into Nirvana, Cathy," I said, "tell me what you're wearing and what your office looks like. What time of year is it?"

"I'm wearing a jeans skirt and a T-shirt. Fridays are catch-up and research days, so I don't have any client meetings. It's May and I'm looking forward to the summer when we can spend more time outside with the baby. My office is light and bright—natural cherry wood, com-

---

[1] Thanks to Bert Whitehead for teaching me about using visualizations with clients. Bert's book is listed under Resources at the end of Chapter 2.

fortable chairs, soft lighting, a big window looking out over the back yard. I clipped a picture of my ideal space from a magazine article on home offices."

"It sounds great," I said. "Mike, it's your turn."

"It's Saturday morning and I'm loading up the Range Rover. Our two-year-old is in the back yard trying to kick a ball around, and he or she—I can't tell—looks up to see what I'm doing. I'm wearing shorts. It's summer—say late June. Cathy's inside packing some toys for the trip and checking around the house to make sure we haven't forgotten anything. In about an hour, we'll all get in the car and head to a resort near the Appalachian Trail. We're meeting friends there, and I'm going to try hiking with our child in a baby carrier. I'm planning to get in some golf, but nothing much is scheduled. Things are going well enough at work that I feel I can get away for a while and not have the department go down the drain."

"That's a very clear vision, Mike," I said. "I feel like jumping on the Web and checking out Appalachian hiking lodges.

"Now, I'm not a psychologist so I don't intend to analyze your visions and relate them to some particular childhood experience. I do think they're very interesting, though. Your visions are similar in several ways. You both thought about a house and a child, the weather's warm, and you both mention outdoor activities. You're both looking forward to some down time, but Cathy spent more time talking about her work."

"I was thinking about that," said Cathy. "In my ideal world, my work and family are somewhat combined. For example, I'd like to have my office at home—close enough so I can take breaks to be with my children, but separate enough that I can concentrate on work and really get things done."

"That's interesting," said Mike. "I like what I do, but when you told us to picture a great moment, I didn't think of work right away. I thought of play—getting ready for a vacation."

"One of the reasons I asked you to do a visualization exercise was to crystallize some of your five-year goals," I said. "Your lists are valuable guides for the future, but the visualization tells the story of what your life will look like when you have achieved your goals."

"I think I get it," said Mike. "When I wrote 'new house, new baby, new car, vacation' on my list, I really didn't think too hard about what that meant. When I visualized packing the car for a family vacation, it seemed real."

"Now you know what you're aiming for," I said. "The trick is to get there. I have confidence in you two because you have such clear visions of what you want.

"There are a few things you can do to anchor your visualizations. Keep talking to each other about that best day five years from now and add a few more details each day. In two weeks, I'd like you to buy a small gift for each other that symbolizes your partner's visualization. It should be inexpensive and small enough to go on a bedside table or a dashboard or a desk. The purpose is to have a visible reminder of your dream.

"The topic for our next meeting is cash flow. I'll see you in a few weeks."

What Cathy and Mike Learned

1. Financial planning isn't only about numbers and charts and graphs.

2. Writing down and discussing your goals with your partner make them more concrete and achievable.

Recommendations for Cathy and Mike

1. Complete a timeline worksheet for major goals.

2. Complete the visualization exercise and buy each other a small gift.

Your Homework

1. Set aside time with your partner for a goal-setting exercise and go through steps 1 through 7 described at the beginning of the chapter.

CHAPTER 4

How Your Cash Flows

I f you read no other chapter in this book, read this one. Cash flow is where it all begins. Wise spending decisions can set you on a path to financial security; uncontrolled spending will sabotage your progress or even sink your financial plan.

You'd think we'd all be pros at managing our cash flow because we've had so much practice at it. If you received an allowance while you were growing up, you could trace the dollars from your pocket to the mall or, perhaps, to the piggy bank. Your first paycheck may have been divvied up among the gas station, the Gap, and fast food restaurants. Cash flowed in and it flowed out.

It's more complicated now. You earn more money and you have many more obligations and choices. The price tags are higher, too. Although a chunk of your money is still spent at the mall, you're also purchasing some very big items like cars and a home. And now that you're part of a couple, you can't make all your spending decisions on your own.

Getting a handle on your cash flow is a three-step process:

- Figure out what's really important to you and your partner and how you want to spend your money.

- Review how you've been spending in the past—both individually and as a couple.

- Set up and stick to a spending plan. Although some couples successfully use Quicken® and other software tools to budget and track their spending, you don't need to be a fanatic about classifying every penny of every expenditure. You do, however, need some benchmarks.

Your Spending Style

Before you and your partner start working on a spending plan, take a step back and decide what kind of spenders and savers you want to be. Here are three examples:

- The Fun-Fun-Fun Couple. These people live above their means, spending more than they make and financing the gap with credit cards and loans. They can be great friends, always willing to go out and have a good time or throw a party. They have the latest gadgets, the coolest clothes, the best vacation photos. Often they earn high salaries and they work hard, so they feel they're entitled to nice things and fun times. They're counting on the next raise or bonus or gift from their parents to bail them out. The credit card offers keep arriving, so they figure they're not in deep trouble yet.

Of course, their "live-for-today" lifestyle can only go so far, and eventually they either have to cut way back and start repaying their loans or, in extreme cases, declare bankruptcy. The bottom line is you can't consistently live above your means without dismal consequences. Fun-fun-fun couples can get very grumpy when creditors start calling at work or their mortgage application is denied.

- The Teetering Couple. These people live just within their means. They go paycheck to paycheck, not saving a dime but avoiding severe debt problems. They pay their bills but never have any extra money at the end of the month to put aside for gifts or home repairs or their next car. Every year they put their vacation expenses on a credit card and then chip away at the balance over the next several months. By the time the debt is paid off, it's time to take another vacation.

The Teetering Couple is not on solid financial ground. With little or no savings to back them up, they are vulnerable to economic downturns or emergencies. Every so often, they will experience a moment of panic—what if one of them got laid off, or this year's bonus didn't come through, or the car needed a major repair?

Overall, they're not satisfied with how they handle their money. They can't figure out where it all goes every month, and they're uneasy they haven't done much to save for retirement or build up an emergency stash. But they hear all the stories on the news about average Americans who are staggering under a mountain of credit card debt, so they figure they must not be doing so bad. After all, they're living within their means, aren't they?

Still, there's that nagging doubt. Maybe they should start putting some money aside each month. The next time they get raises, they vow to enroll in their retirement plan. Then again, retirement is far away and it would be so nice to upgrade the home theatre system.

- The Aha Couple. This couple figured out that the only way they were going to reach their goals was to live below their means. They didn't start out that way. They realized their friends who spent more than they earned were headed for trouble, but that wasn't their own situation. They reasoned that as long as they weren't mired in debt themselves, they were probably doing okay. Then one evening they sat down to figure out how they spent their money. In an "aha" moment, they realized that by shaving a few expenses and making some smarter spending choices, they could free up some money each month to funnel into savings. Some could go into a money market account for a vacation or new car and some could go into retirement plans or IRAs. Suddenly, it all made sense. It wasn't good enough simply to live within their means. In order to reach financial security, they had to spend less than what they made and sock away the difference. Aha!

You may have recognized yourselves as one of those three couples. However, it's more likely you're a hybrid couple. When you think about all the reasons you fell in love with your partner, his or her spending habits probably didn't figure high on the list. One of you may get it and be an "Aha," while the other is still living the "Fun-Fun-Fun" life. Or one of you may feel that "Teetering" is okay for now, while the other is squirreling money away just in case.

Your whole approach to spending may be different as well. You may be a "tracker"—recording each expense in a notebook or entering that day's double latte purchase in Quicken® every night. Or you may be oblivious to day-to-day spending, never balancing your checkbook, letting bills pile up unopened on the kitchen table. As you might expect, the tracker often sticks to a spending plan, and the oblivious spender frequently blows the budget, but it doesn't always work that way.

In any case, if you think agreeing on a vacation spot with your partner is tricky, try meshing different spending styles. The tracker can drive the oblivious spender crazy. *What fun is it to spend money if you agonize over every purchase and second-guess every dollar we spend?* asks the oblivious spender. *Do we always have to plan and discuss, plan and discuss? Loosen up and live a little.*

Meanwhile, the tracker is concerned and frustrated. *Of course we can spend money, but we should know how we spend it. If we need something, we should buy it, but do we really need another kitchen doodad? It's not like either of us cooks. And what's wrong with postponing our ski trip to get better hotel rates? There may still be snow on the ground in April.*

Reaching Money Bliss

Even if you have only recently become a couple, you have probably had at least one conversation about spending money. If you're lucky, the conversation was calm and rational. Many couples, however, have discovered money is a touchy subject—one that can rapidly escalate into accusations and hurt feelings.

After all, money isn't just the cash in your wallet or the balance in your checking account. We often value ourselves, and others, in terms of how much money we have accumulated or how high our salaries are. For most couples, that means there's an imbalance right off the bat because chances are you have chosen different career paths and you earn different salaries.

Then there's the fact that we all have different money backgrounds. Cathy and Mike found out in their goal-setting session that their childhood money experiences were not at all alike. Even children raised in the same home by the same parents will have different attitudes toward money. Think about your own siblings. If you and your partner clash over spending habits, there are several ways to defuse the arguments. You each have to be willing to give it a try and agree not to dredge up past arguments or hurtful words. Here are seven money harmony exercises. Please feel free to try these at home.

1. Recognize your own money personality. The first step is to come to terms with your own relationship with money. Be honest with yourself. Are you happiest when you come out of the mall with a fistful of shopping bags or pick up the check at dinner with friends? Or does sending in a contribution to your IRA make your day? Are you a tracker who gets great satisfaction when

your checkbook balances and the colorful pie charts pop up on the computer screen? Or are you an oblivious spender who revels in recreational shopping? Next time the Sunday paper arrives, check yourself—do you peel the news section off first and dive in, or do you grab the advertising supplements just in case there's some great deal on something you really want, or need?

2. Share your feelings. Just as Mike and Cathy did, talk about your childhood money experiences with your partner. Open up about how your past may influence your current feelings about money. What are your deepest money fears? Are you worried you'll make mistakes investing? Do you squirrel away money because the bag-lady image haunts you? Is spending a reward for good behavior and saving a chore? Or is spending the way you were taught to show your love? If holidays meant a pile of gifts for everyone in the family, it will be hard to hold the line on spending at that time of year. Listen to your partner and talk things over but don't offer advice and, above all, don't judge.

3. Fund the big picture first. Couples often agree on long-term goals and basic values, but they get mired in the day-to-day struggles and lose their focus. Get back to the basics. Try a joint goal-setting session, similar to the one Mike and Cathy had, to identify what's important for both of you. Discuss the big picture together. What do you need to make you feel more secure financially? Are you saving for a house? Is there a special vacation you would both like to take? Then crunch the numbers to figure out how much you'll need to set aside each month to reach those goals. Next, set up automatic payroll deduction or monthly contributions to savings accounts. It's amazing how much stress is relieved when you know your future is being funded. And how much fun it is to take a trip together when you can pay cash from your vacation fund with no post-vacation credit card hangover.

4. Keep some money separate. Sometimes couples argue because they feel their partner is second-guessing every purchase. Just as you need privacy in other parts of your life, you need some private spending money. Each of you should have a "no questions asked" sum of money each month, especially if you pool your money together into one account. The amount will vary

with your circumstances, but even $20 a month means you can have a meal out with friends and not feel guilty that you are jeopardizing the house fund. If each of you has control over a sum of discretionary money, some of those arguments will vanish.

5. Walk in the other person's shoes. If you're a hoarder and your partner's a spender, agree to switch roles for a week or a month. The hoarder can promise to purchase something on impulse or even have a small spending binge. The spender can promise to make an extra deposit to a savings account or open a mutual fund account and make a contribution. If one partner has always paid the bills, have the other partner take over for a few months. This works particularly well when the spender takes over as bookkeeper—as long as the bills get paid. If one of you has sole responsibility for recording expenses on a spreadsheet each month, have the other partner do the data entry. Or, if neither of you has a system for tracking expenses, set one up together.

6. Sharpen your money skills—together. Sometimes arguments get started because you feel uneasy about your ability to handle money. Every spending decision can be stressful if you don't know if you're on track to reach your goals, or you're not sure how much house you can afford, or you don't have a clue how to choose your investments. Consider taking a personal finance course together at a local community college. Or go on the Web and fill out some worksheets and read some articles. I have listed some resources at the end of each chapter. But whatever you choose, do it together. And beware of the freebie seminars presented by local brokers and commissioned planners. Any educational information imparted is just a veneer; the real purpose of these events is to sell products.

7. Bring in a neutral party. Sometimes even with the best intentions it's hard to work things out on your own. It may help to get an unbiased second opinion on your spending situation. A competent, objective financial planner whom you both trust can help you define your goals and lay out a strategy to meet them. A planner can help you identify problems and suggest ways to deal with them. If your money clashes have deteriorated to the point that you can't have a calm discussion about spending, consider consulting a psychotherapist who specializes in couples and finances.

Dump the Budget; Get a Spending Plan

It's time to get to the nitty-gritty of cash flow. But instead of going through the steps of setting up a budget, I'm going to show you how to prepare a spending plan. To-may-to, to-mah-to; budget, spending plan. Is there really any difference? I think there is.

When I say the word "budget" to my clients, they immediately think of cutting back, reducing expenses, doing without. I have even had new clients tell me they postponed hiring me until they had taken a big vacation or bought a new car because they figured I would put them on a strict budget. It's sort of the reverse of straightening up the house before the cleaning lady arrives.

Budget is a negative word, suggesting scrimping and belt-tightening. Spending plan, on the other hand, is a positive term because it focuses on how you spend your money, not how you cut back. When you prepare a spending plan, you start with your values and goals. Those are your guiding stars.

Think of a world in which you had an infinite supply of money. You wouldn't need a plan because you could spend as much as you wanted on whatever you wanted. But that's not the way the world works. So we start by identifying the things that are important to us and then we make trade-offs. We keep the car another year so we can take a family vacation because time away together is valuable and our old car can last a while longer. If a professional, up-to-date wardrobe is essential to your job, you may cook at home more and eat out less. If charitable giving is more important to your family than expensive holiday gifts, direct your dollars accordingly. Your spending should simply be a reflection of your values. Focus on how you *spend* your money, not where you scrimp.

You've probably noticed how friends or relatives who make about the same amount of money seem to spend it in very different ways. If there's no accounting for taste, there's also no accounting for how people spend their money. I have worked with couples who are content driving a sedan they've owned for a decade even though they could afford a new car every couple of years. They'd rather give generously to charity or take a nice vacation each year.

Spending plans are definitely not one-size-fits-all. The key is to agree with your partner on the broad areas of spending and make sure your plan is consistent with what's important to you both. So step one in preparing a spending plan is to go through the goal-setting exercise in the previous chapter. Then review the worksheet at the end of this chapter and mark each of the categories with an A, B, or C. An A means a basic subsistence expense—rent, electricity, water gasoline, health insurance, and so on. Mark a B next to each expense that isn't absolutely necessary for keeping body and soul together but is important for the way you both want to lead your lives. Cs are reserved for nice-to-have items. Cable, cell phones, lunch out, and health club dues may be Bs for some people and Cs for others. A few categories may end up with more than one letter next to them. You may mark an A and a C next to clothing because the basics are essential and the new leather jacket you've been eyeing is a nice-to-have. Or groceries might be both an A and a B expense because gourmet cooking is a passion, and expensive ingredients push your food bill above what the basics cost. Always include a row for "no questions asked" money for each of you.

Reconstructing the Past

The next step is to figure out how you're currently spending your money so you can judge how close a fit there is between your dreams and reality. Couples who know how they spend their money each month tend to be more successful at meeting their financial goals than those who don't. If you already track your expenses on personal finance software or a spreadsheet, go to the head of the class. If you're like most of us, you may know how much you pay for some fixed expenses like rent or mortgage, and have a vague notion of your monthly utility bills or grocery expenses, but very little idea of how much you spent on clothes or vacations or gifts last year.

Reconstructing the last 12 months of spending sounds daunting, but I recommend that you try it. If you tend to put everything on a credit card (that you pay off each month, ideally) or flash your debit card for most expenses, your job will be a lot easier. Year-end spending summaries issued by some credit card companies are a great help.

Here's how to figure out what you've spent:

(1) Gather all your checkbook registers, bank statements, and credit card statements for the past 12 months. Divide them into 12 monthly stacks. (An accordion file with monthly dividers might help.)

(2) Pick a tool to help you sort and analyze the data. Programs like Quicken® or Microsoft Money® are terrific, but if you've never used

them, you might try to use a low-tech way to enter the old data and save the software for your new plan. It's too tempting to get bogged down with setup issues at this stage. Besides, the key to using those programs effectively is to properly identify the categories—the "buckets" into which each expense goes. It's easier to figure out your buckets when you have some spending history in front of you.

A notebook-and-pencil system can work, although you may grow weary of adding up numbers. I have found that a spreadsheet does the trick nicely. (For an example, see Table 4.1).

(3) Go through your check registers and credit card statements month by month and record each expense in the appropriate column. Since you're doing this together, one can read the month and expense and one can enter the data. Add up all the columns and rows.

(4) Do a reality check. Compare your monthly expenses to your monthly take-home pay. If your take-home pay equals $50,000 a year and your expenses total $40,000, either you have $10,000 stashed away in a forgotten coffee can or you haven't accounted for everything. Maybe you neglected to add in a few trips to the ATM, or forgot to include expenses charged to a store or gas credit card that you only use occasionally. On the other hand, if your expenses are higher than your take-home pay, you dipped into savings, received gifts, or added to credit cards to cover the difference.

If you frequently pay with cash, you may end up with a chunk of miscellaneous expenses the first time through. It's good to have a general idea of how you spend your cash, but accounting for every penny is a drag. Instead, keep careful track for a month so you get a feel for your typical expenditures—$20 a week for lunches, $2 a day for coffee, $1 a day for a newspaper, and so on. Then just multiply times 12 to get an annual cash benchmark.

Now you have a spending history. Before we go to the next step, let's check in with Mike and Cathy. Their homework assignment was to go through the steps I just described. Let's see how well they reconstructed their spending history.

"That was some assignment you gave us," said Mike. "The only thing that saved us was that Cathy had put most of the old credit card and bank statements in the filing system you gave us."

"One of our New Year's resolutions last year was to start entering everything in Quicken®," said Cathy, "but that only lasted a few months. It would have been a lot easier if we had kept it up."

Table 4.1: Yearly Expenses

Category	Frequency	Pmt	Jan	Feb	Mar	Apr	May	Jun	Jul	Aug	Sep	Oct	Nov	Dec	Total
Rent	Monthly	EFT*	750	750	750	750	750	750	750	750	750	750	750	750	9000
Groceries	Monthly	Check	24	120											
			78	12											
			112	62											
			42	14											
			256	208											
Car Insurance	Semi-Annually	Check				460						460			960

*EFT = Electronic fund transfer. For example, rent is withdrawn from your checking account automatically each month.

"Before you show me the numbers," I said, "let me ask you a basic question. Do you think you need to change anything? In other words, if you both kept spending the way you're spending, would you be pretty happy?"

"No," said Cathy immediately. "I think too much money slips through our fingers and we're not saving enough."

"I think we do all right," said Mike. "Once Cathy finishes her degree and starts working full time, we can start saving more."

"That's true, but our spending always seems to go up when our income increases. I don't think we pay enough attention to how we spend our money," said Cathy. "We'll head out to the hardware store to pick up some picture hangers, and we'll walk out with a new lamp and a drill. Or we'll go to the movie theatre in the mall and end up buying a couple of books, a few CDs, have some coffee, and by the time we've paid for the movie and popcorn, we've had a $100 night out."

"Where's your sense of fun and spontaneity?" asked Mike. "Can't we just go out to the movies once in a while and not worry about the budget?"

"I like going to the movies and to the mall," said Cathy, "but I tend to get buyer's remorse when we unpack the shopping bags."

"It sounds like some tweaking might be in order," I said. "Were there any surprises when you added up the numbers?"

"I can't believe how much we spend on gifts," said Mike. "I know we're pretty generous with our families, but where did all the rest of the money go?"

"I had forgotten how many friends got married or had babies or both," said Cathy, "and we can't show up empty-handed at a wedding or baby shower."

"I also noticed your dry cleaning bills were bigger than my clothes budget some months," said Mike.

"I can't wear khakis and golf shirts every day the way you do," said Cathy.

"The discretionary items are the hardest to get a handle on," I said. "Couples are often amazed at how much money goes out the door—or on the credit cards—for gifts, entertainment and dinners out.

"Now that you know how you spent your money last year, let's see how you prioritized your spending into A, B, and C categories."

"I've got the list right here," said Mike. "Our essential expenses— the ones on the A list—are:

- Rent
- Electricity, gas, and water
- Gasoline and car repairs
- Groceries
- Health insurance
- Car and renter's insurance
- Car payments
- Student loan payments
- Credit card payments
- Discretionary spending money for each of us

Our B items—the ones we want to keep in the budget even though they're not absolutely essential—are:

- Cell phones
- Cable
- Mike's 401(k) savings
- Online Internet service

The C stuff—the extras—are:

- Health club
- Parking—because I can park for free if I walk several blocks to the office
- Books and newspapers—we can use the library or go on line.

"We had a bunch of expenses that fit in a couple of categories," continued Mike. "We thought clothes, haircuts, and our out-of-pocket medical expenses were A/B expenses. We'll always spend something in these categories each year, but the question is, how much? I'm thinking about getting braces, so that would really add to our medical expenses."

"We had a lot of B-C categories, too," said Cathy, "and that's where things got interesting. We agreed that these expenses make our lives better, but we didn't always see eye-to-eye on how much we should be spending."

"I didn't expect your spending habits to be identical," I said. "You would be a very odd couple if that were the case. Let's see the B-C list.

These are items on the bubble. You'd like to keep them in the budget, but you don't know how high a priority to assign to them. Is that a fair description?"

"That's the way we saw them," said Cathy, "and it's a long list."

- Home furnishings
- Eating out
- Vacations
- Gifts
- Charitable contributions
- Saving for a home
- Building up an emergency fund.

"Let's pick a couple of these categories and talk about why they're in the B-C list," I said. "How about starting with "Saving for a home"? You both said you wanted to buy a home in the next five years, so shouldn't that be a B expense?"

"We put it on the B-C list because we don't agree how much to save," said Cathy. "I'm really anxious to get out of our apartment, so I'd like to put a bunch of money in a house account every month. Mike isn't in such a rush, right?"

"Sure, I'd like to have our own house," said Mike, "but I don't see it happening for a while. I don't know what we would cut out to free up more money for the house fund. We're spending just about everything we make, except for my 401(k) contributions. Cathy's only working part time while she's in school. I say we wait until Cathy gets her MBA before worrying too much about the house."

"We're scheduled to talk about home and car purchases in an upcoming meeting," I said, "so let's defer that topic. We'll figure out how much house you can afford and how to save for it. Let's look at another B-C category, like eating out."

"We like to eat out," said Cathy, "especially if it's at the end of a long day or we're getting together with friends. But it seems like a logical place to cut back."

"How often do you go out each month?" I asked.

"We probably go out for dinner on our own twice a week," said Mike, "and we meet up with friends about once a week. We like to go to a restaurant and then to a movie or concert or sometimes to a club."

"It really adds up," said Cathy, "especially if we go to a nice restaurant."

"One of the tricks to coming up with a realistic spending plan is to find ways to reduce spending without feeling deprived," I said. "What if you changed the routine a bit and decided you and your friends would all go out to a nice restaurant once or twice a month, and a couple of times a month you'd eat at someone's apartment or home? You could take turns hosting an informal dinner or you could do potluck."

"Now there's a word from my parent's era," said Mike. "I'm not sure potlucks would work with our friends. We're not great cooks."

"It doesn't have to be coq au vin," I said. "The host couple could make something simple, like pasta, and the other couples could bring bread, salad, wine, and dessert. Trust me—it can be fun as well as profitable. I'll bet each couple could save $100 a month.

"Even if you got Chinese take-out occasionally, you'd save money compared to going to a restaurant. Some of my clients have really gotten into this eat-at-home trend. They have theme dinners and experiment with new recipes. One group even took a couple of cooking lessons together at a local restaurant. Then when you do go out to a restaurant, you can splurge a little."

"I guess that might work," said Mike slowly. "Peter just got a gas grill, and he's been talking about his great rib recipes."

"We'll have to organize these dinners ahead, so it will take some extra time," said Cathy, "although come to think of it, we wasted a lot of time last weekend phoning back and forth just to decide on a restaurant."

"The key is to substitute another fun activity for one you are cutting out," I said. "If your new activity is more of a chore, you won't stick with it even if you are saving money."

"I'm beginning to see how this works," said Mike. "Let's talk about our gift budget."

"Good choice," I said. "I think you both mentioned you were surprised at the amount you're currently spending. Can you think of some ways you could squeeze a few extra dollars out of that category?"

"I don't think we can scrimp on wedding gifts for our friends," said Cathy. "They gave us nice gifts when we got married. I wouldn't mind cutting back on birthday presents for friends, though. It gets expensive and sometimes it's a pain to shop for that special gift."

"Talk to your friends," I said. "They might be very receptive to the idea of scaling back. After all, they're saving for houses and babies and paying back student loans, too. You might also talk to your families. Instead of getting individual gifts for everyone, you might give family presents—like a gift certificate for a local restaurant."

"When we were children, my mom asked us to give her certificates for gifts of time, as she called them, instead of buying presents for her," said Cathy. "We would write out promises to clean out the garage or weed her garden. I thought it was pretty corny."

"Sometimes corny works," I said. "You could offer to babysit for friends with a new baby. When I had young children, that was one of the best gifts I received. Keep the booties—give me a night out with my husband. I think you could come up with some terrific ideas.

"Those are just some suggestions of how you might shave your spending in a few categories. Just don't try to tackle everything on your list immediately. Most people can't stick to a diet if they cut out every one of their favorite foods. It's the same way with spending. If you focus on a couple of categories each year, you'll do just fine."

"I feel like I have to rethink a lot of my spending habits," said Cathy. "It's almost like some of my spending is on automatic pilot. We buy gifts for everyone in the family each year because we've always done it that way. There are other ways to celebrate holidays and show we care."

"Don't get mushy on me now," said Mike. "But I see what you mean."

"If you think about the messages we get everyday from newspapers, magazines, TV, and radio," I said, "it's all about spending. Get the new and improved doodad, save by buying, prices have never been lower. Think about the last time you heard the media encouraging you to save and invest your money."

"Well, there are a lot of ads now for brokerage firms and banks," said Mike.

"You're right," I said, "but most of those ads are not really about saving and investing. They're more about moving the money you have already saved to firms or advisors who can sell you products and reap commissions. Occasionally, you'll hear an ad encouraging individuals to fund their IRAs or open a savings account. But the spend-spend-spend blare is deafening."

"The advertising supplements in the Sunday paper are heavier than the news sections," said Cathy. "Sometimes I yearn for simpler times."

"There are organizations that advocate a simpler life style," I said. "If you're interested in learning more, a good place to start is the book

Your Money or Your Life by Joe Dominguez and Vicki Robin. You don't have to start wearing berry-dyed shirts or eat lentils every day to make your life a little less costly and a bit simpler."

"Thanks," said Cathy. "I may look into that. May I ask a question about another category? We put discretionary spending money on our A list. Although we make a lot of spending decisions together, we keep separate accounts so we already have no-questions-asked money—it's whatever is left over after paying our joint expenses and individual bills."

"Great timing, Cathy," I said. "The question of how you handle your accounts is a perfect segue to our next topic."

One Account, Two Accounts, Three Accounts, More

There are lots of ways to organize your money, and how you do it can influence your spending. According to the 1950s sitcoms, the husband would bring home his paycheck and either the wife would take over from there and pay all the bills or the husband would control the money and dole out an allowance to his wife for household expenses. There was one source of income and one account, so there was just one pool of money.

Times have changed. Couples often have two incomes, their own retirement and savings accounts, some joint expenses, and some individual expenses. There are several different ways couples can choose to handle their money.

Some couples still pool their incomes and pay all their expenses out of a single joint checking account. Usually one partner is the keeper of the checkbook and pays the bills. The other partner uses an ATM card to get cash and may have a blank check stuck in a wallet for emergencies. The couple may also have a joint credit card account, with individual cards. Mike and Cathy, however, are typical of many young couples, keeping more than one account.

"It would be nice to have just one checkbook to balance," said Mike, "but I know I would forget to tell Cathy when I took cash out of the account."

"You have just identified both a plus and a minus of the one-checkbook approach," I said. "Some couples feel a strong sense of partnership with this system—what's mine is ours and what's yours is ours. It's tricky, however, to designate discretionary money for each of you unless you set aside some cash each month. And one partner gets to duck the responsibility of paying bills unless you rotate the checkbook. There are other minuses to this system."

"I can think of one," said Cathy. "I trust Mike absolutely, of course, but if we both dumped our money into one checking account, one of us could empty out the account pretty easily."

"That's right," I said. "Or if one of you defaulted on a loan, assets you own jointly might be vulnerable."

"So if one of us skipped out on a debt, our joint checking account could get nabbed?" asked Mike. "I hadn't thought of that. "

"I mentioned it only as something else to keep in mind when you pick a system," I said. "You said you keep separate checking accounts. How does that work?"

"We each have a credit card as well as our own checking account," said Cathy. "Mike makes more money than I do, so he pays the rent and the utilities. I pay for groceries and most other household expenses. We aim for about a 75-25 split. At the end of the month, I add up all the bills I've paid. If I've paid more than about 25 percent of our total expenses, Mike writes me a check."

"Cathy's got things working like a well-oiled machine," said Mike. "I just write a check when Cathy tells me to."

"You agreed to this system, Mike," said Cathy. Anyway, we each pay our own expenses such as clothes, gas, car repairs, haircuts, and lunches."

"How do you pay for big expenses like vacations?" I asked.

"We try to split the big stuff 75-25 as well," said Cathy. "When we go on vacation, Mike might pay for the airfare and hotel and I'll pay for meals and incidentals, for example."

"There are several advantages of paying for things the way you two do," I said. "You share expenses proportionally to your income, which is usually the fairest way. You each have discretionary money and you share bill-paying responsibility, although it sounds like Cathy keeps track of who pays for what. By keeping separate accounts, you are also each building your own credit history. Is there anything that doesn't work well?"

"Going out for dinner or to the movies can get complicated," said Mike. "We don't like splitting the bill in the restaurant so we alternate paying, but then we have to keep track of who paid last."

"And I get tired of adding everything up each month to see if we hit our target split," said Cathy. "Plus, remember when the vacuum cleaner broke last month, Mike? You ended up paying for a new one, and I still owe you for my share."

"Have you thought about keeping your individual accounts and opening a joint household checking account?" I asked. "You could estimate how much you typically spend on shared expenses each month. If you each contribute your proportional share and then pay household and entertainment expenses out of that account, you won't need to keep track of who paid for what. Of course, the downside is someone will have to agree to make sure the household bills get paid. To make the job easier, you can arrange to have your utilities and rent deducted automatically from your account or set up electronic bill paying with your bank."

"I like the idea of having a household account," said Cathy, "especially when we buy a house and have more expenses. We could give it a try, Mike."

"Sure," said Mike. "As long as we keep our individual accounts. I'll look into electronic bill paying so we don't have to write so many checks."

"Try it a few months and let me know how it's working," I said. "That takes care of checking, but what about savings accounts? Retirement accounts like 401(k) plans and IRAs are held in individual names, of course, but you may wish to open a joint money market account for your house fund and other big-ticket items. If you set up automatic monthly deposits from each of your checking accounts, it will make saving a lot simpler."

Your Emergency Stash

We've mentioned how important it is to keep some cash set aside, but how much is enough?

There are several reasons to hold cash. First, you need it for making monthly transactions, like paying your rent and buying groceries. That's the money in your checking account. Next, you need to earmark some cash for planned expenses that don't happen every month, like a vacation or holiday gifts or quarterly estimated taxes. If you have some money to invest, you might park it in a savings account while you're researching your investment choices. Finally, you should stash some emergency cash aside for unexpected events like a big car repair, or a hiccup in business income due to a late payment, for example.

The rule of thumb is to keep three to six months' worth of living expenses in an emergency fund. If you and your partner have stable jobs and steady income, three months' worth should be enough.

I recommend putting about half of your emergency fund in a very safe and readily accessible place like a bank or money market account. A credit union account is also a good option, and you're likely to earn slightly more interest there than at a bank.

The other half of your emergency fund can be parked in something that is still relatively safe but will earn more interest than a savings account. Mutual funds that invest in short-term bonds fit the bill nicely. Look for a fund offered by a no-load mutual fund company that offers a free checkbook. The Vanguard Short-Term Bond Index fund and the Vanguard Short-Term Federal Bond fund (*www.vanguard.com*) are both excellent choices if you can meet the $3000 minimum investment. TIAA-CREF (*www.tiaa-cref.com*) and T. Rowe Price (*www.troweprice. com*) have short-term bond funds as well, and you can open an account for no minimum initial purchase as long as you set up automatic contributions of at least $50 a month.

Short-term CDs and savings bonds are also good choices. They are super-safe, although they aren't as flexible as bond funds because you can't dip in and out of them as easily.

Focus on stability and easy access when choosing places for your emergency money. The stock market is not a good place because it's too volatile. If you stick to bank and money market accounts, CDs, savings bonds, and short-term bond funds, you won't make a fortune on your emergency cash, but it will be there when you need it.

"How much emergency cash do you recommend that we keep?" asked Cathy.

"I recommend that you keep three months' worth of living expenses in a safe place like a credit union account," I said. "Because you're self employed, Cathy, you'll need to set aside additional money to pay your quarterly taxes, fund your retirement account, and cover your expenses if you have a lean month.

"Let's start with your emergency fund. Based on the numbers you put together for this meeting, it looks like you spend about $2600 a month after taxes, excluding 401(k) contributions and other discretionary items. Three months' worth would be about $8000."

"We're a long way away from that," said Mike.

"You could start regular contributions to a joint credit union account until you get to about $4000—half your $8000 goal," I said. "If you could add about $160 a month and earn 2.5 percent, you'd reach $4000 in a couple of years. That's not bad. Following your 75-25 split rule, Mike, your share would be $120 a month, and Cathy's would be $40."

"You said I also have to build up my own account," Cathy said.

"That's right. I recommend self-employed individuals deposit one-third of their profit each month in a savings or money market account with check-writing privileges. Every quarter, you can write checks from that account to pay your taxes and make a contribution to your IRA," I said. "That should also give you a cushion to help smooth out your cash flow."

"So every month after I pay expenses, I should put two-thirds in my regular checking account and one-third in my credit union savings account?" asked Cathy.

"That's the idea. Set it up the way that's most convenient for you," I said. "The ability to make electronic transfers between accounts will make it a lot easier."

"There's another cash management tip I'd like to mention," I said. "It's a good idea to set aside some money regularly for expenses that don't hit each month, like vacations and gifts. Figure out how much you spend per year on these expenses and put aside one-twelfth of the total each month."

"This sounds like a Christmas Club account," said Cathy. "I remember my grandma had one at her bank. She'd put in a little bit each month, and then pay for her holiday bills out of that account. She was always so proud of it."

"It's the same principle," I agreed. "Your vacations and holidays will be much more relaxing if you have saved ahead of time. It also easier to stay on budget."

"Don't tell me we need another account," said Mike.

"You can combine your emergency account and your vacation/gift account. The joint savings account you plan to set up at the credit union would work fine," I said. "You will get nickeled and dimed on bank fees if you open too many accounts. Just remember how much of the account is earmarked for emergency expenses."

Putting It All Together

"If we adjust a few numbers in your spending plan, we can free up some money from entertainment and gifts so you can start building a joint emergency fund and Cathy can contribute to her retirement plan. Now we have a spreadsheet with two columns—the left-hand side shows what you spent last year and the right-hand side is a first draft of a spending plan for this year. (See Figure 4-1.)

"This is only the beginning, though. After you two have a chance to review your spending categories, you can come up with a working spending plan. Then you can translate the annual spending plan into a monthly plan.

"I didn't include saving for a house in this draft, so that will have to be incorporated later. You'll probably tweak your spending plan several times over the next few years."

"I know you said the way we spend our money is a very personal decision," said Cathy, "but I'm still curious if we're spending about the right amounts in the right categories. Aren't there some rules of thumb, like you shouldn't spend more than a certain percentage of your income on groceries or rent?"

"The Bureau of Labor Statistics does a survey of consumer spending and publishes the results on their Web site at *www.bls.gov*," I said. "You can compare your spending with averages for people in your age range or income level."

Tracking Your Spending

Once you have a spending plan in place, what's the best way to make sure you're sticking to it?

There are several ways you can track your income and spending. Software programs like Quicken® and Microsoft Money® are great because you can also balance your accounts and do some analysis of your spending habits. It takes a bit of time to set things up, but once you do, the month-to-month updating should not be difficult. You can download bank and credit card statements right into personal finance software.

The lists of categories—called the chart of accounts—that come preloaded into the programs are a good starting point, but you will

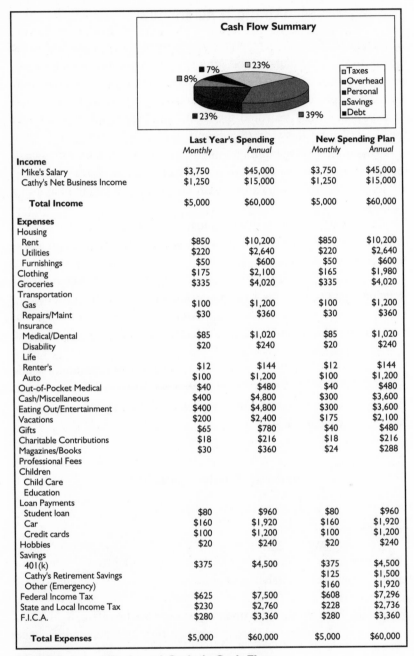

	Last Year's Spending		New Spending Plan	
	Monthly	*Annual*	*Monthly*	*Annual*
Income				
Mike's Salary	$3,750	$45,000	$3,750	$45,000
Cathy's Net Business Income	$1,250	$15,000	$1,250	$15,000
Total Income	$5,000	$60,000	$5,000	$60,000
Expenses				
Housing				
Rent	$850	$10,200	$850	$10,200
Utilities	$220	$2,640	$220	$2,640
Furnishings	$50	$600	$50	$600
Clothing	$175	$2,100	$165	$1,980
Groceries	$335	$4,020	$335	$4,020
Transportation				
Gas	$100	$1,200	$100	$1,200
Repairs/Maint	$30	$360	$30	$360
Insurance				
Medical/Dental	$85	$1,020	$85	$1,020
Disability	$20	$240	$20	$240
Life				
Renter's	$12	$144	$12	$144
Auto	$100	$1,200	$100	$1,200
Out-of-Pocket Medical	$40	$480	$40	$480
Cash/Miscellaneous	$400	$4,800	$300	$3,600
Eating Out/Entertainment	$400	$4,800	$300	$3,600
Vacations	$200	$2,400	$175	$2,100
Gifts	$65	$780	$40	$480
Charitable Contributions	$18	$216	$18	$216
Magazines/Books	$30	$360	$24	$288
Professional Fees				
Children				
Child Care				
Education				
Loan Payments				
Student loan	$80	$960	$80	$960
Car	$160	$1,920	$160	$1,920
Credit cards	$100	$1,200	$100	$1,200
Hobbies	$20	$240	$20	$240
Savings				
401(k)	$375	$4,500	$375	$4,500
Cathy's Retirement Savings			$125	$1,500
Other (Emergency)			$160	$1,920
Federal Income Tax	$625	$7,500	$608	$7,296
State and Local Income Tax	$230	$2,760	$228	$2,736
F.I.C.A.	$280	$3,360	$280	$3,360
Total Expenses	$5,000	$60,000	$5,000	$60,000

FIGURE 4-1   **Mike's and Cathy's Cash Flow**

probably add or subtract some categories to match your spending plan. The key to using those programs is to consistently categorize your expenses. If one month you put eating out expenses under "Dining" and the next month you put them under "Entertainment," you won't have a good idea of how much you spend in restaurants during the year. Also, make sure you split out credit card statements or big trips to warehouse stores among the different categories. You don't have to split each grocery bill into household cleaning products, food, and paper supplies—you'll drive yourself nuts. But if you buy a new DVD player and groceries at one store, don't just lump the whole bill in groceries.

Of course, you can always set up your own spreadsheet, although it's more difficult to balance your accounts that way. Some people feel more comfortable with a pencil-and-paper system, especially at the beginning. You can purchase a blank budget book in an office supplies store that already has category listings preprinted. Each day or week, you record how you spent your money in each category and then add it up each month. That system can work for a while, but it's a lot of writing and adding.

A relatively new Web-based program you might want to take a look at is called Mvelopes. It's based on the system some of our parents or grandparents used when they divided up their cash each month into a set of envelopes, each with a separate category. The rent money went into the rent envelope, the grocery money went into another envelope, and so on. When the envelope was empty, you just stopped spending on that category, or you took money from another envelope. Mvelopes uses the same principle, but the envelopes are electronic. You can also pay your bills electronically with this system.

Doing your homework and gathering data on how you spent your money last year makes it much easier to put together a spending plan. Then you'll need to tweak your new spending plan to adjust for changes in your personal or financial situation. Next time we'll talk about credit and debt.

What Cathy and Mike Have Learned

1. Cash flow is the heart of your financial plan.
2. The first step in developing a spending plan is to reconstruct your spending for the past 12 months.

The Other Side of the Equation

When we talk about cash flow, we zero in on spending, but we shouldn't neglect the income side. After all, there are two ways to improve your cash flow—control expenses and increase income. Over your lifetime, the second will be more significant.

There are several ways to increase your income. Developing your human capital by getting an advanced degree or taking specialized courses is one way. Working with a mentor, applying for advanced positions within your current company or at a new firm, and negotiating raises are other ways to boost your income. Don't be afraid to set aggressive goals and then figure out a path to those goals.

3. Some expenses are essential, some are important for your quality of life, and some are nice-to-haves.

4. Whittling down expenses in a few categories can free up extra cash for other goals. Make sure you don't feel deprived or you won't stick to your plan.

5. An emergency fund should be kept in a safe, liquid account.

6. Once a spending plan is in place, track actual spending with personal finance software, a spreadsheet, or even pen and pencil.

Cathy's and Mike's Recommendations

1. Develop ways to creatively reduce eating out and gift expenses. Consider eating in with friends occasionally and talking to your family about reducing gifts at holidays.

2. Consider opening a joint checking account for household expenses.

3. Start automatic contributions into a credit union savings account to build up an emergency fund.

4. Choose a method to track your spending.

5. Adjust your spending plan as necessary.

Your Homework

1. Figure out your and your partner's spending styles.

2. If you're fighting about money, try some of the suggestions listed earlier in the chapter.

3. Develop your own cash flow strategy by reconstructing your last year's spending. Use the A, B, and C system to identify areas that need attention, and draft and track a spending plan.

4. Review your system of managing your money to see if it's working for you. Do you need to add or consolidate bank accounts?

5. Build an adequate emergency fund.

6. Don't neglect your human capital.

Resources

1. *www.bls.gov* for a comparison of how others spend their money.

2. *www.quicken.com*, *www.microsoft.com/money*, and *www.mve lopes.com* for ways to track your spending.

3. Mellan, Olivia, *Money Harmony: Resolving Money Conflicts in Your Life and Your Relationships*, Walker & Co., 1995 and *Overcoming Spending*, Walker & Co., 1997.

4. Hayden, Ruth, *For Richer, Not Poorer—The Money Book for Couples*, Health Communications, 1999.

5. Dominguez, Joe and Robin, Vicki, *Your Money or Your Life*, Penguin, 1999.

5

Borrowing Wisely

W e get mixed messages every day—get skinny but try this fabulous chocolate, have fun but keep your nose to the grindstone—but some of the most confusing messages are about credit and debt. The buzz is everywhere that Americans are overloaded with debt and millions have filed for bankruptcy, but there doesn't seem to be any shortage of companies willing to lend us more money. We hear stories of couples who are barely staying afloat after borrowing thousands of dollars, yet credit card companies continue to stuff our mailboxes with applications, and stores keep inventing new ways for us to buy now and pay much later. If we're so immersed in debt, why are we offered so many opportunities to get in even deeper? Has the story been blown out of proportion?

The story is real—personal debt is a serious problem, and overborrowing is dragging many young couples further and further away from financial security. If a chunk of your paycheck goes to pay off stuff you bought months or years ago, it will be hard to fund your retirement accounts or save for your next purchases. Trying to reach your financial goals when you're overloaded with debt is like trying to win a horse race with jolly Old King Cole in the saddle.

The choices you make with your partner about when and how much to borrow are some of the most important financial decisions you'll make together. If you're already struggling, it's time to face your debt and work out a plan to deal with it. If you're just getting started together, it's the perfect time to set some ground rules about when to borrow and when to pay cash.

You may be surprised, but I am not advocating a debt-free existence. Paying off debt was the number-one goal for many of our older relatives. Families had mortgage-burning parties when they made their last house payment. But times have changed and it's not only hard to live debt-free, it isn't necessarily the smartest thing to do. Some debt can push you closer to your goals while other debt just drags you down. The trick is knowing which is which.

First, let's review the basics. When banks and stores and car dealerships extend credit, they're making it possible for us to buy things even though we don't have the cash in hand. When we accept their credit, we get to drive a car or take a vacation or become a homeowner before we've saved the money to pay for them. Creditors let us enjoy now and pay later.

Of course, the privilege of accelerated consumption comes at a price: the interest you pay for the use of someone else's money. Sometimes it makes sense to pay that price, and sometimes it doesn't. Some debt is good and some is bad.

Good debt finances things that grow in value and last longer than the debt. Home mortgages and student loans are the best examples of good debt because they finance appreciating assets—your home and your human capital. If we couldn't go to college until we had saved up four or five years' worth of tuition and room and board, most of us would get no further than high school. Only the very wealthiest would be able to afford college, much less medical or law school, and because they had the most education, they would command the highest salaries. The gap between rich and poor would grow wider.

When you get a college education, you reap the return on that investment for years. Student loans help you get your education while you're still young. The sooner you have your diploma, the sooner you'll enjoy the benefits of your degree. Analysis of U.S. Census data has shown that individuals with bachelor's degrees make twice as much money, on average, as high school graduates and four times more than those who didn't finish high school. Workers with advanced degrees earn even more.

Mortgages are also good debt. Without access to a mortgage, most of us would never own a home. We would be lifelong renters, never building equity, never controlling the asset we live in. If you saved $300 a month in an account earning 5-percent interest, it would take you almost five years to accumulate $20,000—enough to put 15 percent down on a $134,000 house. If you had to save the full purchase price, it would take 21 years, and that's assuming the price of the house never increased. If you factored in inflation, you would have to start saving for your house as soon as you got out of school and, if you were lucky, you could buy the house just about the time you qualified for Social Security. You'd be paying rent all your life just so you could buy your retirement home. Mortgages let us buy a home even though we've only saved a small portion of the cost.

And here's the icing on the cake—student loans and home mortgages carry some of the lowest interest rates of any debt around. Plus, home mortgage interest—and, in some instances, student loan interest—is tax deductible, and you can stretch out repayment for decades, if you like. Lenders offer more favorable terms on home mortgages and education loans partly because they know they have a good thing going. Your mortgage is guaranteed by the house, and most homes increase in value during the term of the mortgage. Companies offering student loans know college-educated people tend to earn more, so there's a better chance the lenders will get their money back.

Then there's bad debt. When you take a trip to the Bahamas, charge it to your credit card, and pay off the card over the next three years, you've incurred bad debt. As a rule, any time the debt lasts longer than the item or service purchased, it's bad debt. Most consumer debt is bad because dinners out and stereo equipment and jeans aren't worth much after you've bought them, used them, or consumed them. When you finance consumer purchases with credit card debt, you're living above your means. You're buying things you can't afford, and by the time you pay for them, most or all of their value is gone.

Car loans fall somewhere in the middle of the good-bad debt continuum. Most of us would not be able to purchase a car without a loan, and unless you live in a big city with good public transportation, a car may be the only viable way to travel to work. Yet a car is definitely a depreciating asset.

When borrowing for a car, it's wise to sign up for a loan that lasts at least two fewer years than the time you expect to own the car. Once the loan is paid off, if you accumulate those extra payments in a savings or money market account, you'll need to borrow less the next time you buy a car. By the time you are on your fourth or fifth car, you should be able to pay cash.

So those are the basics—good, bad, and not-so-bad debt. But what if you and your partner have very different ideas about debt? You may have an aversion to debt, and your partner might be more of a "live-for-today-worry-about-paying-tomorrow" sort.

Your attitudes toward credit and debt, of course, are very closely linked to your attitudes about spending. The big spender is also likely to be the big debtor. How do you mesh different attitudes, and when do your partner's habits affect your ability to spend and save? Let's tick down the various types of borrowing available to you and see how you and your partner can manage your credit wisely, together. Then we'll get together with Cathy and Mike to work out a strategy for handling their debt.

Credit Cards

Credit card debt is widespread and very expensive. The studies are all over the map, but it has been estimated that Americans carry an average of $8000 of credit card debt. If that doesn't sound like a lot, it should. If the interest rate on your card is 15 percent and you're making payments of $150 a month, it will take seven-and-a-half years (and over $5300 in interest) to pay off the $8000 balance. The $2000 vacation you put on the credit card really cost you over $3300, and that great leather jacket you bought on sale for $175 may not seem like such a bargain at its true price of almost $300.

Seven-and-a-half years is a very long time to pay off a credit card, but if you cut up your cards and you faithfully make your payments, you will eventually be free of credit card debt. For many people, however, that's not how it works. As the debt is paid off, the amount of available credit increases and the tendency to overspend takes over. You may know the syndrome—write a check for $150 to the credit card company and then charge another $200 on the card. You're not treading water; you're getting dragged under.

Credit card debt is just about the worst kind of debt. The interest rates are high, it's usually used to finance things that are worth less or are even gone by the time the bill arrives, it's very easy to accumulate, and the interest isn't tax deductible.

Let's say you're counting on a bonus to pay off your credit card. If you owe $8000, you'd better wish for a $13,000 bonus because that's what you'll need in order to end up with $8000 after taxes. Let's cast it in a more positive light. If you have been making $300 monthly payments on your credit card debt and you pay it all off, you have just given yourself a $6000 a year raise! That's how much of your salary, including taxes, was being siphoned off to meet the monthly payments.

Despite all the negatives associated with credit cards, there are some times when charging your purchase makes sense. Here's a list of credit card uses—some make sense and some don't.

1. In lieu of an emergency fund. It's much better to stash away some money in a true emergency fund or even set up a personal loan with a credit union than rely on credit cards to bail you out. On the other hand, if you haven't had a chance to build up a savings account or the emergency is severe enough to deplete your stash, your credit cards might be a temporary lifeline.

2. To pay for things purchased by phone or on-line. It's often hard to recover your money if you return an item paid for by check or money order, or never receive the item. If you put the purchase on your credit card, you have more leverage because you can refuse to pay until the dispute is resolved.

3. To build up a credit history. This is a good use—if you pay off the balance in full each month.

4. To rent a car. It's hard to rent a car without a credit card.

5. To access some cash for a hot investment. You guessed it—this is a bad use of credit cards.

6. To rack up perks like frequent flier miles. This strategy only makes sense if you pay off your balance in full each month. Otherwise, the finance charges cancel out the perks. You have to charge about $30,000 to get a free airline ticket worth about $300. If you carry an average balance of $5000 on a 15-percent credit card, you'll pay $750 interest each year, plus the $50 or so annual fee for airline cards.

7. To consolidate your purchases on one statement for easier tracking. Again, if you pay off the balance each month, this can be a good use of credit cards. Some couples put their groceries, gas, entertainment, clothing, and even some utilities on their credit

card each month, pay the balance automatically out of their checking account, and download the information into their Quicken® program. It's a great system.

8. To pay for trips and clothes and entertainment that you can't afford to pay cash for. You know the answer to this one. Bad idea.

There are enough good reasons on the list to justify holding a credit card and using it wisely. But which one is right for you? It depends on how you intend to use the card. Here are the four features you should pay attention to when shopping for a credit card:

1. Interest rate. A card's interest rate is often expressed as the Prime Rate (the rate banks charge their most favorable customers) plus a certain percentage. As the Prime Rate moves up or down, so does your credit card interest rate. Often credit card companies offer a teaser rate that is lower than the normal rate for the first few months or on balances transferred from other cards and then the rate floats up. Your rate can increase if you skip a payment or get your check in late a few times. Make sure you know how the regular (nonteaser) rate is figured.

2. Annual fee. Some cards are free; some carry an annual fee as high as $150. Fees only make sense if you charge a lot to your card each month and get good rewards.

3. Grace period. If you pay your card off in full every month, you can carry a balance interest-free between the time you charge new purchases and your payment is due. This "free" time is called the grace period. On the other hand, if you don't pay off your card each month, interest continues to accumulate on the existing balance as well as new charges, and you lose the grace period.

4. Rebate and frequent flier programs. Some cards offer cash back, some will accumulate miles toward free flights, and some give you discounts or special perks, like free shipping, at selected stores.

If you pay off your balance every month, you don't care much about the interest rate, but you should look for a card with a long grace period and low or no annual fee. If you charge a lot to your card and pay it off each month, you may benefit from a rebate or other special program. Alternatively, if you tend to carry a balance, a low interest

Separate or Joint?

I believe in sharing, but when it comes to credit cards, you and your partner may wish to keep things separate. If you have a joint card, you're each liable for the other person's spending habits while you're together, after you separate or divorce, and even after death. You might start with a joint checking account for household expenses to test the waters. If that works well, you can apply for a joint credit card for purchases you make together such as items for the home or a vacation. But keep the credit limit on the joint card low, and hang on to at least one individual credit card so you can continue to build up your own credit history.

rate is the feature to home in on. Shop carefully—a high annual fee can offset the benefit of a low interest rate. If you carry an average of $3000 on your card, you're better off with a 15-percent card with no annual fee than a 13-percent card with a $75 annual fee. To figure out how much your card is really costing you, just multiply the interest rate by your average balance and add in the amount of the annual fee. Web sites like *www.bankrate.com* and *www.nolo.com* can help you sift through dozens of credit card offers to locate the ones that fit your spending pattern.

Credit Card or Debit Card?

Different types of cards have different rules. When you charge a purchase to your credit card, you buy now and pay later. When you use your debit card, the money comes out of your checking account immediately, just like a check. Which is better for you? It depends.

If you pay off your balance each month, credit cards are a convenient way to track your spending. Your purchases are summarized each month on your statement, and you only need to make one entry in your check register each month—when you pay your bill. You also get to hang on to your money longer. If you buy a shirt on the 20th of January and your bill arrives February 8th and payment is due February 28th, you'll enjoy a float of almost 40 days.

If you don't pay off your credit cards monthly, you may be better off using a debit card. Some couples like the discipline of a debit card because you can only spend what you have in your account (plus any overdraft allowances). Just make sure you record each purchase in your checkbook.

And don't forget to read the fine print. Your liability for a lost or stolen card may be different for a debit card than for a credit card. Your liability for unauthorized purchases on a credit card is limited to $50, although if you notify the company immediately you generally won't owe anything for unauthorized purchases. Debit card rules vary, but you generally get less protection. In many cases, you may be responsible for footing the bill for purchases someone else made if you don't notify the bank within 60 days of losing your card. With either type of card, you're better off reporting a missing or stolen card immediately.

Many credit card companies recommend that you contact them before traveling outside the country or charging unusual purchases or amounts to the card. If the credit card issuer suspects someone else is using the card, they may suspend the card. If you're close to home, a phone call can usually free up the card, but if you're traveling overseas it may be difficult to reach the company to let them know it's really you.

Tapping Your Home Equity

For many couples, the equity in their home—that is, the difference between what the home is worth and what they owe on the mortgage—is a tempting source of extra cash. You can set up a home equity line of credit for little or no cost, the interest rate is typically lower than credit card rates, and the interest is tax deductible. What could be better?

Sometimes it makes sense to siphon off part of the equity you have built up, but beware—the consequences of misusing home equity credit are considerably harsher than those of overspending your credit cards. The reason is simple. The collateral for a home equity line or loan is your house, so if you skip a few payments, you may lose your house. If you're delinquent on your credit card bill, you can wreck your credit, but the credit card company can't repossess your vacation or nights out on the town. Now you know one of the reasons credit card rates are so high—if you don't pay, the credit card companies are often stuck.

There are several ways you can use the equity in your home:

1. To enlarge or remodel your home. There's something appealing about having your home help finance its own improvement. Using your equity to pay for a home project makes the most

sense if your home will increase in value by about the amount of the loan. I don't recommend borrowing $20,000 to install gold-leaf tiles in the bathroom of your $150,000 house. Borrowing $20,000 to expand and remodel an avocado green kitchen, however, can be money well spent. If the project is extensive—and expensive—you may decide to refinance your house when the work is done and roll the home equity loan into the new mortgage. You'll take advantage of a longer loan term and a fixed interest rate if you do.

2. To pay back student loans. All things being equal, it's wise to substitute low-interest debt for high-interest debt, and deductible-interest loans beat nondeductible loans. So why not pay off student loans with a home equity loan? I have two objections to that strategy. First, if you consolidate your student loans, you can lock in an interest rate close to or lower than the going rate on home equity loans. Second, and more importantly, if you run into a cash flow jam because you lose your job, for example, you can usually adjust your student loan repayment schedule and lower your monthly payment. You may be able to stretch out the payments on your home equity line of credit as well, but if you're suddenly jobless, the bank can yank your loan.

3. To consolidate and pay back credit card debt. This is the biggie—the one the ads on TV and the fliers in your bank statement tout. Again, on the surface it makes sense. Why pay 15 to 25 percent nondeductible interest on your credit cards when you can pay 5 to 10 percent deductible interest? And stretch out the payments to boot? The catch is you're putting your house on the line. If you've racked up credit card debt, you have been living beyond your means. If you pay off your credit cards with a home equity loan, you are making two big bets—that you will faithfully repay your home equity debt and that you won't run up the credit cards again when the freed-up credit limits beckon you. Too often couples who pay off their credit card debt with the equity in their home act like that debt has magically disappeared. They continue overspending and soon they have a mortgage payment, a home equity payment, and a credit card payment every month and they're stretched more than ever. It's like plugging a hole in a leaky bucket but still leaving the faucet on. The bucket's

soon going to overflow. You're much better off mapping out a strategy to repay your credit card debt with regular payments and preserving your home equity and your home.

4. To finance a car. This is another case of substituting deductible for nondeductible debt. It can be a reasonable strategy if you have an emergency fund and a solid financial situation and you pay off the loan in no more than 4 or 5 years. There's a real temptation to stretch out the payments over 10 or 20 years or even to lump the car purchase into a refinanced mortgage. If you do that, the tax deduction doesn't make up for all the extra interest you'll pay over the life of the mortgage.

5. As a stand-in for an emergency fund. Setting up a home equity line of credit to cover unexpected expenses is a reasonable tactic, but I don't recommend making it your first line of defense. Cash that's in a savings or money market account should be your mainstay emergency fund because it's always there when you need it. Loans or lines of credit can be revoked—sometimes when you need them the most.

If you have talked things over with your partner and have decided you want to tap into your home equity, here are a few guidelines. Your first decision is choosing between a home equity loan or line of credit. A loan typically carries a fixed term and a fixed rate of interest. Home equity loans make sense if you are financing a particular item or project like a home remodeling job. A line of credit offers more flexibility because you can dip into it and pay it back as often as you like. The interest rate, however, is variable, so your monthly payment may bounce around. If a line of credit suits your situation, shop for a rate of "Prime + 0 percent." That means you will get the same rate of interest the bank charges its best customers. You shouldn't have to pay more than about $50 a year to keep the line of credit open.

Whether you go for a loan or line of credit, look for a deal with no closing costs. The bank will usually cover the appraisal and other closing costs as long as you keep the line open for a specified period, even if you don't use it. However, rules change from bank to bank, so check out your options. You can go wherever you get the best deal, which may not necessarily be the bank that holds your mortgage. The *www.bankrate.com* Web site is a good resource for researching home equity lines and loans.

Student Loans

It generally makes sense to pay off bad debt quickly and good debt more slowly. So as nice as it would be to get out from under student loans, you're generally better off aggressively paying down your credit card debt and consumer loans and getting a head start on building your nest egg. Don't neglect your student loans, however. Pay on time; even better, have the payments deducted automatically from your checking or savings account. Those good habits will help you build a solid credit history, and you may get a break on your interest rate.

Three other features of student loans make them more manageable than credit card debt. First, if you are married and your joint adjusted gross income is less than $100,000 or if you're single and your income is less than $50,000, you can deduct up to $2500 of student loan interest from your taxable income even if you don't itemize. Deductibility phases out at higher incomes and is not available at all for joint filers who make more than $130,000 or singles who make more than $65,000. Under the old rules, interest was only deductible for the first five years of repayment; now there is no time limit. If you are married and file separately, you lose the deduction.

Another benefit of student loans is their flexibility. Lenders of federal student loans (like Stafford loans) offer several different repayment options and the ability to switch among them. In addition to a standard 10-year repayment schedule, you can choose an extended schedule that stretches the term to as long as 30 years, a graduated plan that starts with low payments that gradually increase, and income-contingent and income-sensitive plans that ease the repayment burden if you have a low-paying job. If you're in a real financial squeeze, look into deferments or forbearances—options that allow you to pare down the payments or even stop them for a while.

Some employers will help you pay off your student loan. Americorps workers (*www.americorps.org*) can receive more than $4700 to apply to existing student loans. The pay is low, but the public service work may fit with your career plans. There are also programs to help doctors, nurses, and teachers who work in underserved areas pay back their student loans. Information on such a program for nurses is at *bhpr.hrsa.gov.*

Finally, although federal student loans are issued with a variable rate, by consolidating your loans you can lock in an interest rate that will remain in effect for the life of the loan. Debt consolidation has been a particularly hot topic recently as interest rates have tumbled to their lowest levels in decades. If you haven't consolidated yet, check out one of the Web sites that offers information and calculators; *www.directloan.gov* and *www.salliemae.com* are both good choices. Chances are you can lower your payments and keep them low by locking in an interest rate. You may find out as early as May what the new rate will be in July of that year, so you can choose between consolidating immediately under the existing rate or waiting until the rate changes in July. Consolidation is only available for federal student loans (mainly Stafford, Perkins, and PLUS). If you have private loans, try negotiating a lower rate directly with your lender. If you and your spouse both have student loans, don't consolidate together. Your federal student loans are forgiven if you are permanently and totally disabled or if you die, but if you've consolidated your loans together, your spouse will still be liable for repaying all the loans.

Predatory Lending

It's hard to think that such an ugly term could be associated with those cheerful, brightly lit cash advance stores that have sprung up in strip malls all over the country. But predatory lending is an accurate description of the business these operations do. They lend money at exorbitant rates of interest for short periods of time, and they target the people least able to afford them. Predatory lenders typically take advantage of loopholes in usury laws to charge loan-shark rates of interest.

Most of the time, I give pros and cons of financial choices, but not in this case. My advice here is clear and simple—steer clear of predatory lenders. There are four main categories:

• Refund anticipation loans (RAL). Many tax preparation firms—particularly the big national chains—charge their customers between $35 and $90 to get their tax refund immediately, rather than wait for the check from the IRS. According to a study cited by the Consumer Federation of America (CFA), the annual percentage rate on these very short-term loans range between almost 100 percent to over 2000 percent. If you want a fast refund, skip the hefty charge and instead file electronically and have your refund deposited automatically in your bank account—usually within 10 to 14 days.

• Check-cashing "services." You will be charged from 1 to 10 percent to cash a check at a check-cashing outlet—less for a paycheck and more for a personal check. Instead, open a bank account and cash your checks at your bank for free.

• Payday lending. These are probably the most insidious of the predatory lending practices. By writing a postdated check, a customer can get cash immediately. In a typical transaction, a customer writes a check for $115, and the payday company turns over $100 in cash. Then the company holds the check until payday and either cashes it or rolls it over for an extra charge. Again, the loans are for very short terms (7 to 14 days) and the interest rates are sky high—from over 200 percent to over 1800 percent, according to the Consumer Federation of America. The ads suggest that this is a great source of cash for ordinary people who need a little extra money for the holidays or school supplies. The truth is, once you get sucked in, it's very easy to get trapped. If you're so desperate for cash you can't wait until payday, chances are you won't be able to afford to pay back the loan when get your paycheck. So you end up rolling the loans over and over, and the interest snowballs. If you face an emergency, talk to your bank or credit union about a short-term loan instead.

• "Home equity" loans that exceed the value of the house. The pitch seems legitimate enough—get cash out of your home. But read the fine print. If the creditor is offering to extend a loan that, combined with your current mortgage, exceeds the value of your house, just say no. These loans involve your house in a very risky game. The interest rates are high so the payments are high; if you sell your house soon after you get the loan or during a soft real estate market, you'll need to come up with extra cash to pay off the loan. Missed payments can jeopardize your house. On top of it all, the interest isn't even fully deductible.

Those are the basics. Let's check in with Cathy and Mike and see how they're managing their borrowing.

Paying off Debt

"I see you have brought recent credit card, student loan, and car loan statements," I said. "How do you two feel about your debt situation?"

"It doesn't keep me up at night," said Mike. "We make our payments on time, and I don't think we're overloaded with debt, do you Cathy?"

"Not really," said Cathy. "Is there a rule of thumb about how much debt you should carry?"

Steps to Take if You're in Serious Debt Trouble

If you're taking cash advances from one credit card to pay another card, or you're fending off calls from creditors, sending in payments late, or even skipping payments, you're in trouble. Instead of ignoring your problems, take action.

First, communicate with your lenders. Try to negotiate a lower rate of interest or stretched-out payments. Then continue to pay on time, even if you can't afford the whole payment.

If you are still drowning in debt, contact the Consumer Credit Counseling Service, a nonprofit organization that helps individuals and families manage their debt. Funding for these organizations comes from the credit card companies, so the emphasis is on repayment. You can find an office near you through *www.nfcc.org* (the National Foundation for Credit Counseling Web site). And by all means, don't pay anyone to "clean up your credit history." These companies tend to charge exorbitant rates for work you can do yourself. There is no magic wand you can wave to make up for past borrowing mistakes.

Declaring bankruptcy is the absolute last resort. Although it may seem like a way to make a fresh start, bankruptcy hangs over your financial picture like a dark cloud. The bad news stays on your credit history for 7 to 10 years, and during that time you will pay significantly higher costs for loans you acquire, including mortgages. When you add up all the extra charges and higher interest rates, bankruptcy will most likely cost you more over the long run—not less.

"It depends on the kind of debt," I said. "For example, your total house payment shouldn't be more than about 25 percent of your gross monthly income. The rule of thumb on consumer debt—credit cards and car loans—is a little squishier. Some advisors say your payments can safely add up to as much as 15 to 20 percent of your monthly pay, but I prefer to keep them to 10 percent or less. If you go higher than that, it's very difficult to fund your other goals.

"You two are paying $160 a month on Mike's car loan, $80 a month on Cathy's student loans, and $100 a month on your credit cards. That's about 7 percent of your monthly income."

"So we're okay, right?" asked Mike.

"Using the 10 percent rule of thumb, you're fine," I said. "But you're also saving for a house and trying to put money into an emergency fund, so even 7 percent might strain your spending plan. Of the three loans I listed, I would classify one as good debt, one as bad debt, and one somewhere in the middle. Any guesses about which is which?"

"I can't imagine you'd call credit card debt 'good'," said Cathy, "so that leaves either my student loans or Mike's car loan. I'll say my student loans are the good debt."

"That's right," I said. "You're going to school to learn how to do more complex work, attract larger clients, and make more money, right? The student loans allowed you to go back to get you MBA before you saved up the whole price of tuition."

"Why isn't my Jeep loan good debt?" asked Mike.

"The Jeep is a depreciating asset—it loses value each year—so I don't put it in the same category as student loans or a home mortgage," I said. "Nevertheless, I know it's a necessary loan because you need transportation. Let's just call it neutral."

"I have a debt question that has been bugging me for a long time," said Cathy. "I always hear you are supposed to pay off your high-interest debt first, and it doesn't make sense to have money stuck in a savings account paying 2 or 3 percent while you have credit card balances at 12-percent interest. Shouldn't we get rid of our credit card debt before we focus on building up an emergency fund? Maybe we should even cut back on Mike's 401(k) contributions until we pay off our debt. We haven't been earning 12-percent a year on those investments."

"The rule of paying off high-interest debt more quickly than low-interest debt is a sound one," I said. "When you pay back a credit card with a 12-percent rate of interest, it's as if you earned 12 percent on your money because you save that much in interest. You'd rather earn 12 percent than 10 percent, so you're better off paying back a 12-percent credit card faster than a 10-percent one.

"The choice between paying down debt and saving for the future is less obvious, though. There are three problems with postponing saving and investing until you are debt free—or at least credit-card-debt free. First, you push important goals like buying a house further out in the future. That means paying more rent instead of building equity, and, since houses continue to increase in value, you end up reaching for a moving target. Second, when you postpone investing, you lose the powerful advantage of time. When we have our retirement planning meeting, you'll see how a delay of 8 or 9 years can cut the future value of an investment in half. Finally, once you pay off your credit cards, it's just human nature to look at all that freed up credit as a buying opportunity. I'm not saying you two will give in to the temptation, but it's not unusual to run the credit cards up again, pay them off again, and start charging again. If you did that, 5 or 10 years from now you'd still be caught in the credit card payoff cycle, and you wouldn't have started saving for your long-term goals."

"So how do we decide how much to pay off on our credit cards each month and how much to put aside for investments?" asked Mike. "I'm not even sure how to start figuring that out."

"That's one of the challenges of financial planning," I said. "In order to succeed, you have to move several goals forward at the same time, even if some goals get pushed more aggressively than others. You're a computer guy, Mike. Isn't that like parallel processing instead of serial processing—working on several tasks at once rather than working on the tasks sequentially?"

"I think I see what you mean," said Mike. "So how do we divvy up our money among all our goals?"

"A good place to start is the spending plan we put together at our last meeting," I said. "We shaved a few categories like entertainment and cash expenses to free up some money to fund Cathy's retirement plan and build up an emergency fund. We left the loan payments and your 401(k) contributions, Mike, as they were. So your spending plan already reflects a strategy of working on several goals at once.

"Now let's do a reality check. According to your balance sheet, you owe $1800 on your credit card, Mike, and you owe $2800 on yours, Cathy. What are the interest rates on those cards?"

"I brought the statements with me," said Cathy. "The interest rate on my card is 10 percent and on Mike's it's 12 percent."

"You're paying $100 a month on both cards," I said. "One strategy is to pay the minimum payment on your card, Cathy, and the rest of the $100 on Mike's. It looks like your minimum is $56, so $44 could go to Mike's card. At that rate, and assuming you immediately pay off any new purchases, of course, Mike's card would be paid off in 53 months. Your balance at that time, Cathy, would be $634. With Mike's balance gone, you could put the full $100 a month toward that card, and it would be paid off in another 6-and-a-half months. So, by paying $100 a month, you would be free of credit card debt in about 59 months—just under five years."

"That's a very long time," said Cathy. "Is that really the best strategy?"

"Let's look at the flip side," I said. "During those 59 months, Mike plans to continue contributing $375 a month to his 401(k) plan, you'll contribute $125 a month toward your nest egg, Cathy, and you plan to put $160 a month into a money market account for emergencies and other expenses. Assuming you earn 8 percent a year on retirement investments and 2.5 percent on your money market, I can calculate how much more you'll have in those accounts by the time you've finished paying off your credit cards.

"Mike, you'll have over $27,000 more in your 401(k) plan. Cathy, you'll have almost $9000 in your nest egg, and you'll have accumulated over $10,000 in your joint money market account. Not bad at all. Ignoring other changes for the moment, if you stick with this strategy, your assets will increase $46,000 in less than 5 years and your liabilities will decrease $4600. Your net worth will be over $82,000—more than double what it is now."

"That does sound pretty good," said Mike.

"I agree," said Cathy, "but it still seems like we should be able to pay off our credit card debt faster. What about all those offers for 0-percent cards we get in the mail. Shouldn't we apply for one of those?"

"Many credit card companies offer teaser rates to attract new customers," I said. "If you apply for a card with a low rate for transfers of existing balances, look for one that keeps the special rate in effect until you pay off the balance. If you plan to hang on to the card, find out what the rate is for new purchases.

"If you transferred Mike's $1800 balance to a 0-percent card, I would modify the strategy and just make the minimum payment on Mike's card—around $30 a month—and pay the remaining $70 a month against your balance, Cathy."

"How long would it take to pay off our cards if I got a 0-percent card?" asked Mike.

"You'd pay off your card in 4 years, Cathy," I said, "and it would take another 4 months to finish paying off Mike's card, so you'd be credit-card debt fee in 52 months. That shaves 7 months and over $700 in interest off your timeline. The key is to keep paying the same amount each month until you've paid off all your credit cards. You can try out different payment strategies on an on-line calculator." (See Figure 5-1.)

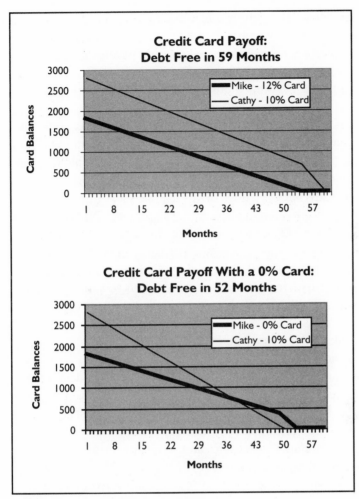

FIGURE 5-1 Credit card payoff

"Why don't we apply for a card with a teaser rate for me, too?" asked Cathy.

"You could," I said. "There's a downside to turning over your credit cards regularly to take advantage of teaser rates, aside from the hassle of changing automatic payments like health club dues or on-line fees. Your credit score will suffer slightly if there are repeated inquiries on your record, and each time you apply for a new card, the credit card company checks you out.

"As an alternative to getting a new card, you could call your existing credit card company and ask them to reduce your rate of interest. If you have been a good customer, making your payments on time, you may get a reduced rate just by asking."

"Now that you mentioned our credit score," said Cathy, "I heard you can find out your score on-line."

"You can get a copy of your credit history as well as your score from *www.myfico.com*," I said. "The cost is about $20, and you get a response immediately along with information on how to interpret and improve your score. I recommend that you get your scores every year or two, especially since you hope to buy a home soon. Check over your credit history information to make sure it's accurate. You may also see some old credit cards on your report you'd forgotten about and need to close."

"When I graduated from college, I applied to a bunch of cards at stores that were offering a10-percent discount on your first day's purchase," said Mike. "I probably have a stack of cards in my desk drawer. I'll go ahead and cancel them."

"Great idea. Make sure you cancel your cards in writing so your report will show the cards were closed by the consumer.

"So, to summarize, you two are in pretty good shape debt-wise," I said. "You just need to stick to a strategy of paying off your existing credit card debt and don't load any more purchases on the cards unless you can pay them off immediately. Just continue to make regular payments on your student loans, Cathy, and your car loan, Mike, and keep funding your retirement plans and emergency fund."

"I like looking down the road to see what our net worth might look like if we stay on track," said Cathy. "It makes the rewards of paying off our debt a little more real."

What Cathy and Mike Have Learned

1. Good debt finances assets that grow in value; bad debt lasts longer than the item financed.

2. In general, it's smart to pay off bad debt faster than good debt and higher-interest debt faster than lower interest debt.

3. Don't wait to invest and save until you've paid off all your debt. You need to make progress on lots of goals at once to reach financial security.

Recommendations for Cathy and Mike

1. Set up a system for paying off credit card debt—either the plan we worked out or another strategy involving new credit cards with teaser rates.

2. Continue to contribute to retirement plans and emergency fund while you're paying off debt.

3. Try negotiating directly with the credit card company to get a better interest rate on an existing card.

Resources

- *www.nolo.com*—great information on credit cards, bankruptcy, student loans, and other credit and debt topics.

- *www.ftc.gov*—the Federal Trade Commission Web site, containing tips on dealing with identity theft and telemarketers.

- *www.nfcc.org*—to locate an office of Consumer Credit Counseling Service near you.

- *www.myfico.com*—to order a copy of your credit score and credit reports.

- *www.smartmoney.com*—good debt management worksheets.

- *www.financialrecovery.com*—tips for getting out of debt

- Hunt, Mary. *Debt-Proof Living*. Broadman & Holman. Nashville. 1999.

CHAPTER 6

Managing Your Risk

Once upon a time, when you lived at home with your parents, you probably didn't think much about insurance. Then you started driving and car insurance popped up on your radar screen. That may have been your first experience with the insurance industry, but it will be far from your last.

Insurance is your safety net and a vital piece of your financial plan. The tricky part is knowing the right kinds and amounts of insurance to hold. You could just walk into an insurance agent's office for help, but you'd be smart to do some homework before you sign up for a policy. Although there are plenty of smart, ethical insurance agents who work hard for their customers, some agents push expensive products that are unsuitable for young couples. Recent lawsuits have highlighted such practices as characterizing life insurance as a retirement pension in order to make the sale. Some agents tout themselves as financial planners, even though they really only know about insurance and don't have the training or experience to handle comprehensive planning. If you go to an insurance agent for your financial planning, chances are you'll walk away with insurance products for college saving, investing, and retirement, even though there are much better—and less expensive—solutions for those needs.

Before I sound totally negative on the industry, let me emphasize that a good insurance agent can be an important ally as you chart your path to financial security. But be a wise consumer. Armed with some basic knowledge, you will be in a much better position to judge whether your agent is giving you the straight stuff. And always ask questions. Ask why your agent is recommending a particular policy compared to other options. Ask your agent to obtain a few quotes from different companies, if possible, and to compare the policies. Insurance can be complex, but if your agent can't explain the terms and cost of a policy in straightforward language, find another agent.

And don't buy a product you don't understand. I have met young couples who purchased expensive, complicated products when a simpler, cheaper policy would have met their needs much better. They were convinced that they would be irresponsible spouses or parents if they didn't follow their agent's advice. Or an agent had persuaded them that a particular product would feather their retirement nest even though they didn't really understand the mechanics of how that would happen.

Let's go back to the basics—why even bother with insurance? We buy insurance because life is full of risks. We're stuck bearing the consequences of some of the risks we take: Will going back to graduate school be a good investment? Will the mutual funds I picked in my 401(k) perform well? And, not least of all, will my partner and I live happily ever after?

There are other risks, however, that we can transfer to someone or something else—in this case, to an insurance company. Every time we get in a car, we take a risk, so we buy auto insurance to reduce the financial consequences of an accident. We buy disability insurance to provide a stream of income in case we can't work, and we sign up for health insurance so we won't get stuck paying large medical bills if we are ill or injured.

The premiums we pay are a small fraction of the benefits we would get if disaster struck. The insurance companies make money because they charge premiums to a large pool of individuals, knowing that they will only have to pay out benefits in a small number of cases. You pay your homeowner's insurance premium every year even though you're only likely to have a claim every eight years or so. You rest easier knowing you'll receive financial help in case of a disaster, and the insurance companies thrive because they can collect more in premiums than they have to pay out in claims. It's a win-win situation.

The basic rule of insurance is don't risk what you can't afford to lose. That means you should insure against events that would result in financial disaster to you or your family even if there's only a small probability that the event would occur. Only a tiny number of houses burn down each year, so it's highly unlikely your house would be hit. If yours did burn, however, and you had to pay to replace your house and all your possessions out of your own pocket, you might never recover financially.

On the other hand, if a loss would be disastrous and there's a high probability it would happen, insurance companies will not be eager to sell you a policy. If you're an amateur skydiver, you might have trouble finding affordable life insurance.

You can buy insurance for minor mishaps, but it usually doesn't make sense. Just about every time you purchase a piece of electronic equipment at a major chain store, you're offered insurance to extend or enhance the warranty. In general, just say no. As inconvenient as it might be if your Walkman failed in mid-jog, your financial plan would not be thrown into disarray if you had to dip into your own funds to replace it. So save your insurance bucks for the big stuff.

This chapter is not meant to cover the waterfront on insurance. Instead, I'll focus on what young couples should look for and what to steer clear of when getting insurance. Later we'll join Mike and Cathy to see how their insurance safety net looks.

Life Insurance

Do You Need It?

There are lots of different reasons to buy life insurance—some sensible and some not very smart. If you had infinite resources, you could load up on all kinds of life insurance and never worry about how to pay the premiums. In the real world, your resources are limited and you need to spend your premium dollars wisely.

The number-one reason to purchase life insurance is to replace a stream of income—your paychecks—if you were to die prematurely. Before you became part of a couple, you probably didn't need life insurance because no one besides you relied on your income. Now you need life insurance if your partner or family depend on your income for living expenses. Here are three different life-insurance scenarios for young couples:

1. *You and your partner earn fairly equal incomes, you rent an apartment together and have no children.* You may need a limited amount of life insurance to cover final expenses and help

pay some bills while your partner adjusts. If you get some life insurance as a benefit at work, you probably don't need to buy any more.

2. *You and your partner earn fairly equal incomes and have no children, but you recently purchased a house together.* Unless your partner could cover the mortgage payments and other house expenses without your income, you need some life insurance. The exact amount you carry will vary according to your circumstances, but an easy rule of thumb is to have enough insurance to pay off the mortgage. If your partner didn't have a mortgage payment, he or she might be able to stay in the house and cover the extra living expenses even without your income. Some couples decide to carry a smaller amount of life insurance—less than the mortgage balances—because they believe neither would want to keep the home if one of them died. Even if this is your philosophy, be sure to carry enough insurance to give your partner time to sell the house and find another place.

3. *You and your partner have a young child or children.* Unless your children have a trust fund that would pay all their expenses through college, you and your partner each need sufficient life insurance to replace your income until your children become independent. If you are a stay-at-home parent, you need enough life insurance to cover child-care and housekeeping expenses while the children are young. Depending on how big your family is and where you live, you may need insurance to cover $20,000 to $40,000 worth of expenses each year until the children can take care of themselves.

What Kind of Life Insurance Do You Need?

There are two main types of life insurance—term and permanent. Term life insurance is often called plain vanilla insurance because it's the simplest, cheapest kind and has no investment value. If you die while the policy is in force, your beneficiary will receive the death benefit. If you drop the policy, your coverage will end. It's as simple as that. If you purchase level term life insurance, your premium will stay the same each year for the term of the policy. You can buy level term insurance for 5, 10, 15, and even up to 30 years. Unless you are worth millions and might have an estate tax problem when you die, term life insurance is your best bet.

The other kind—permanent life insurance—includes whole life, universal life, variable life, and universal variable life insurance. Permanent insurance is part life insurance, part investment. When you pay your premiums, a portion goes to cover the life insurance component and a portion is invested—either in interest-earning assets, in the case of whole life or universal policies, or in stock and bond mutual funds, in the case of variable policies. You can usually access the investment portion—called the cash value of the policy—by borrowing against it or by surrendering (cashing in) the policy.

At first blush, it might seem like permanent life insurance is a better deal because it can last your whole life and it allows you to accumulate an investment. It's not. The fact is, most couples don't need life insurance for their whole life—they need it while they have dependent children or while they're still accumulating their nest egg. Once you've retired, the need for life insurance usually disappears.

Although your agent may not point these out, there are some very big gotchas associated with permanent life insurance. These policies typically cost 8 to 10 times more than term policies providing the exact same amount of insurance coverage. A healthy 30-year-old female would pay about $100 a year for $100,000 of 20-year level term life insurance or about $800 a year for the same amount of permanent life insurance.

The extra fees and commissions built into permanent insurance policies drag down the performance of the investment portion. Your cash value will grow much more slowly than comparable investments in true retirement plans or in most mutual funds—especially during the first few years. The agent who sold you the policy gets a commission just about equal to your first year's premium, and ongoing fees can chip off as much as 2 to 3 percent of your return each year after that. Now you know why many agents push permanent policies over term policies—they make a lot more money off of them. If you are still considering purchasing a permanent policy, take a look at the annual cash value projections your agent will show you and notice how long it will take to build up a significant investment.

Even if you have accumulated some value in a permanent life insurance policy, accessing your money is not easy. You can borrow against the investment portion, but you'll pay interest, and the rate you earn on your investment may be reduced. If you want to get the cash value out without borrowing, you'll either have to give up the policy or reduce the coverage.

Agents are often quick to point out that your investment inside an insurance policy grows tax deferred. That's true, but there are plenty of better ways to defer your taxes, including investing in 401(k) plans, IRAs, or tax-efficient mutual funds. If you cash in the policy, you'll owe ordinary income taxes on the earnings. Compare that to investing in a Roth IRA, for example, where you can pull out your original contributions any time you like, tax free, or cash in your earnings after age 59½ tax free.

The bottom line is to keep your insurance and your investments separate. Purchase level term life insurance and invest the extra money you would have spent on a permanent policy in a Roth IRA or other tax-advantaged investment.

What if you have already purchased a permanent life insurance policy and now you're wondering if it was such a good idea? The best thing to do is get an objective analysis of your options either from another insurance agent or from an independent financial planner who does not sell insurance. The Consumer Federation of America, a non-profit consumer advocacy group, will prepare an unbiased analysis of your policy for a small fee. Consult their Web site at *www.con sumerfed.org* for details.

How Much Do You Need?

If you have decided you need life insurance, and term insurance is the appropriate kind, you still have one more decision to make—How much do you buy? The answer varies from couple to couple, but here are a few guidelines. Life insurance is meant to replace a stream of income, so the larger your paycheck, the more insurance you'll probably need. If you have already accumulated a substantial nest egg, you'll probably need less insurance. If your children are small, you'll need more insurance than if they are in high school or college because you have a longer period of time to cover.

One rule of thumb for estimating how much life insurance you need is to add the amount required to pay off your debt plus the amount you'd need to fund college for your children, plus five times your salary.[1] Using this rule, a 30-year old earning $40,000 a year who has a $140,000 mortgage and two toddlers might need $450,000 of life insurance. If he

---

[1] Thanks to John Ryan, owner of Ryan Insurance Strategy Consultants in Colorado for sharing this rule of thumb.

receives life insurance equal to one times his salary at work, he might look for a 25-year $400,000 level term policy to fill the gap. If he is healthy and doesn't smoke, his annual premium will be about $400.

The best way to estimate how much life insurance you need is to do some number crunching on your own. Several Web sites have easy-to-use insurance calculators. I have listed a few at the end of this chapter, but be careful when using them—the calculators are usually linked to insurance-selling sites and tend to produce very high numbers.

Disability Insurance

As important as life insurance can be to your family's financial security, disability insurance is even more crucial when you're young. You're at a much greater risk of becoming disabled than dying during your working years. In fact, the disability rate is seven times higher than the death rate for individuals between 30 and 40. Disability results in a double whammy: your income is hit because you can no longer earn a full—or perhaps even partial—paycheck, yet your expenses may be even higher than before.

Seven Things to Consider When Buying Term Insurance

1. Choose a level term policy with guaranteed renewability. Your premium will remain the same for the duration of the term, and you will be able to renew the policy at the end of the term, although at a much higher premium.

2. Choose an initial term that is slightly longer than the number of years you think you'll need life insurance. If you have a baby, consider locking in a 25-year or 30-year term in case your child goes to graduate school or you have more children. When you're young, the additional cost of buying a policy with a longer term is minimal.

3. Make sure your insurance company is financially sound, especially if you're buying a long-term policy. You can check your company's rating on www.ambest.com. Look for an A rating or better.

4. Look for a policy with a conversion option available during the entire term. This feature allows you to convert your term policy to a

Unless you have a huge nest egg or trust fund, if you earn a paycheck, you need disability insurance. Unfortunately, many young couples have inadequate or no coverage. We tend to worry about our savings and investments but don't protect our ability to contribute to those accounts. We focus too much on the golden eggs and not enough on the golden goose.

Long-term disability insurance pays you a monthly income if you are unable to work due to an illness or injury covered by the policy. Typically, you can obtain coverage for no more than 70 percent of your income. Companies are reluctant to insure you for more because if you could get a full paycheck by being ill or injured, there would be a strong incentive to claim a disability instead of staying in the work force. If you were disabled, there wouldn't be much financial motivation to get well and go back to work.

Typical long-term disability policies have a waiting period of 60 to 90 days before benefits are paid. Ideally, the policy would pay full benefits if you were unable to perform the duties of your own occupation, even if you could do other work. Such policies are either very expensive or difficult to obtain; more common are policies that pay

universal life policy or another form of permanent insurance and can be useful if you need life insurance beyond the original term but have become uninsurable.

5. Skip the waiver of premium rider. For an extra charge tacked on to your premium, the insurance company will waive your premium if you are disabled. The annual cost of term life insurance is not onerous and if you become disabled, you should be able to continue to pay the premium.

6. Comparison shop on the Web. A couple of good sites for term life insurance quotes are www.insure.com and www.quicken.com.

7. Even if you get quotes on the Web, you may still wish to work with an agent to purchase your policy. The cost will probably be the same, and an independent insurance agent can help you through the process, especially if you have a medical condition that may make it difficult to obtain life insurance. Your agent's knowledge of different companies' underwriting requirements will help your search.

full benefits for a short period of time (two years or less) if you cannot perform your own occupation and then partial benefits if you can do some other kind of work. Most insurance companies only offer long-term disability coverage to individuals who are earning income—it is very difficult to obtain a policy for a stay-at-home parent. Social Security provides disability benefits to individuals who have worked sufficient number of quarters in the time frame required. However, in order to qualify for benefits, you must be totally disabled or have a terminal illness, so don't rely on Social Security exclusively.

If you are employed, check out your benefit package. Some employers offer good disability coverage for their employees; some offer partial coverage, and some skip it completely. You may have the option of increasing your coverage through payroll deduction. If so, buy as much as you can. Benefits you receive under an employer-paid plan are taxable to you. If you pay the premiums yourself, the benefits are not taxed.

Some companies also offer short-term disability insurance, although many companies allow employees to save up sick and vacation leave to cover a short-term illness or injury. Your emergency fund will also come in handy if you need to cover a short-term disability.

If you are self-employed or your employer offers partial or no long-term disability coverage, shop for a policy immediately. As Cathy will find out later in this chapter, it's expensive insurance unless you compare it with the cost of replacing your paycheck if you're disabled.

Health Insurance

Health insurance can also be pricey, but it's another piece of your safety net you cannot afford to skip. Without insurance, a severe illness, a surgery, or a hospital stay could wreck your financial future. If you are self-employed, or your employer doesn't offer coverage, shop for an individual or small-business policy. Although you can get quotes on the Web, you'll probably benefit from working with an agent who can guide you through all the jargon.

There are three main types of health care plans:

• Fee-for-service (traditional indemnity) plans. Under these plans, you pay the first expenses each year—called a deductible—out of your own pocket. After you have met the deductible (typically between $100 and $2000), the insurance company will pay 80 percent of the "usual, customary and reasonable" (UCR) costs of your medical care and you pay the remaining 20 percent. If your doctor's or hospital's fee are higher than the UCR costs, you pay the difference. You can choose your own doctor and hospital, and you can usually consult a specialist without obtaining permission from a primary physician. There is extra paperwork involved in obtaining reimbursement, and these plans do not typically cover checkups and other preventive care.

- Health Maintenance Organizations (HMOs). When you sign up with an HMO, you choose your doctors and hospitals from a list provided by the HMO. You don't have to meet a deductible or fill out any paperwork to get reimbursed. Instead, you pay a small copayment for each service or prescription. HMOs usually provide comprehensive services, including preventive medicine. Your primary care physician serves as a gatekeeper, and you must get permission from him or her to consult a specialist. If you obtain care outside the network, except for extreme emergencies, you pay the full bill. The physicians in HMOs have a financial incentive to limit expensive procedures or tests and to control access to specialists. As a result, there have been numerous—and vocal—complaints about inadequate care from HMOs.

- Preferred Provider Organizations (PPOs). These plans offer some characteristics of a traditional insurance plan and some of an HMO. If you consult a physician from a network list of providers, you pay a copayment. If you choose to go outside the network, you will pay a deductible first and then a percentage of the cost of the services. Like HMOs, PPOs offer preventive care and a minimum of paperwork if you stay inside the network. Like traditional plans, you do not need permission from your primary physician to obtain services outside the network. Many consumers like the additional flexibility offered by PPOs.

How do you choose a plan if you are shopping for an individual policy or your employer offers you more than one option? It depends on your circumstances. If you have young children or are planning to start a family, the preventive care coverage offered by HMOs and PPOs is attractive. It's usually cheaper and less hassle to pay a copayment at each check-up than to meet a deductible and submit paperwork for reimbursement. On the other hand, unless you are willing to switch physicians, it only makes sense to sign up for an HMO or PPO if your physicians and hospitals are in their network. By combining some of the benefits of HMOs with the flexibility of traditional insurance plans, PPOs have become the most popular type of health care plan in the United States.

Changing Jobs? Know Your Health Insurance Options

If you are leaving a job and may have a gap in health insurance coverage, get to know **COBRA**. **COBRA** stands for the Consolidated Omnibus Budget Reconciliation Act of 1985, and it guarantees your right to continue to participate in your former employer's group health plan for up to 18 months after you leave your job. You and your family are eligible for coverage if the company you left employed at least 20 people and you were not fired for gross misconduct. (Some companies, such as nonprofit firms, are exempt from **COBRA** rules.) **COBRA** can be a great stop-gap if you are between jobs, are self-employed and haven't shopped for a new policy yet, or have a waiting period at your new employer. It doesn't come cheap, though. You are required to pay the full cost of coverage and your former employer may tack on a 2-percent administrative charge as well. Your employer was probably subsidizing your premium when you were employed, so coverage under **COBRA** might be quite expensive. Nevertheless, it beats going without health insurance.

Property and Casualty Insurance

Until now, I have been describing ways to insure your lives and your health. Let's switch gears and talk about purchasing insurance for your things and for protecting yourself from liability associated with those things. Property and casualty insurance provide you with a financial safety net if disaster struck your home, your possessions, or your car. The three main categories are renter's insurance, homeowner's insurance, and automobile insurance. Each type of insurance will help you replace your possessions—your house, furniture, clothing, and so on—if they were destroyed by a fire, storm, theft, or other peril covered by the policy. The policies also have a liability component that offers protection for your assets if your negligence causes damage or injury to others. Just like health and disability insurance, it's the kind of insurance you can't do without.

- Renter's Insurance. If you rent rather than own, you need renter's insurance to protect your possessions against damage and theft and to protect your savings against the consequences of a negligent act. Some

The second acronym to know is **HIPAA**—the Health Insurance Portability and Accountability Act of 1996. One of the problems individuals faced when they switched health insurance was that the new insurer often didn't cover pre-existing conditions for the first 12 months. As long as you have had health insurance for at least 12 continuous months and have not had a lapse of more than 63 days, **HIPAA** guarantees that you will get credit for that time and will not have to wait out a new 12-month waiting period before pre-existing conditions are covered. If you have less than 12 months of coverage under your belt, your wait is reduced proportionally. **HIPAA** also guarantees that you can't be excluded from group coverage because of health conditions. The law doesn't provide perfect health insurance portability—changing between individual, as opposed to group, policies is trickier.

Both laws can help you maintain your health insurance coverage. At the risk of becoming acronym-happy, you can think of **COBRA** as a way to avoid a lapse in coverage so you can make sure you qualify for **HIPAA** guarantees.

policies cover your clothes, furniture, stereo, computer, and other equipment at actual cash value—what they're worth at the time of the loss. Instead, ask for replacement cost coverage, which will pay to replace or repair your damaged possessions. A sofa purchased five years ago for $600 might have an actual cash value of $200 and a replacement cost of $850. You would want the insurer to pay $850 if your sofa were destroyed. Renter's insurance will cover a minimal amount of jewelry and other pricey possessions. Check your policy, and if you own more jewelry, for example, than is covered in the basic policy, you'll need a separate rider. Renter's insurance typically covers you, your family, and your pets. The cost for renter's insurance depends on where you live and how much stuff you own; typical premiums run between $100 and $400 a year.

• Homeowner's insurance. Like renter's insurance, homeowner's insurance covers your possessions and your liability for negligent acts. It also covers your house as well as other buildings on your property like a detached garage or storage shed. Just as with renter's insurance, replacement cost coverage will provide you with more protection than actual cash value. Agents often recommend that you make a written inventory or even a videotape of your possessions, noting the prices of unusual objects. Store the information in a safe deposit box or other off-site location. There's a special version of the standard home-owner's policy that covers condos and another version that covers historic or older homes that are particularly costly to reconstruct. You'll generally pay more to insure your home and possessions against floods and earthquakes.

• Automobile insurance. It will probably cost you more to insure a $15,000 car than it will to insure a $100,000 house stuffed with $50,000 of possessions. Why? The car moves and the house doesn't. Every rush hour in every big city, cars are dinged, dented, and wrecked. Houses never suffer a fender bender.

There are plenty of ways to save on car insurance, but you don't want to cut corners the wrong way and leave yourself exposed to financial risk. Let's take it by parts. There are five types of coverage included in your car insurance:

- Liability coverage will pay for damages and legal defense if you are involved in an accident that is your fault. Don't scrimp on this part. Each state has minimum amounts you must carry, but at least $300,000 is recommended. If you can afford more, buy more.

- Medical payments coverage typically pays for medical expenses for you and your family and for passengers riding in the insured car.

- Uninsured (and underinsured) motorists coverage protects you if you are injured by a driver with no or inadequate insurance or by a hit-and-run driver.

- Collision coverage pays for damage to your car if it's involved in an accident, no matter who caused it. You can save money on your premium by raising your deductible to $500 or even $1000. Just make sure you beef up your emergency fund to cover the higher deductible. Insurance companies pay very little for damage to an older car, so if you're driving a junker, forego the collision insurance.

- Comprehensive insurance pays for damage to your car caused by something other than a collision with another car, like a rock thrown through the windshield or a tree that lands on the hood.

Your car insurance may also provide coverage for damage to a rental car. Check with your agent.

If you already have renter's or homeowner's and car insurance in place, you can add an extra layer of liability protection by purchasing an umbrella policy. A policy providing a million dollars of coverage typically only costs between $100 and $200 per year.

That's it for Insurance 101. Let's return to our conversation with Mike and Cathy and answer any questions they may have.

Cathy and Mike's Insurance

"I think I understand less about insurance than any other part of financial planning," said Mike as he and Cathy sat down at the table in my office.

"I know something about life and disability insurance from my work in human resources," said Cathy, "with the emphasis on 'something.'"

"Don't underestimate yourselves," I said. "You may know more than you think. We're going to cover four different kinds of insurance today—life, disability, health, and property and casualty. Let's start with life insurance. One way to begin is to imagine what would happen if one of you weren't around."

"You mean if one of us died?" asked Mike. "There's a gloomy start to a meeting."

"It is," I agreed, "but working through different scenarios is part of financial planning. Cathy, would you like to start? What would you do if Mike died?"

"I would have to go to work full time in order to afford the rent and other expenses," said Cathy. "I might not be able to finish my MBA."

"In order to complete your studies, you would probably need to replace Mike's income for about a year," I said, "but after that, you wouldn't need ongoing financial support. Is that accurate?"

"Yes," said Cathy. "We don't have a house or children, so Mike probably doesn't need much insurance."

"My company provides life insurance equal to one times my salary," said Mike. "Would that be enough?"

"Cathy would receive the insurance benefits income-tax free," I said, "so $45,000 in insurance proceeds is worth more than $45,000 in salary. That would probably cover a year's expenses, plus some extra bills you might have, Cathy. I think that's enough life insurance to allow you to postpone full-time work until you finished your MBA. What about you, Mike?"

"If something happened to Cathy," said Mike, "I think I could live off my salary. I signed up for $10,000 worth of life insurance for Cathy at work. That wouldn't be enough if I got stuck paying Cathy's student loans, though."

"You wouldn't be on the hook for her student loans," I said, "because those are forgiven at death. Cathy, you have some credit card debt, so your assets would probably be used to pay those off. I'd say a small amount of life insurance—about $10,000—is probably sufficient."

"What if we had a house?" asked Cathy. "I would want to make sure Mike wouldn't have to move out—at least not right away."

"When you have a house, you may wish to carry enough life insurance to pay off the mortgage," I said. "The remaining spouse would still have utilities, property taxes, and upkeep to pay, but those expenses would be manageable if there were no mortgage payment."

"Some friends of ours got mortgage insurance when they bought their house," said Mike. "Is that a good idea?"

"You'll get bombarded with offers of mortgage insurance when you buy a house," I said, "but I advise getting plain level term life insurance instead. Mortgage insurance coverage decreases as the mortgage gets paid off, it's typically more expensive than term life insurance, and it can only be used to pay off the mortgage. The only exception to my skip-the-mortgage-insurance rule is if one of you is not healthy enough to get affordable term insurance. Then, mortgage insurance may be a way to get some coverage without having to answer medical questions. You're both healthy, so term insurance is a much better option. We'll talk more about term insurance later.

"Although you might need more insurance when you buy a house, the biggest adjustment will come when you have children. If you have dependents, you'll need enough life insurance to replace your paychecks if something happened to you."

"Since we're planning on having a family," said Cathy, "I'd like to go ahead and talk about getting more life insurance now. We're young and healthy—we may as well explore our options."

"I have heard that you need life insurance equal to seven times your income if you have children," said Mike. "That's supposed to be enough to cover all the expenses while they're growing up plus college."

"It's a rule of thumb I have heard before," I said, "but every family's situation is different, so it's better to crunch the numbers for your case. Several personal finance and insurance Web sites have calculators. I like those that base insurance need on income replacement and not on a list of expected expenses. Too often that method results in a wish list and an inflated amount of recommended insurance. The purpose of life insurance is to replace a paycheck, not to enrich the survivors.

"Let's assume you had two young children, and we calculated that you each needed $500,000 life insurance. The next decision would be to choose the appropriate kind."

"An insurance expert came to our office a few months ago," said Mike. "He was pushing universal and variable life insurance. He said you can build up investments as you pay the premiums. It sounded pretty good."

"He will also build up his commissions if he sells you a policy," I said. "Universal and variable life insurance are two types of permanent insurance. You're right—they're part insurance and part investment. Although that may sound like a good combination, you pay dearly for the investment component. The premiums for permanent insurance are 8 to 10 times more than premiums for the same amount of term insurance—partly because some of your premium gets invested and partly because the commissions and ongoing fees are so high. You are much better off with term life insurance, which is plain insurance without the investment piece."

"But term insurance is only temporary," said Cathy. "Don't we need insurance that will last all our lives?"

"Most people don't need permanent insurance," I said. "Once your children have grown up and become independent and you have built up your own investments, your need for life insurance will greatly diminish or even disappear. When you retire, there is no paycheck to replace. And, when you stop working, you'll both be living off your nest egg. If there's enough for two to retire, there's enough for one. The smart thing for you two is cheap term life insurance."

"Do we choose the term?" asked Mike.

"Yes," I said. "I recommend you pick a long term—probably 30 years. If you have a couple of children over the next few years, it will be that long before they're all out of college. You can drop or reduce your insurance earlier if you wish. The advantage of locking in a longer term is that your premium will stay the same over that period."

"Let's cut to the nitty-gritty," said Cathy. "How much will term insurance cost?"

"Less than you probably think," I said. "I went on line and got some sample quotes. A $500,000 30-year level term policy would cost about $430 a year for you, Cathy and $475 a year for you, Mike."

"Why is Cathy's cheaper?" asked Mike.

"She's younger and she's a female," I said, "so, statistically, she's likely to outlive you, Mike. Cathy's premium is lower because there's less chance the insurance company will have to pay a benefit."

"I think the agent who came to our company said a $100,000 variable life insurance policy would cost over $800 a year," said Mike. "I would pay almost twice as much for a policy that only provided one-fifth the coverage. We could only afford to buy a small amount if we went with variable life insurance."

"Now I see why term insurance makes such sense," said Cathy. "I'd much rather save the extra money on our own instead of investing it with an insurance company. Especially after I saw the information Mike brought home. The investment part of the policy grows slowly at first, and there are surrender charges if you cash out during the first few years."

"I have another option that I almost forgot to mention," said Mike. "One of my buddies at work said he was going to skip the insurance the agent was selling and just buy extra term insurance through our benefits program. I could pay for the premium through payroll deduction and wouldn't have to answer any health questions. And that's term insurance, so should I do that instead of buying my own policy?"

"It's worth taking a look at," I said, "but you may pay more than you would with your own policy because you'll get lumped in with less healthy people on your employer's policy. Plus you can lock in the premium on your own term policy—the insurance at work will cost more as you get older. Finally, if you switch jobs, you lose insurance provided at work. It's not a problem if you're still healthy and can get a good policy on your own, but you're taking a chance. Compare the costs before you make a decision."

"It sounds like we should shop for our own policies," said Cathy. "Is there something we should look out for?"

"You should check out the financial strength of the insurance company," I said, "especially if you choose a policy with a long initial term. You want the company to be around and paying benefits for the whole time you hold the policy. You can look up your company's rating at *www.ambest.com.*

"Although you won't need to increase your life insurance right away, I agree with Cathy. It doesn't hurt to start the process. There's a list of Web sites in your binder that offer free instant life insurance quotes. I recommend you get some quotes for 30-year term life insurance for each of you. You can fill out an application on line, but I think sitting down with a knowledgeable, trustworthy insurance agent is a better idea. I'd be happy to give you some names of agents if you'd like."

"We'd like to see your list so we can get started," said Mike.

"Health insurance is next on my list. Ready to tackle that?" I asked.

"This is an area I know something about," said Cathy. "Mike's employer offers an HMO and a PPO plan. We chose the PPO because I like being able to go out of network if I want to see a specialist who isn't on the list. I also checked out the maternity and newborn benefits, and they're very good. I think we're set."

"It sounds like you are," I agreed. "Your choice was a little easier because you knew you wanted to be covered on Mike's plan, Cathy. If you both had health insurance at work, you would want to compare costs and benefits of staying on your employer's plan versus becoming a dependent on your spouse's plan. If you choose your spouse's plan and then change your mind, you'll generally have to wait for an open enrollment period to get back on your employer's plan. Some couples decide to participate both in their own health insurance and in their spouse's program. That's an expensive option—particularly since employees are bearing more of the cost of health insurance than a few years ago. The policies will likely have a coordination of benefits clause that will prevent you from double-dipping, so it's not clear the extra cost is worthwhile.

"It's important to check your coverage regularly. Mike, does your company also offer long-term disability insurance?"

"Yes it does," said Mike. "Cathy looked over the policy and thought it was a pretty good deal."

"I brought some information about your benefits just in case," said Cathy. "After a 90-day waiting period, 67 percent of your salary would be covered if you were disabled. During the first year, you'd get full benefits if you couldn't perform the duties of your job. After that, you'd only get the full 67 percent if you were totally disabled and couldn't work at all. If you could work part-time or at a lower-paid job, you'd be eligible for a residual benefit. You're covered until age 65 and the company pays the full premium."

"I'm glad she understands this stuff," asked Mike. "I have a question. Why does the insurance stop at age 65? I could get disabled at age 70."

"The purpose of disability insurance is to replace a portion of your paycheck if you're unable to work," I said. "Disability coverage generally ends when you're retired and there's no paycheck to replace. Some policies will extend coverage for your lifetime, but employer-paid plans commonly end at age 65."

"I agree with Cathy's analysis that the plan sounds pretty good," I continued. "Does the company offer any short-term disability benefits?"

"It looks like they'd pay 50 percent of your salary for 60 days," said Cathy. "That means we'd have to foot the bill for the other 50 percent of your salary plus the rest of the waiting period. That could be expensive."

"I've already saved up a bunch of sick leave," said Mike, "so it wouldn't be that bad."

"Good," I said. "Accumulated sick and vacation time can help you bridge the gap. You still might come up a bit short, though, so chalk up another reason for keeping an emergency fund.

"Cathy, do you have disability insurance?"

"I'm embarrassed to admit it," said Cathy, "but I don't. I know how important it is—even more so than life insurance at our ages—but I've just put off getting it. Besides, I don't think I'd be eligible for very much coverage because I'm self-employed and I'm only working part-time."

"Self-employed people can have a harder time getting a policy," I agreed, "especially if their earnings are volatile or they've just started their business and don't have a long earnings history. In your case, Cathy, I'd look for a policy that allows you to purchase additional coverage when your earnings increase. There are even some policies that allow you to increase your coverage after you are disabled."

"What should I be looking for when I get quotes?" asked Cathy.

"Ideally, you'd like to get own-occupation coverage for at least two years, or longer if you can," I said. "You'll also want the highest benefit you can get—probably 70 percent of your earnings—and the benefits should be adjusted annually to keep up with cost of living increases. It would be nice to shave the waiting period to 30 days, but your cost would soar, so 60 or 90 days is more realistic. The policy should be guaranteed renewable to age 65 and, if you can afford it, noncancelable, which means the premium stays the same. My rule of thumb is the premium should be no higher than 4 to 5 percent of the annual benefit. If your benefit is 70 percent of $15,000 or $10,500, your annual premium shouldn't be more than about $500."

"That's a lot to remember," said Cathy. "I'm glad you put all that in our recommendations sheet."

"It's hard to compare long-term disability insurance policies because there are so many variations," I said. "I recommend working with an experienced agent whom you trust. Some agents sell both life and disability insurance, and some specialize in disability insurance.

"One more suggestion and we can move on to renter's insurance," I said. "I wouldn't delay getting a policy, Cathy, since you and Mike are planning to start a family."

"I won't," said Cathy. "Feel free to nag me at our next meeting if I haven't started lining up some insurance."

"Great," I said. "I noticed you wrote in your initial questionnaire you have renter's insurance. How much coverage do you have?"

"I looked it up before we came," said Mike. "We have $25,000 of insurance on our personal possessions and $300,000 of liability coverage. We pay about $200 a year."

"I put my jewelry on a separate rider," said Cathy, "after you suggested that at our first meeting."

"It sounds like you two are on top of things," I said. "Do you have replacement cost coverage on your possessions?"

"You bet," said Mike. "Our agent explained how little we'd get if we were only reimbursed for what the stuff is worth now. Several things we bought a few years ago have depreciated a lot. "

"A stack of baseball cards suddenly comes to mind," said Cathy.

"Nice try," said Mike, " but I meant my computer and our television. Besides, those baseball cards are worth way more than I paid for them. Or they will be soon."

"In any case," I said, "replacement cost coverage is the way to go. By the way, Cathy, since you use your spare bedroom for your office, I recommend increasing your insurance to cover your computer and office furniture. Do clients ever come to your home?"

"No," said Cathy. "I meet them at their offices. I would hate to have to keep the apartment clean day after day."

"Then you probably don't need more liability insurance," I said, "but it's a good idea to talk to your agent about upping your property coverage.

"Last on the list," I continued, "is car insurance. I see you brought in the declarations page so we can check your coverage. You each have $100,000/$300,000 liability limits, which means you are covered up to $100,000 per individual and $300,000 per accident if the accident is your fault. That's good coverage."

"Car insurance is so expensive," said Mike. "Any suggestions on how we could save a few bucks?"

"I noticed you have a $250 deductible on your collision coverage," I said. "You could save money by increasing that to $500. I also recommend asking your agent if you could save money by getting your car and renter's insurance from the same company. Your cars are relatively new, so you still want to carry collision coverage. Ask your agent about any other discounts you might be eligible for, like a good driver rate.

"It doesn't hurt to ask for a few quotes to see if you can get a better deal. In fact, that's a general insurance rule. Every few years you should do some comparison shopping to see if you can save some money without reducing your coverage. But if you're planning on switching companies, always make sure you have the new insurance in place before you cancel the old."

"Our friends got a new Honda Civic and their insurance premium went way up," said Cathy. "I could see if it was a Mercedes, but a Honda?"

"When you're shopping for a new car, check out insurance rates at the same time," I said. "Some cars are prime targets for car thieves and other cars are expensive to repair, so insurance on them can be pricey. You shouldn't make your decision solely on insurance costs, of course, but it's a factor to consider.

"So, to summarize, you need to fill a few gaps in your safety net—most importantly getting Cathy a disability policy—and tweak your car insurance. Your renter's policy looks good, but I would ask your agent about coverage for Cathy's office in the home. I'd start exploring your term life insurance options as well.

"We've spent most of the meeting talking about insurance you need. Before we wrap up, let's spend a few minutes on insurance you don't need. Some insurance duplicates coverage you already have, and some is just not worth the premium."

"I keep getting offers from credit card companies for insurance that will pay off my credit card debt if I'm disabled or die," said Mike. "I always throw that stuff away."

"Good decision," I said. "You can skip those special-purpose policies like credit life insurance that the credit card companies push or travel insurance sold at airports. Accidental death and dismemberment insurance is cheap because the insurers know they rarely have to pay a benefit. You're better off with an appropriate amount of term life insurance from a sound company. You can get nickeled and dimed with those small policies, and you'll end up with an expensive patchwork quilt of coverage."

"What about special health insurance for cancer?" asked Cathy.

"I'd also save your money and just get good solid health insurance," I said.

"I've got one," said Mike. "When I was born my parents bought a small life insurance policy for me. It wasn't worth much, so I cashed it in when I started college. Should we buy life insurance for our baby when he or she is born?"

"Excellent question," I said, "and there's a fair amount of debate about this one. Some agents recommend getting some life insurance on a newborn or a young child because it's inexpensive and you can lock in some coverage if the child later becomes uninsurable. My opinion is that very few children grow up to be uninsurable adults, and you'd have to buy a big chunk of insurance when they're young to really make a difference by the time they're adults.

"But here's the bottom line. We buy life insurance to replace our earnings. Unless your child is a movie star or a fashion model for Baby Gap, there are no earnings to replace. Some parents buy enough life insurance for their children to cover final expenses. That's okay if you don't have any savings that you could tap into. I still think you're smarter adding to your emergency fund rather than writing a check for an insurance premium for your child. I know—there's that emergency fund again. It can really make a difference in your financial security. I remember the wife of the president of a bankrupt company lamenting their lack of liquidity. I guess they hadn't followed the guidelines on stashing away emergency cash."

"So the moral of the story is, get insurance for the big stuff and save your own money for the little stuff," said Mike.

"You're becoming a regular financial planning wizard," I said. "That's a great way to sum it all up.

"Next stop on our journey is how to buy houses and cars."

What Cathy and Mike Have Learned

1. Insurance is your safety net, but you need to be careful to choose the right kinds and the right amounts of insurance.

2. Life insurance is important if someone depends on your earnings.

3. Term life insurance is much cheaper and almost always more appropriate for young couples than permanent insurance.

4. Disability insurance is crucial for young couples because you are much more likely to be disabled than die during your working years.

5. Property and casualty insurance should be checked every few years to make sure that coverages are correct and to explore ways to save money premiums.

Recommendations for Cathy and Mike

1. Research and purchase long-term disability insurance immediately (Cathy).

2. Begin researching purchase of term life insurance (Cathy and Mike).

3. Get additional coverage for home office, if necessary (Cathy).

4. Ask insurance agent about advisability and cost of umbrella policy (Mike and Cathy).

Your Homework

1. Check your life insurance policies. Are they the appropriate kind? Do you have the right amount? Do some research and then sit down with a trusted, knowledgeable agent.

2. Check your long-term disability insurance. If you don't have coverage up to 70 percent of your earnings, talk to an agent about buying insurance on your own.

3. Review your health insurance options at work. If you are self-employed, make sure you have adequate coverage, and get new quotes every two or three years. If you leave employment, check into your options under COBRA to maintain coverage.

4. Review your property and casualty insurance. Make sure you have replacement coverage on your possessions and your coverage is adequate. Look for ways to shave your premium without reducing coverage. If you have an office in your home, make sure it's covered. Consider buying an umbrella policy, particularly if you are a high-earning professional, like a doctor or dentist. An umbrella policy will not provide professional liability coverage but can protect your home and other assets if you are sued in connection with a car accident or an accident in your home.

Resources

1. General articles on insurance: *www.insure.com* and *www. smartmoney.com*.

2. Instant quotes: *www.insure.com*, *www.tiaa-cref.com*, *www. quicken.com*.

3. Insurance calculators: *www.quicken.com*, *www.vanguard.com*.

4. General information on insurance: Check with the department of insurance in your state for free booklets and insurance guides.

The Big Stuff—Buying a House and a Car

With the possible exception of your children's college education, your home and cars will be the biggest purchases you make. Although the Internet has facilitated the buying process for these items, you'll still spend a lot more time deciding how much to spend and what to buy than you do on smaller purchases like furniture and computers.

The bigger price tag is part of the reason, but, especially in the case of houses, there are many more decisions you have to make, and comparison shopping is complicated by the wide array of choices. Even after you have narrowed down a price range, the type of house you want, and several acceptable neighborhoods, how do you compare a 2000-square-foot older house with hardwood floors and plaster walls with an 1800-square-foot new house with state-of-the-art appliances? A bag of oranges is a bag of oranges, and the price will probably be the deciding factor; that's not the case with a house or a car.

Then there's the financing issue. At the same time you're car- or house-shopping, you need to be researching ways to pay for your purchase. You can buy or lease a car, use the dealer's financing or arrange your own, and, depending on special promotions, choose a low interest rate or a cash rebate. Home mortgages are even more complicated because, in addition to deciding how much to put down and how long to stretch your repayment, you will also face a dazzling array of interest rate options.

It's easy to get overwhelmed, but, as with any financial decision, if you understand the basic terms and take the process step by step, you have a better chance of making a choice that fits your goals and your situation. We'll start with home buying.

Buy or Rent?

Home ownership may be the American dream, but it's not right for everyone. If your finances are shaky or your job isn't secure, you're probably better off renting until your situation stabilizes. Home ownership brings significant—and often unpredictable—costs, and if you jump in before you have adequate reserves or steady employment, you could jeopardize your house and your credit record.

Even if your financial situation is sound, renting may be more in tune with your lifestyle. If you plan to move in a couple of years, renting is a smarter choice. It usually takes at least two years to break even on the extra costs of home ownership such as mortgage closing costs, real estate commissions, and moving expenses.

You may prefer the flexibility of renting if your personal situation is in flux. If you are considering moving in with a partner or expanding your family, you might rent for a while. Or you may have recently moved to a new area and like the idea of trying out a neighborhood before making the big decision to buy. You may decide to rent if you want to be in a particular school district or neighborhood and can't afford to buy a house there yet.

Some couples continue to rent because they don't want to take on the responsibility of owning and maintaining a home. This strategy fits their lifestyle, but they end up missing out on the substantial advantages of home ownership. If you fit in this category, I recommend comparing the costs and benefits of renting versus owning so you have a good idea of the impact of your choice on your overall financial picture. Couples who own their home are generally in a stronger financial position after a few years, even if they have to pay someone to help clean or maintain the house.

The Advantages of Owning Your Home

The first thing most people think of when asked about the benefits of owning a home is the tax advantage. There's no doubt that the tax savings are significant, although that's only one of the many benefits. But, since taxes are at the top of most people's lists, we'll start there.

1. Tax savings. The mortgage interest and property taxes you pay on your principal residence and your vacation home are deductible from your income. Interest on up to $100,000 of home equity debt is tax deductible as well, no matter how you use the money. Points paid to reduce the interest rate of the loan are generally deductible. Check out IRS Publication 936 for all the rules.

There's also a very sweet tax break awaiting you when you sell your home. Under current law, up to $500,000 profit on your house ($250,000 if you are single or married filing separately) is tax free as long as the house was your principal residence for two out of the last five years. You don't need to roll the profits into another house to get the tax benefit, and the IRS will give you a break if you had to move before meeting the two-year rule due to illness or job change or other specific circumstances. It's a great benefit—you could buy a house today for $200,000, sell it in two years for $700,000, and you and your spouse could pocket the $500,000 gain tax free. Of course, only a few of us make that much money on our house in a lifetime, much less in two years, but in an average real estate market, a $200,000 home will double in value in 18 years and the profit will be tax free when you sell it.

2. Leverage. Probably the most significant benefit you get when you own a home is the ability to control a growing asset while only investing a small piece of the purchase price. When you buy a house, you only really own part of it—the down payment plus the principal you have paid back on the mortgage. The bank holding the mortgage has a claim on the rest. Yet you control the whole house, and when you sell it you get all the profit. That's a very good deal. Without leverage—in this case in the form of a mortgage—you would have to own the whole asset in order to get the whole profit.

Let's say you and a friend bought an antique table at a garage sale for $400 and you each contributed $200. If you sold it later to a dealer for $600, you'd split the proceeds and you'd each get your original $200 back plus $100 of the profit. On the other hand, if you bought a house for $100,000, put $20,000 down, got a mortgage for $80,000 and sold it five years later for $120,000, you'd get your $20,000 down payment back plus you'd get to keep the whole $20,000 profit. You would repay the mortgage to the bank (and after 5 years on a 30-year mortgage you'd still owe most of the original $80,000), but you wouldn't share the profits with the bank. You might conclude that a 20-percent profit in five years is a pretty good return. That's the percentage the house increased in value. In fact, your rate of return is a whole lot more—you doubled your money in five years because you invested $20,000 and you made $20,000 profit. (See Figure 7-1.)

3. Diversification. When you buy a house, you add real estate to your investment portfolio and reduce your overall risk. The investments in 401(k) plans and IRAs tend to be financial securities—stocks, bonds, and mutual funds. When inflation escalates, existing bonds lose value and stocks decline because companies' profits get squeezed. Real estate, however, tends to hold or increase its value during inflationary times. The key to diversification is mixing assets that react differently to economic and market conditions. Real estate balances out other investments because it usually "zings" when stocks and bonds "zang."

4. Inflation Hedge. Because real estate tends to do better than other investments during periods of rising prices, it helps insulate your portfolio against inflation. If you have a fixed mortgage, inflation gives you another bonus. Your monthly payment is fixed, so you'll pay the same number of dollars month after month while the prices of other things continue to increase. Your mortgage payment gets cheaper in real terms—that is, after adjusting for inflation. If you bought your house five years ago and your mortgage payment was $1000, today you're still making $1000 payments even though a $2 loaf of bread now costs $2.30, and a Chevy that cost $10,000 when you bought your

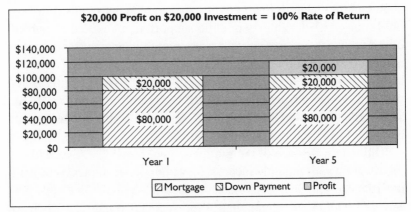

Figure 7-1   Making a Profit on Your Home

house now goes for over $11,500. Other expenses of owning a home such as property taxes and repairs continue to go up, but that mortgage payment stays nailed at $1000. That's why we hear of couples who bought a house 10 or 15 years ago and are making $600 monthly payments on $250,000 homes.

5. Enjoyment. Your mutual funds won't keep you warm and dry, and you wouldn't invite your friends over to watch your stock certificates, but your house is one investment you can enjoy every day. And a house isn't only about shelter—it's about stability and being able to express your personality and lifestyle. Renters have to live by the landlord's rules.

How Much House Should You Buy?

If you think home ownership fits with your financial picture and lifestyle, the next step is figuring out how much you can afford. One rule of thumb suggests that you should buy a house that is between two and two-and-a-half times your annual gross salary. If your partner's and your combined income is $72,000, you might look for houses in the $144,000 to $180,000 range.

Mortgage lenders use two different rules to determine your eligibility, sometimes known as the front-end ratio and the back-end ratio. To satisfy the front-end ratio, your total monthly house payment (including principal, interest, property taxes, and insurance) must equal no more than 28 percent of your monthly gross income. If you pass that test, the lender will verify that your house payment plus all your monthly student loan, credit card, and car payments, plus any obligations such as alimony or child support, don't exceed 36 percent of your monthly income. If your gross monthly income (your income before taxes) is $6000, you could afford a house payment of $1680 as long as your other loan payments didn't exceed $480 a month. If you have a $350 car payment and owe $200 a month on credit cards and $150 a month on student loans, your maximum house payment would be limited to $1460 to satisfy both ratios.

Ultimately, the size of the mortgage you'll qualify for depends on four factors: your monthly income, prevailing interest rates, your creditworthiness, and your other debt. As Figure 7-2 shows, a couple who earn $6,000 a month could qualify for a $213,000 mortgage with a 6 percent interest rate but only a $174,000 mortgage at 8 percent interest.

Case 1: $6,000 monthly income; less than $480 other loan payments

Case 2: $6,000 monthly income; $700 other loan payments

	Case 1			Case 2		
	6%	7%	8%	6%	7%	8%
Principal + Interest	$ 1,280	$ 1,280	$ 1,280	$ 1,060	$ 1,060	$ 1,060
Property Taxes	350	350	350	350	350	350
Insurance	50	50	50	50	50	50
Total House Payment	$ 1,680	$ 1,680	$ 1,680	$ 1,460	$ 1,460	$ 1,460
Mortgage Amount[1]	$213,493	$192,394	$174,443	$176,799	$159,326	$144,461
House Price[2]	$266,867	$240,492	$218,054	$220,999	$199,158	$180,576

[1] 30-year fixed mortgage

[2] With a 20% down payment

FIGURE 7-2 How Much House Can You Afford?

If that same couple had $700 in additional debt, they could only qualify for a $144,000 mortgage at 8 percent—equivalent to a $180,000 house.

Lenders pay a lot of attention to your credit score when determining your creditworthiness, but they also check into your employment status and your reserve money as well. One mortgage broker told me he looks for a cash reserve in a money market fund or savings account equivalent to three months of mortgage payments before he'll go forward with a mortgage.

Those are the rules for qualifying for a mortgage. But should you look for a house as expensive as your mortgage broker or banker says you can afford? Not necessarily. Mortgage lenders will only close the deal if they feel confident they will get paid every month; they do not factor in your other financial goals, like building a college fund or a retirement nest egg, or even taking a nice vacation once in a while. Your broker or banker is not giving you financial planning advice when he or she approves you for a loan—you're responsible for factoring in the other pieces of your plan before shopping for a house.

I recommend using the rules of thumb and ratios as a starting point. Then go back to your spending plan and plug in some different mortgage payments to see how much house fits in your plan. Don't forget to adjust for increased utilities, repair and maintenance, and furnishing expenses when including a house in your spending plan, and make sure you adjust your tax bill to reflect your homeowner tax breaks.

Coming Up with a Down Payment

Even if you and your partner have stable jobs, low debt, and an emergency fund, you may have trouble buying a house if you haven't been able to scrape together a down payment. In order to buy a $150,000 house—around the average price in the United States—you'll typically need a $30,000 down payment to get the most favorable mortgage rate and avoid extra expenses. You would have to earn over $40,000 and save your entire after-tax salary to accumulate a $30,000 down payment in one year. Thankfully, there are other ways to get over the down payment hurdle, particularly if you are a first-time home buyer. Here are some ideas.

1. Pay PMI. Many lenders will allow you to put down less than 20 percent of the price of the house if you agree to pay a monthly premium for Private Mortgage Insurance (PMI). The amount you'll pay

varies between about .3 and .7 percent of the mortgage each year. On a $180,000 mortgage you might pay $75 a month. Unlike interest, the payment is not deductible from your income, and it does not reduce your mortgage balance. It's simply a premium for insurance to protect the lender for the difference between the amount you put down on the house and the standard 20-percent down payment.

Once you have accumulated 20-percent equity in your house, you can usually dispense with PMI. As you make payments on your mortgage, your equity will increase. However, if you put 5 percent down on a $190,000 house, it will take about 10 years to pay back enough principal to get to the 20-percent mark because so much of the early payments goes to interest. As your home appreciates, you will also build equity. Most homes will appreciate fast enough to eliminate PMI in about 5 years if you put 5 percent down initially. You may have to pay for an appraisal and other fees before the bank will let you get rid of PMI, so keep an eye on property values in your neighborhood so you'll know when to make your move.

The Homeowner's Protection Act of 1998 provides for automatic cancellation of PMI for most mortgages signed after July 29, 1999 when the homeowner reaches 22-percent equity. The percentage is based on the original purchase price of the house. Check the Consumer Alerts section of the Federal Trade Commission Web site (*www.ftc.gov*) for details.

2. Get a piggyback loan. Mortgage lenders may arrange two loans for you—a conventional mortgage and a shorter-term loan for a down payment. The advantage is you can buy a house with little or no down payment and skip the PMI. The downside is you will have hefty payments for several years while you're paying off both loans. Typically, lenders extend these loans to young professionals such as physicians and attorneys who have high earning potential. Piggyback loans can be reasonable options if the payments fit in your spending plan and you have secure employment.

3. Get an FHA or VA loan. The Federal Housing Administration (FHA) offers mortgages to homebuyers who pay as little as 3 percent down. The house must pass a comprehensive inspection to qualify and generally must not be more expensive than the median price of homes. The buyer pays a mortgage insurance premium. Eligible veterans of the U.S. Armed Forces can buy a home with little or no down payment and no mortgage insurance through the Veteran's

Administration (VA) loan program. Ask your mortgage lender for details on these programs.

4. Take advantage of special programs for first-time or low- or moderate-income homebuyers. Several government and private programs have sprung up to help people who may not qualify for a conventional mortgage to buy houses. Such programs as AmeriDream and Partners in Charity are described on the *www.fhaloan.com* Web site. Fannie Mae (*www.fanniemae.com*) offers help for prospective homebuyers with less than perfect credit histories and the U.S. Department of Housing and Urban Development (*www.hud.gov*) has Teacher Next Door and Officer Next Door programs to provide special low down payment arrangements on HUD-owned homes to teachers and law enforcement officers. Check with local community organizations and lenders about first-time homebuyer programs in your area.

5. Share your equity. Many mortgage lenders will not allow you to count a gift from a relative as part of your down payment. As an alternative, a friend or relative might agree to share the equity in your home by supplying all or part of the down payment. In exchange, you agree to repay the investment and a portion of the increased value of the house in a certain number of years. Shared equity arrangements provide an opportunity for a friend or relative to help you out and still earn a nice return.

Getting a Mortgage

Accumulating a down payment may be your biggest hurdle, but choosing a mortgage may give you your biggest headache. There are many different types of mortgages, and without a crystal ball you can't know in advance which will be perfect for you. You can, however, use what you know about your situation to sort through your options.

Your first choice is fixed versus adjustable. Fixed mortgages lock in an interest rate and a payment for the term of the loan; adjustable rate mortgages (ARMs) lock in an interest rate for a specified period, and then your payment adjusts up or down to match a change in interest rate. There is no clear consensus on which is preferable, but here are some guidelines.

If you are confident that you will only be in the house for a short time (three to five years, for example), you may do well with an ARM. The initial rate will be lower than a fixed rate—often between .5 and

1.5 percent less—so your monthly payment will be smaller. If you are considering an ARM, find out how long the initial period lasts before the payment can be adjusted, how often after that an adjustment can be made, which index the interest rate is pegged to, and whether there are interest rate caps on individual adjustments as well as an overall cap that sets a maximum interest rate for the loan. If you are considering a 5-percent ARM that can adjust after three years and every year thereafter with a periodic cap of 2 percent and an overall cap of 11 percent, your interest rate could float up all the way to 11 percent in six years under a worst-case scenario. If you think you might be in the house six or seven years, consider choosing an ARM with a longer initial term or less frequent adjustment periods.

Fixed-term mortgages eliminate the uncertainty associated with ARMs but come with a higher rate of interest. If you intend to stay in your house several years or you just prefer to avoid the risk of higher mortgage payments, a fixed term is a sensible choice. Personally, I prefer the peace of mind that comes with a fixed mortgage, especially since my house payment is the largest expense in my budget. When mortgage interest rates are unusually high—in double digits—ARMs can be attractive, but when interest rates are low, it makes sense to lock in a fixed rate.

Another variation is the 7-year balloon mortgage. The loan payment is calculated as if it were a 30-year mortgage, but the balance is due after 7 years. At or before the 7-year mark, you either have to come up with the cash to pay off the mortgage or, more likely, refinance with a new mortgage. Although the interest rate is slightly better than with a fixed-rate mortgage, I wouldn't want to be forced to refinance on the mortgage company's time schedule, especially if mortgage rates have gone sky high. If you think you're going to be in the house for more than 7 years, you're probably better off with a conventional fixed mortgage.

Once you've chosen between fixed and adjustable, you still have to pick the term of your mortgage. The typical terms are 15 years (180 payments) or 30 years (360 payments). You'll save lots of interest with a 15-year mortgage, and your interest rate will probably be slightly lower, but your monthly payment will be significantly higher because you pay off the loan twice as fast.

I endorse the rule that says as long as you can earn more on your investments, on average, than the interest rate you pay on your mortgage, you're better off taking a longer mortgage and using the money you save on a lower monthly payment to fund your nest egg.

Here's how that works. Let's say you're planning to buy a $150,000 house and put 20 percent or $30,000 down. Your two options might be a 15-year mortgage at 6.75 percent and a 30-year mortgage at 7 percent. Your monthly payment (not including property tax or insurance) on the 15-year mortgage would be $1062, and you would pay $71,000 in interest over the life of the mortgage. Your monthly payment on the 30-year mortgage would be $798, and you would pay $167,000 interest. If you only look at the amount of interest you'll pay, your choice would be easy—take the 15-year option. You have to look at the whole picture, though. For simplicity, let's assume you have $1062 a month to spend on a mortgage or invest or a combination of both. If you pay $1062 a month on your mortgage, after 15 years, you'll have no mortgage, but you won't have a nest egg, either. If for the next 15 years you invest the entire $1062 a month at 8 percent, you'll end up with $367,500. (See Figure 7-3.)

Alternatively, if you chose the 30-year mortgage and invested the $264 savings ($1062 minus $798) each month for 30 years at 8 percent, you'd have $395,000 in your nest egg at the end of 30 years, plus you would have paid off your mortgage. Even though you paid a lot more interest with the 30-year mortgage, your nest egg is 7 percent bigger than if you had chosen the 15-year mortgage. If you had earned 8.5 percent on your investments, your nest egg advantage would increase to almost $52,000 with the 30-year mortgage. This analysis does not take into account the extra tax savings you get with a longer

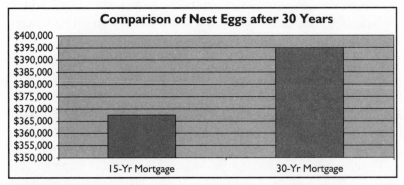

FIGURE 7-3   Comparison of Nest Eggs after 30 Years

mortgage, particularly in the first several years. That would tip the scales even further toward the 30-year option.

Even though I'm a fan of longer mortgages in order to keep your payments down and increase your leverage, there are two circumstances when the shorter mortgage makes more sense: if you can't earn more on your investments than the interest rate on your mortgage or if you'd just blow the extra cash you'd have if you stretched out your mortgage.

Paying Off Your Mortgage Early

The same rules that apply to choosing a mortgage are useful when deciding whether to speed up payments. Some advisors recommend making extra payments to save interest over the life of the mortgage. They point out that when you make an extra payment against the principal of a 7-percent mortgage, for example, it's as if you paid yourself 7 percent. That's true, but if you can earn more than 7 percent on your investments, you're better off investing the extra money rather than paying down your mortgage.

If you still intend to pay down your mortgage more quickly, first make sure you have fully funded your retirement plans and you have paid off higher interest debt like a credit card balance. Then set up a do-it-yourself system. You can add a little bit to your normal payment each month or make an extra payment each year. Either way, make sure your lender applies the money to the principal of the loan—each time you pay back a chunk of principal, you eliminate the interest you would have paid on that amount. And, by all means, skip the biweekly payment schemes your lender may offer. You'll get charged an up-front fee plus a service fee with each payment, adding up to hundreds of dollars in just a few years. You can get the same result for free by making an extra payment once a year.

When Refinancing Makes Sense

When it comes to your mortgage, you hold the cards. If your interest rate is as good or better than prevailing rates, you can just hang on to what you have, and if rates drop you can dump your old mortgage and get a new one. The old rule of thumb was interest rates had to drop 2 percent or more to make refinancing worthwhile. That's not the case anymore. Instead, compare your monthly savings to the amount you'll pay to refinance to see how long it will take you to break even. Generally, if you can break even in 24 months or less, and you plan to stay in the house at least that long, it's smart to refinance.

For example, if you had the $120,000 7-percent mortgage described above and interest rates fell to 6 percent, your mortgage payment would drop from $798 to $719 a month—a savings of $79 a month. If your closing costs were $1200, you'd break even in 15 months. As long as you didn't plan to move in the next year and a half or so, refinancing would be a good deal. Just remember that if you're several years into your mortgage when you refinance, in effect you're restarting the clock on your loan.

If you've decided to refinance, you may wish to get an estimate from your current lender first, but I recommend you comparison shop. The Bankrate Web site (*www.bankrate.com*) is a good place to get information on lots of lenders. Don't just focus on the new interest rate—get an accurate estimate of closing costs as well. You shouldn't pay more than about 1 percent of the mortgage balance to refinance, plus any escrow payments.

Can Cathy and Mike Buy a House?

It's time to check in with Cathy and Mike. They are eager to buy a house but aren't sure they can afford one yet.

"I'm a little nervous about this meeting," said Cathy. "I'm tired of renting, but Mike and I have been going to open houses and I'm not sure we can afford the kind of house I want."

"I guess we're suffering from sticker shock," added Mike.

"Let's start by figuring out how much house you can afford," I said. "According to one rule of thumb, with a combined income of $60,000, you should be able to buy a house costing between $120,000 and $150,000."

"Could we get a mortgage for the full amount?" asked Cathy.

"Generally, you should try to put 20 percent of the price of the house down and mortgage the rest," I said. "That means a $24,000 to $30,000 down payment for a house in that price range."

"We're sunk," said Mike. "We could only come up with a few thousand dollars at most. Do we really have to put 20 percent down?"

"Not necessarily," I said. "There are several programs available to first-time homebuyers who can't put a full 20 percent down. I'll give you a list of places to contact. But first we should figure out if you qualify for a mortgage big enough to finance a house costing that amount, and then we'll need to see if the payments fit in your spending plan.

"The first test is the front-end ratio. In order to comply, your total monthly house payment cannot be more than 28 percent of your gross monthly income. Your gross monthly income is $5000, so $1400 is your cap. Assuming property taxes and insurance total $270, your principal and interest payment would have to be $1130 or under. Interest rates are about 7 percent, so you could qualify for a 30-year, $170,000 mortgage."

"So we pass the first test," said Cathy. "Hurray. What's next?"

"In order to pass the second test, your total monthly payments must not exceed 36 percent of your monthly income. In your case, your total payments can't be more than $1800 a month. You pay $80 a month on student loans, $160 for Mike's Jeep and $100 toward credit cards, so that leaves $1460 for the total house payment. At 7 percent, you would qualify for a 30-year $180,000 mortgage."

"Does that mean we can afford a more expensive house than your first estimate of $120,000 to $150,000?" asked Mike

"That only means a lender could qualify you for that size mortgage," I said. "We need to look at your spending plan and see how payments that size fit in. I prepared a side-by-side comparison of your current plan and a new plan with a $1460 monthly payment for principal, interest, taxes, and insurance. I also had to adjust your federal tax bill. The mortgage interest of $12,500 and property taxes of $2,600 push your total deductions above the standard deduction. By itemizing, you'll save about $1,400 in federal taxes. I'm afraid even with the tax break, you're almost $500 short each month." (See Figure 7-4.)

"Couldn't we figure out how to save $500 a month?" asked Cathy.

"I don't see how we can do that, Cathy," said Mike. "We already shaved $100 a month from eating out and entertainment and $100 a month off our cash expenses in order to free up money for your retirement plan and emergency cash. I don't want to be house poor."

"I hate to be a wet blanket," I said, "but the picture's slightly worse than that. I haven't added private mortgage insurance, extra utilities, or a repair fund. Many real estate professionals suggest you count on spending 1 percent of the value of the house each year just keeping it up. I think you're probably about $700 short a month."

"We could buy a cheaper house, Mike," said Cathy.

	Current Spending Plan		With Mortgage	
	Monthly	Annual	Monthly	Annual
Income				
Mike's Salary	$3,750	$45,000	$3,750	$45,000
Cathy's Net Business Income	$1,250	$15,000	$1,250	$15,000
Total Income	$5,000	$60,000	$5,000	$60,000
Expenses				
Housing				
Rent/House Payment	$850	$10,200	$1,460	$17,520
Utilities	$220	$2,640	$220	$2,640
Furnishings	$50	$600	$50	$600
Clothing	$165	$1,980	$165	$1,980
Groceries	$335	$4,020	$335	$4,020
Transportation				
Gas	$100	$1,200	$100	$1,200
Repairs/Maint	$30	$360	$30	$360
Insurance				
Medical/Dental	$85	$1,020	$85	$1,020
Disability	$20	$240	$20	$240
Life				
Renter's	$12	$144		
Auto	$100	$1,200	$100	$1,200
Out-of-Pocket Medical	$40	$480	$40	$480
Cash/Miscellaneous	$300	$3,600	$300	$3,600
Eating Out/Entertainment	$300	$3,600	$300	$3,600
Vacations	$175	$2,100	$175	$2,100
Gifts	$40	$480	$40	$480
Charitable Contributions	$18	$216	$18	$216
Magazines/Books	$24	$288	$24	$288
Children				
Child Care				
Education				

FIGURE 7-4   **Fitting a Mortgage into Mike's and Cathy's Spending Plan**

	Current Spending Plan		With Mortgage	
	Monthly	Annual	Monthly	Annual
Loan Payments				
Student loan	$80	$960	$80	$960
Car	$160	$1,920	$160	$1,920
Credit cards	$100	$1,200	$100	$1,200
Hobbies	$20	$240	$20	$240
Savings				
401(k)	$375	$4,500	$375	$4,500
Cathy's Retirement Savings	$125	$1,500	$125	$1,500
Other (Emergency)	$160	$1,920	$160	$1,920
Federal Income Tax	$608	$7,296	$493	$5,919
State and Local Income Tax	$228	$2,736	$228	$2,736
F.I.C.A.	$280	$3,360	$280	$3,360
Total Expenses	$5,000	$60,000	$5,483	$65,799

FIGURE 7-4 **(Continued)**

"We didn't like any of the houses we looked at that cost less than $150,000," said Mike. "We can keep looking, but I don't want to live in a dump."

"I know how much you want to buy a house, Cathy," I said, "and I agree home ownership makes sense for your long-term financial picture. But I recommend you build up your emergency fund and accumulate at least a small down payment before you jump in. In the meantime you can look into programs that offer assistance to first-time buyers."

"And we can keep going to open houses so we'll have a better idea of what we want," said Mike.

"I guess so," said Cathy. "I'm really disappointed. So many of our friends have already bought homes. If I were working full time, we'd be in better shape."

"You'd have a higher income this year if you weren't going to school," I agreed, "but you're close to finishing your MBA, and the advanced degree will boost your income for the rest of your life. I think you're doing the right thing by getting more education now."

"So the plan is to keep making contributions to our retirement plans, and add $160 a month to our emergency fund as we intended," said Cathy. "I'm going to take another look at our spending plan to see how we can put aside some money for a down payment."

"That's a great idea," I said. "A new house is in your future, I have no doubt."

Car Buying Basics

For some people, cars are simply transportation—a way to get from Point A to Point B. For others, their car is their prized possession, an extension of their personality. Although our attitudes about cars differ, we all face the same facts: Cars are expensive to buy and keep, and they lose their value with use. The cost of a car plus insurance, gas, maintenance, and repair represents a significant chunk of our cash flow. And we have to keep replacing them.

As with any big purchase, a little research can save a lot of money. Pricing and availability used to be mysteries guarded closely by car dealers. Thanks to the Internet, car buyers can find out invoice prices, comparison shop with a few clicks of the mouse, even research the history of a used car. Although most people still buy their cars from dealers, more and more are gathering information off the Internet first.

Before you buy your next car, think about how you use a car. Which features are essential and which are simply nice to have? When you have a list of cars that fit your specifications, start researching prices. In addition to looking up the invoice price and average purchase price for each car on your list, find out how rapidly the car depreciates and how much you're likely to spend to maintain it. Insurance is one of the biggest ongoing costs of owning a car—find out how much you'll pay to insure the cars you're considering.

Look into different ways to finance your car. Credit unions or even your local bank might offer a better rate than the dealer.

Armed with cost and financing information, you're ready to head to the dealer and start negotiating. Forget how much the monthly payment will be or how many free car washes you'll get or what kind of financing your dealer can arrange until you've nailed down the purchase price. Don't be shy about walking away and talking to another dealer. You may have more leverage if you shop at the end of the month when dealers are trying to meet their quotas.

Lease or Buy?

The fanfare over car leasing seems to have died down a bit, but the papers still carry plenty of ads touting leases on all kinds of cars. When you lease a car, you pay for the use of the car (the depreciation) plus a financing charge.

Lease payments tend to be cheaper than payments you make when you purchase a car because you're only paying for part of the value of the car when you lease. When the lease is up, the car still has value that you don't own. The car goes back to the dealer and you're left with nothing except memories. When you buy, you typically build up some equity in the car.

Leasing is similar to renting an apartment. At the end of the rental period, you clean up the apartment, hand over the keys, and walk away. Every time your apartment lease ends you either have to sign a new lease or move out.

Certain individuals can make a case for leasing. If you tend to take good care of your car, don't put more than about 15,000 miles a year on it, like to get a new car every two or three years, and have the discipline to save or invest the money you'll save on monthly payments, you could be a candidate for leasing. However, many people lease in order to drive a car they couldn't afford to buy, and they end up with a perpetual car payment—never owning, always renting. Your financial picture will generally be better if you own rather than lease your cars.

Ten Tips for Buying A Car

1. Don't overspend. If the price of your new car is more than about 20 percent of your annual income, chances are you'll need to shortchange some other goals.

2. Don't skimp on auto insurance. Insuring your car is expensive, but you're risking a lot if you go for the bare minimum. Raising the deductible or cutting back on collision coverage is smarter than reducing your liability coverage.

3. Don't focus on the monthly payment when you buy. Car sellers are famous for steering your attention away from the full price and toward the monthly amount. They'll often stretch out the term of the loan to whittle down the payment. Keep your eye on your total price,

and don't sign up for a loan term longer than 60 months—a 48-month loan is even better.

4. Keep the car for at least two years longer than the term of the loan. When the car is paid off, keep making payments into a money market account to build up a down payment for your next car. If you follow this strategy, each time you buy a car you should be able to put a bigger chunk down.

5. Check out your credit union and local banks for car loan rates. Compare rates on *www.bankrate.com*. Your dealer may offer decent terms, but you're better off doing your homework first.

6. Do your research on the Web even if you buy in person. Two Web sites chock full of information on new and used cars are *www.kbb.com* and *www.edmunds.com*.

7. Negotiate. If you've done your homework, you'll know a lot about the price of the car you're considering. Use that information to your advantage.

8. Consider buying a newer used car. According to information on the Edmunds Web site, new cars depreciate about 20 percent in the first year, on average. Cars coming off short-term leases can be good buys.

9. Do the math on rebates and incentives. If you're financing a $15,000 car, which is better—a $1500 rebate or a 0-percent 3-year loan? It depends. An 8-percent 3-year car loan will cost you $470 a month. A 0-percent loan will cost $417 a month, or $1908 less over three years. The 0-percent deal wins. If you only intended to get a loan for half the price of the car, however, you'd do better taking the rebate.

10. Don't be too picky. If you have your heart set on the latest model of a popular car and won't budge on the color or options, you may get stuck with a higher price. The more flexible you are, the more negotiating leeway you'll have.

So read up, check out the Web, know what you want, and don't be swayed by a glib salesperson. You'll get more experienced with every car purchase you make—it's an exercise you'll repeat many times during your life.

What Cathy and Mike Have Learned

1. A mortgage broker may qualify you for a larger mortgage than comfortably fits with your other goals and cash flow.

2. Home ownership usually enhances your overall financial picture, but don't skimp on other goals like retirement funding just to get into a house.

3. There are several programs available to first-time home buyers who can't come up with a 20-percent down payment.

Recommendations for Cathy and Mike

1. Continue to build up your emergency reserve and contribute to your retirement plans.

2. Continue to visit open houses to narrow down your choices of neighborhoods as well as to learn more about how much house your targeted price will buy. Make a list of "must-have" and "nice-to-have" features to make the search easier when you're ready to buy.

3. Look into programs for first-time home buyers in your community.

Resources

- *www.ala.org*—The Web site of the American Library Association contains a list of good Web sites and books for homebuyers.

- *www.pueblo.gsa.gov*—Free information from the federal government about various consumer issues, including home buying.

- *www.bankrate.com*—Mortgage research.

- Irwin, Robert. *Buy Your First Home*. Dearborn Trade, 2001.

- Glink, Ilyce R. *100 Questions Every First-Time Homebuyer Should Ask*. Times Books, 2000.

- *www.kbb.com* and *www.edmunds.com* for car-buying information.

CHAPTER 8

Getting on the Path to Financial Independence

ven if you're not a procrastinator by nature, it's easy to put off saving for retirement. After all, it's so far away and there are so many other ways to spend your money in the meantime. By the time you have finished paying student loans, credit card debt, house payments, car payments, and had a little fun, there's just not much money left over each month.

In Chapter 4, we looked at three ways you can manage your cash— (1) you can live above your means, spending more than you make (at least temporarily); (2) you can live just within your means, not getting into serious trouble but not saving either; or (3) you can live below your means, spending less than you make and socking away the difference in savings and investments. Only the last will set you on a path to a better life and financial security. And that's the secret to funding your retirement—each month siphon off part of your earnings into long-term investments. The earlier you start, the better.

Why is there so much focus on retirement? Pick up any personal finance magazine or visit one of dozens of financial Web sites, and chances are a few articles—if not the entire issue—will be devoted to some aspect of retirement. The topic may seem unnecessarily hyped, but there's a very good reason why you should begin thinking early about your nest egg. The responsibility for a secure future rests on your shoulders. The old days of working 20 or 30 years for one company and retiring with a generous pension have all but disappeared.

You face a greater burden for funding your own future than your parents or grandparents faced.

The traditional way to think about retirement was to picture a three-legged stool that would support you in your golden years. One leg was your pension. However, pensions are rare these days, so it's unlikely that leg will hold you up. The second leg was Social Security. But even a patched-up Social Security system won't guarantee a cushy retirement all by itself.

The third leg of your retirement is your nest egg—your investments. Unless you expect a big inheritance or the lottery to bail you out—and I encourage you not to count on either—your investments will be the leg that holds you up when you're no longer working.

Just as the burden for preparing for retirement has shifted to our shoulders, the definition of retirement has changed. For most of us, our vision of life after work doesn't mean sitting on a porch in a rocking chair. Instead of retirement, we're planning for financial independence—getting to the point where we don't have to earn a paycheck because we've accumulated enough money to support ourselves without working.

If you love your work—and I hope you do—then you may decide to continue working beyond typical retirement age. You may switch careers or you may cut back on your work hours, but you may continue to earn a paycheck because you enjoy what you're doing. However, the goal is to be financially independent so you're free to call it quits and live off your investments if you choose.

So it's as simple as that. The secret to financial independence is to live on less than you earn and stash away the rest for the future. That's the general rule, but let's fill in some details.

Youth Has Its Privileges

Most of us wish we had started planning for the long term much sooner than we did. Mike and Cathy are lucky—and smart—to be thinking about this subject now.

"I know we're going to talk about retirement planning," said Mike, "but we're pretty young, and I just want to make sure I don't have to wait until I retire to enjoy life."

"I'm confident we can put together a retirement savings plan and still allow some room for fun now," I said. "Starting to save now increases the chance that you'll meet your goals. The younger you want to retire and the more you want to spend in retirement, the larger the nest egg you'll need to accumulate while you're working. If you start working at age 24 and want to stop at age 50, you'll need to invest enough in 26 years to last you for 45 years. That's a big undertaking."

"Why 45 years?" asked Mike.

"The life expectancy of Americans born in the 1970s is about 78," I explained. "And your life expectancy increases the longer you live. If you make it to age 65, you have a better than 50-50 chance you'll live past age 85. Advances in medicine and health care will keep pushing life expectancies further out. If you spend all your nest egg by the time you're 80 and you live until you're 100, how will you pay the bills for the last 20 years of your life? I suggest planning for at least age 95."

"I'm starting to feel overwhelmed," said Cathy.

"It's not as bad as all that," I said. "Let's go back to Mike's comment about postponing fun. The trick with financial planning is to strike a balance between your near-term goals—like buying a house, taking vacations, eating out, and having fun—with your long-term goals, like retirement. I think the British call that 'jam today or jam tomorrow.'"

"With a bit of forethought, you can have both. In fact, the two of you have a wonderful advantage. Care to guess what that is?"

"A good plan?" asked Cathy. "Or at least we'll have one soon."

"A good education, so we can continue to get promotions and better pay?" asked Mike.

"Good habits," added Cathy. "We're not seriously in debt and we don't usually go on big spending binges."

"Don't forget my extraordinary mutual-fund picking skills," said Mike with a grin.

"All good answers," I said. "Human capital—your education and experience—plus a good plan and the discipline to stick to it are important factors. I'm not going to bank a lot on Mike's mutual-fund crystal ball, though.

"Your biggest advantage is time. You're young, so you can get a head start. Let's see how lots of time can translate into lots of money."

Double Your Money

"You may have heard the tale of the two brothers," I said. "One starts saving right out of college but stops after seven years. The other brother waits until he's in his early 30s and saves for more than 30 years. Even though the late-starter invests more than four times as much money as the early-starter, his nest egg never catches up."

"I've heard that story," said Cathy, "but it always sounded kind of fishy."

"Not at all," I said. "It simply demonstrates the power of compounding. Let's say you invest $2000 today in a stock mutual fund in an IRA and you earn 9 percent a year.

"At that rate of return, your investment will double in eight years to $4000. In another eight years, your investment will double again to $8000. Every eight years, your investment will double, to $16,000, then $32,000, then $64,000. If you hold on to your investment for 40 years, your money will double five times. You're 27 years old, so in 40 years you'll be 67 and your investment will be worth about $64,000.

"Not bad considering the only money you put in the IRA was the original $2000. But let's say you decided you just couldn't save anything this year, Cathy, or even next year. In fact, you waited eight years from now until you were 35. By then you may have bought a house, had a few children, and were feeling more secure in your consulting business. But you also lopped eight years off your investment horizon. You'll have 32 years until you turn 67. If your investment doubles every eight years, you'll have four doubling periods. Your $2000 investment will only be worth about $32,000 at age 67."

"Let me make sure I understood that," said Cathy. "If I wait just eight years before investing my $2000, you're saying I'll end up with only half the money, right?"

"I'm afraid that's right," I said. "By waiting, you lose your last doubling period—when your investment would have gone from $32,000 to $64,000."

"How did you know Cathy's money will double every eight years?" asked Mike.

"I used a handy tool called the Rule of 72," I said. "If you take the number 72 and divide it by your average annual rate of return, your answer is the number of years it will take for your investment to double. I assumed Cathy would earn 9 percent on her money, so 72 divided by 9 equals 8. If Cathy invested more conservatively and her average rate of return was only 7.2 percent, it would take 10 years to double her money. How much would her $2000 investment be worth in 40 years? Start by figuring out how many times her investment would double."

"I'll try this one," said Mike. "There are four 10-year periods in 40 years, so Cathy's $2000 would double four times. She'd have $32,000."

"I see how the rule works," said Cathy. "But is it really just compounding that produces those incredible results?"

"Incredible, but true," I said. "Compounding simply means earning interest on your interest. If you invested $10,000 today and earned 10 percent interest each year, but you only earned simple interest—that means your interest didn't compound—you'd earn 10 percent of $10,000 or $1000 each year. At the end of 30 years you'd have your original investment of $10,000 plus 30 chunks of $1000 interest payments for a total of $40,000.

"If, however, you earned 10-percent compound interest, the first year you'd earn $1000. In the second year, your 10-percent rate of return would be calculated on your original $10,000 plus the $1000 interest you earned in the first year, so you'd earn $1100. By the end of your second year, your investment would be worth $12,100, and at the end of 30 years it would have grown to over $170,000—more than four times what you earned with simple interest.

"Every time you get a raise, Mike, it's like earning compound interest," I said. "You earn $45,000 now. If you got a 4-percent raise, your salary would increase $1800 to $46,800. If next year you got another 4-percent raise, it would be worth a little more—$1872—because it was applied to a bigger base. The extra $72 was a raise on your previous raise.

"There's another way to look at compounding. Let's say you told me you wanted to have a million dollars in your retirement nest egg in 30 years and you wanted to know how much you'd need to save each year to reach that goal. If you earned 8.5 percent on your investments, you'd have to invest about $8000 a year. Cathy, you'd be a 57-year-old millionaire.

"If a 37-year-old couple wanted to accumulate a million dollars by age 57, they'd have to save $20,600 a year. A 47-year old couple would have to invest $67,000 a year to reach the million-dollar mark by age 57. The longer you wait, the harder it will be to get to where you want to go."

"I'm convinced," said Mike. "We need to save early and save often. But there's one thing you left out. A million dollars isn't going to be worth diddley in 30 years."

"I agree that you can't plan for retirement without taking inflation into account," I said. "You can apply the rule of 72 to calculate the effects of price increases. Just divide 72 by the average inflation rate and your answer will be the number of years it will take for prices to double. If prices double, your nest egg will only buy half as much as it did before. Let's say you had a shoebox full of money, and inflation averaged 4 percent per year. In 18 years (72 divided by 4), that stack of money would lose half its value—that's what happens when prices go up."

"So how much will my million dollars be worth in 30 years?" asked Cathy.

"If you had it stuck in a shoebox and didn't earn any interest on it, it would only be worth about $300,000 in terms of what it would buy. If you put your money in an account earning 4 percent, instead, the interest you made would offset inflation, and your million dollars would still be worth a million dollars. In order to grow your investment, you'll have to earn more than the inflation rate."

Financial Independence

"Okay," said Mike. "We're on board. How much do we need to invest each month so we can retire while we're still young enough to enjoy it?"

"Before we get to the subject of how much," I said, "let's talk for a moment about what retirement means to you. Who wants to start?"

"I'll jump in," said Cathy. "Retirement to me means staying up as late as I like and throwing the alarm clock out the window. I want to travel to exotic places and maybe do some volunteer work. I want to have time to do things I can't do now."

"That all sounds good to me," said Mike. "On the other hand, I can't really imagine ever retiring. It would be nice if I didn't have to do the 9-to-5 thing, and I'd like to be my own boss someday. But quitting work completely—that's just not me."

"Sounds like a pretty active retirement to me," I said. "I didn't hear either of you talk about settling in and spending your golden years whittling on the front porch."

"No thanks," said Mike. "Our grandparents didn't even do that."

"Many people stay very active long after they've quit their regular jobs," I agreed. "So maybe retirement isn't a particularly accurate term. You're not retiring so much as shifting gears. Let's call it financial independence instead. That means accumulating enough wealth so you can live off your investments instead of your paychecks. It doesn't mean you stop working, necessarily, but you have the freedom to slow down or quit if you want to."

"So if I still enjoyed doing consulting work," said Cathy, "I might keep working, but I could cut down on the number of clients because I wouldn't be depending on my work to support me."

"Exactly," I said. "And that opens up all kinds of possibilities. You could arrange to meet with your clients at your home in Aruba or by conference call while cruising the Mediterranean. You might decide to write a column or do some public speaking—in exotic places, of course. When you are financially independent, the world is your oyster."

"Sounds wonderful," said Cathy grinning. "Can I just skip the middle stage and start living that way now?"

"Sure, if you can earn enough to pay all your bills and still stash away money for your long-term goals," I said.

"I think we should keep our day jobs for now, Cathy," said Mike. "But I really like thinking about retirement the way you described it. Instead of planning for a time when we stop doing things, we can focus on planning for a time when we are free to do lots of things."

"I'm excited," said Cathy. "I'd always thought of investing for retirement as something like eating my vegetables. It was good for me but I didn't much like it. Now I'll just keep that mental picture of me dangling my feet in the warm Caribbean Ocean while I'm on my cell phone arranging to meet a client in Oslo. "

"Great," I smiled, "because I have a 25-year jump on you two. Now you won't be surprised if in a few years I e-mail you from my flat in London. So let's agree that even though we may talk about retirement, we're really going to plan for financial independence."

How Much is Enough?

The million-dollar question, or for many young couples, the multimillion dollar question is how much do you need to save to reach financial independence? There's no precise answer because so many things can change along the way. You'll switch jobs a few times and probably even careers. We can't predict exact rates of return or inflation rates, much less how long you'll live or how much money you'll need to live on each year.

There are rules of thumb you can use. Most couples need to save 10 to 15 percent of their income to reach their retirement goals, but the numbers vary widely. Your plan will depend on how soon you want to reach financial independence, how lush a lifestyle you want, and how aggressively you invest your nest egg.

I recommend developing a scenario of how financial independence will look, and then working backwards to calculate how much you'll need to save. This gives you a starting point—even though you'll have to tweak the numbers along the way. Once you have a savings goal, you can set up a system to pull a certain amount out automatically from your paycheck or checking account—the "pay yourself" principle. By funding your financial independence before you pay everyone else, you make retirement saving automatic rather than a day-to-day decision. Your spending decisions can focus on trade-offs like taking a vacation versus remodeling the bathroom instead of taking a vacation versus saving for retirement. You've already taken care of the retirement part, and that takes a lot of stress off your spending decisions.

The first step in constructing a retirement scenario is to make some assumptions. Cathy and Mike want to be financially independent by the time Cathy's 60 and Mike's 62. We'll assume they earn 8 percent on their nest egg—roughly what a balanced portfolio of 60 percent stocks and 40 percent bonds and cash has earned over the past 50 years—and we'll assume inflation averages 3 percent a year. They would like to live on $4000 a month, after taxes, in today's dollars, about $1000 more than what they're living on now. We'll apply an inflation factor later.

Neither Cathy nor Mike is eligible for a company pension, and neither is counting on Social Security to provide much income in retirement. The current system is structured so Social Security benefits replace a smaller percentage of income for workers who earn more. Even if Social Security is viable when they retire, we can leave it out of their scenario without changing the result very much.

Next we need to figure out how much they already have in their nest egg.

"Mike, your 401(k) balance is about $14,300 and Cathy, you have $6200 in your old 403(b) plan, right?" I asked.

"Well, not exactly," said Cathy. "After our house-buying meeting a couple of weeks ago, I was so depressed I decided to cash in my 403(b) plan and add it to our down payment fund. I've been sitting here listening to everything you said today about getting an early start on retirement savings and thinking I might have made a mistake."

"Let's hold off on the scenario-building for a few minutes," I said, "and talk this one through. I can understand why it was tempting to push the house-buying timetable along a little faster. I know how disappointed you were at our last meeting. But cashing in a retirement account is a very expensive fix to the problem.

"Let me ask two important questions—how much did you receive and where is the money now?"

"I just got the check last week, so the money is sitting in my savings account," said Cathy. "The check was for $4960 because the custodian withheld 20 percent for federal income taxes. I had no choice, but at least I don't have to worry about paying more taxes, right?"

"I'm afraid you will owe more taxes," I said. "Generally, 20 percent is withheld for federal taxes when you cash in a retirement account, but you are in the 15-percent tax bracket, and you'll owe a 10-percent penalty because you're under $59\frac{1}{2}$. So your tax bill is 25 percent and you'll owe the difference—another 5 percent or $310—at tax time. Plus, you'll owe state income taxes on the withdrawal. You're in the 5-percent state tax bracket, so that's another $310."

"Uh-oh, Cathy," said Mike. "Have you been adding up all these taxes? It sounds like we'll have to pay another $620 in addition to the $1240 you already had withheld. That means $1860 goes out the door to taxes."

"So the only amount left over for our down payment fund is $4340," said Cathy. "I feel pretty stupid. We still won't have enough to buy a house, and I've lost all that compounding in my retirement account."

"I'm sure it seemed perfectly reasonable at the time," I said. "Fortunately, there's still a way to fix what you did. Are you interested?"

"Absolutely," said Cathy. "Can I just return the money to the plan?"

"I suggest you set up a rollover IRA at a mutual fund company and send a check in with the application," I said. "As long as you get the money back in the plan or in an IRA within 60 days of withdrawing it, you won't be taxed for the withdrawal. There is one catch, though. You'll need to send a check for the full $6200, even though you only received $4960."

"So we lost the 20 percent withheld for taxes?" asked Mike.

"You didn't lose it," I said. "You just loaned it to the government. When you file your taxes next year, you get credit for that withholding, and you'll get the money back. Before you leave today, I'll give you an application form for a rollover IRA. The money can sit in a money market account in the IRA until we talk about investments at our next meeting."

"What a fine mess I've gotten us in," said Cathy, "but at least I can undo it. I guess the only consequence is I'll lose the interest I could have earned on the 20-percent withholding. Oh well. Live and learn."

"Exactly," I said. "You haven't damaged your plan or even postponed any of your goals. This was a very small blip on your way to financial independence.

"Speaking of which, let's get back to our scenario. We can go ahead and count your 403(b) plan assets, Cathy. So your total nest egg is $14,300 plus $6200 or $20,500. You said you want to reach financial independence in 33 years, and we have assumed an 8-percent rate of return so your money will double every 9 years. In 27 years—that's three doubling periods—you'll have about $164,000. In 33 years—slightly more than three doubling periods, you'll have just about $260,000.

"Congratulations—you've already banked a $260,000 nest egg, in future dollars. That's a great start, but it won't be enough to fund the lifestyle you're hoping for. You'll need to keep adding to your retirement fund. You're contributing 10 percent of your salary to your 401(k), Mike, right?"

"Yep. And my company matches half of my contributions up to 6 percent of my salary, so you can add another 3 percent."

"Great," I said. "It's always smart to contribute enough to get the full company match. That's free money. Since they match 50 percent of your contributions, it's like making an instant 50-percent rate of return on your money. That beats any investment you can make."

"I figured the match was a good deal," said Mike. "Should I reduce my contributions to 6 percent to get the match and put the rest of my money someplace else?"

"In your case, I encourage you to keep contributing 10 percent," I said. "It's easy and automatic, you get an instant tax benefit when you contribute, your money grows tax deferred, and you have good investment choices in your plan. Finally, every time you get a raise, your 401(k) contribution will increase as well. There's a lot to be said for the automatic pilot approach."

"What about me?" asked Cathy. "I don't get free money—I don't even have a retirement plan. Until this year, I wasn't making a profit in my company. I don't mean to whine, but sometimes it's hard to be self-employed."

"Trust me," I said. "By the end of this meeting you'll have a plan of your own. You said you thought you'd clear $15,000 after expenses, so let's put you down for 10 percent or $1500. I have also assumed, very conservatively, that you can increase that about 3 percent per year. I'm sure you'll be able to afford bigger contributions as your business grows.

"Now that we have all the assumptions in, let's take a look at the chart." (See Figure 8-1.)

"Am I reading that right?" asked Mike. "If those bars represent our nest egg, it doesn't look like we'll have money beyond our 80s. That can't be good."

"I'm afraid you're interpreting the graph correctly," I said, "and I agree that's not an ideal outcome. Let's explore your options. First, you can postpone your financial independence date. You would have more time to accumulate a nest egg and fewer years to spend it. Alternatively, you can try to earn more on your investments, but even if you were to invest 100 percent in stocks and stock mutual funds, I'd be reluctant to bump up your expected rate of return too far. Let's assume you'll earn 8.25 percent while you're working and 8 percent when you're retired."

"Do we have other choices?" asked Cathy.

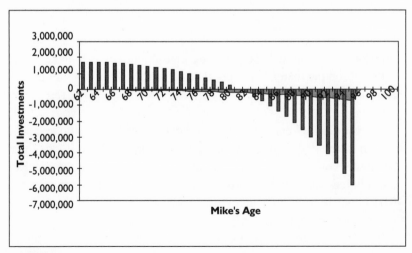

FIGURE 8-1   Retirement planning scenario 1

"Yes. Two more," I said. "You can plan on spending less during your golden years. If you only spend $3500 a month instead of $4000 a month, in today's dollars, your money would last until your mid-90s. That's much better."

"I don't want to scrimp later on," said Mike. "What's our last option?"

"Save more now," I said. "If you can save an additional $2000 a year, you can keep your $4000-a-month spending goal and not deplete your nest egg until your mid-90s. Remember—these are estimates based on the assumptions we made. Small changes now will result in very large changes down the line because our time frame is so long."

"So you're saying we should save the $4500 Mike is contributing to his 401(k) plus the $1500 I'll be putting away, plus $2000, said Cathy. "That's $8000 a year."

"I think $8000 is a good target," I said. "It's about 13 percent of your combined incomes, plus the match on Mike's 401(k) plan."

"I don't think we can swing an extra $2000 right away," said Mike. "Not while we're saving for a house and paying off student loans."

"I agree," said Cathy. "But I bet it won't be too long before we can hit that target. I think we have a plan." (See Figure 8-2.)

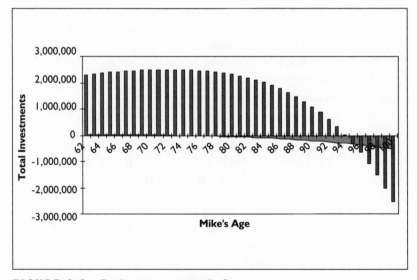

FIGURE 8-2   Retirement scenario 2

401(k) Do's and Don't's

When they were introduced in the 1970s, 401(k) plans were hailed as a boon to workers who wanted to build their retirement funds. In those days, many employers still offered company-funded pension plans, and 401(k) plans were nice "extras." Times have changed. For most young couples, 401(k) plans and IRAs will be their main source of retirement income. That's a lot of responsibility on your shoulders, but don't panic. If you follow some simple rules, you can retire in style.

1. Contribute at least enough to your 401(k) plan to get the full match—it's free money! Even better, contribute the maximum amount allowed each year.

2. Diversify your investments. Choose three to five mutual funds that invest in different parts of the stock and bond market. For broad diversification at low cost, choose index funds. Don't load up on your company's stock—about 5 percent of total investments should be the limit.

3. Don't try to time the market. It's tempting and easy—just pick up the phone or go on-line—but it doesn't work. Stick to your asset allocation and don't move in and out of the stock market.

4. Don't borrow from your 401(k) plan. It sounds like a good idea because you pay yourself back. It's not. Because you pay back the loan with after-tax money, you pay taxes twice—once when you repay the loan and once when you take out money in retirement. If you leave the company, you'll have to repay the loan or get taxed and penalized on the outstanding balance.

5. Roll over your balance into an IRA or a new 401(k) plan when you leave the company. If you cash it in, you could lose one-third to one-half to taxes.

Do-It-Yourself Retirement Planning for the Self-Employed

When saving for retirement—or for anything else for that matter—you always want to get the most benefit from your investments. Take advantage of free money—such as Mike's 401(k) match—and tax breaks.

Self-employed individuals don't get a match unless they give it to themselves, but they do have a choice of tax-deferred retirement plans.

If you work for yourself, you can set up just about any plan you like—including a 401(k)—but it's often not worth paying a bunch of setup and administration expenses for a complex plan. Three types of plans are both easy to set up and administer and will allow you to make significant, tax-deductible contributions: profit-sharing plans, SIMPLE IRAs, and SEP-IRAs. You can set up any of them yourself.

A profit-sharing plan is a little more cumbersome than the others because it's a qualified plan. There's more paperwork involved, but any of the big no-load mutual fund companies or discount brokerages can guide you through it. Profit-sharing plans have some extra features, like vesting for employees and loan provisions. You can contribute a big chunk—up to 25 percent of your profits each year. However, if you have employees, you must contribute the same percentage of their salaries as you contribute of your own. That can get expensive.

The SIMPLE IRA is a great choice if you have employees or your business is quite small and you want to make a significant contribution to your account. You can contribute 100 percent of your income after expenses—the amount shown as "net profit" on your Schedule C—up to $8000. That's your employee contribution—the amount you contribute from your own pay. SIMPLE plans also require you to match contributions dollar for dollar up to 3 percent of salaries (or 2 percent of all salaries, regardless of contributions). As a business owner, you wear two hats—employer and employee—so you match your own contributions by adding another 3 percent. If Cathy set up a SIMPLE plan and made $15,000 profit, she could contribute the full $8000 plus a match of 3 percent of $15,000 or $450.

The third choice is a Simplified Employee Pension plan or SEP-IRA. A self-employed individual can contribute 25 percent of profits up to $40,000 to a SEP-IRA. You're required to contribute the same percentage to your employees' accounts as you do to your own, so the SEP-IRA is not the best option if you intend to add employees. The deadline to set up and fund a SEP-IRA is your tax filing deadline, plus extensions.

You can get free setup kits for small business retirement plans from no-load mutual fund companies like Vanguard, T. Rowe Price, and Fidelity or from discount brokerages like Schwab. Cathy liked the easy setup and flexibility of the SEP-IRA, and because she doesn't plan on hiring any employees, she decided that was the plan for her.

Straight Talk on Retirement Plans

There are three main types of employer plans, and they're all named after a part of the IRS code: 401(k), 403(b), and 457. The plans are similar in many ways—your contributions are deductible from your income, your investments grow tax-deferred, and you are taxed when you take money out of the plan. There are some important differences, though.

If your employer offers a 401(k) plan, you have two decisions to make: how much to contribute and which funds to invest in. When you leave the company or retire, you can take the money (and pay regular taxes, plus a 10 percent penalty if you're under 59-1/2) or you can roll over your investments into an IRA or another plan.

If you work for a nonprofit organization like a school or hospital, your employer may offer a 403(b) plan instead. The rules are generally the same as for a 401(k) plan, but most nonprofits don't sponsor a single provider of investments. Instead, you'll get a list of approved plan providers, and it's up to you to choose one.

The list will probably be chock-full of insurance companies who offer annuities. That's why 403(b) plans are often called Tax-Deferred Annuities or Tax-Sheltered Annuities. Once you select a provider, you'll have to choose among the mutual funds available in that annuity. When mutual funds are wrapped up in an annuity, you pay extra fees for the insurance company's cut—typically between 1 and 1.5 percent of your balance each year. That may not sound like very much but if you are earning 8 percent on your investments, the insurance company is getting 15 percent of your earnings each year. Ouch.

You can bypass the insurance companies if your employer offers a twist on the usual plan called a 403(b)(7) plan. This option allows you to invest directly in no-load mutual funds, skipping the extra fees. Vanguard, Schwab, T. Rowe Price, Fidelity, and several other mutual fund companies and discount brokerages offer 403(b)(7) plans. If your employer's list doesn't include a 403(b)(7) option, ask for one.

If your only choices are insurance companies, I recommend you choose a company with very low fees. TIAA-CREF has very low-cost annuities and excellent investment choices.

Finally, state and local governments frequently offer 457 or Deferred Compensation plans. These are similar to 401(k) plans except that they are nonqualified plans so you don't have to pay a 10-percent penalty if you pull the money out before age 59½.

The Power of Tax Deferral

From time to time, articles pop up questioning the wisdom of tax-deferred retirement plans such as 401(k) plans. The reasoning goes something like this—you'll have to pay taxes when you take the money out, and you may be in a higher tax bracket in retirement so you're just building up a huge tax liability. You may even hear about "planners" who encourage clients to forego company-sponsored retirement plans and purchase expensive life insurance instead. It shouldn't be surprising that their goal is a fat commission and not your financial security.

Here's the real story: even though you're just deferring—and not avoiding—taxes, plans such as 401(k), 403(b) and 457 plans are still a great way to save your retirement dollars. When you defer taxes, your nest egg grows faster, and even after you pay taxes on the withdrawals, you'll be better off.

Let's say you invested $1000 directly in a mutual fund, and $100 in dividends and capital gains were distributed the first year. If you're in the 25-percent tax bracket, you'll pay $25 in taxes and only have $75 to reinvest. Even if you reinvest the entire $100, you're $25 poorer because you had to take the money to pay the taxes from another account. On the other hand, if your $1000 was invested in a 401(k) plan, the entire $100 distribution is reinvested with no taxes due. Your nest egg grows faster when you don't have to siphon money off for taxes each year. (See Figure 8-3.)

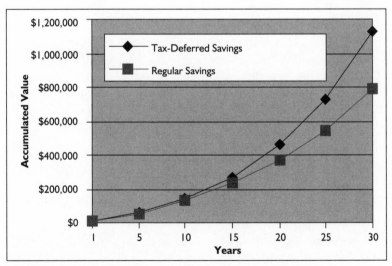

FIGURE 8-3   **The Advantage of Tax-deferred Savings**

To Roth or Not to Roth

"I know you're not quite ready to commit to that last $2000 of retirement savings," I said, "but let's go ahead and talk about the best place to invest it. I recommend an IRA."

"Suits me," said Mike. "Can we open a joint IRA and take turns contributing to it?"

"I'm afraid that's not the way it works," I said. "IRA stands for Individual Retirement Account and the account has to be opened for an individual, not a couple."

"I know IRAs have tax advantages," said Cathy, "but we'll have to tie up our money until retirement, right?"

"It depends," I said. "There are many flavors of IRAs—traditional IRAs—deductible and nondeductible—and Roth IRAs. We'll save the Roth IRA for last.

"In general, anyone who has earned income can contribute to a traditional IRA, but if you're covered by a retirement plan at work, you can only deduct your contribution if your income is less than $70,000 ($50,000 for singles). If you're not covered by a retirement plan, you can deduct your IRA as long as your joint income is less than $150,000.

"If you can subtract your IRA contribution from your taxable income, your money goes further. Deducting a $2000 IRA contribution can save you about $400 in taxes in your tax bracket. That's an extra $400 you can invest.

"Traditional IRAs are taxed when you withdraw the money. In general, if you pull the money out before age 59½, you'll get hit with a 10-percent penalty as well as ordinary taxes."

"Who invented these rules?" asked Cathy. "If our adjusted gross income is over the $70,000 threshold you mentioned, what are our options?"

"As soon as you set up your SEP-IRA, Cathy, you'll both be covered by retirement plans," I said, "so you won't be eligible for a deductible IRA. You could still fund a nondeductible IRA, but you wouldn't get a tax break up front, and you'd be taxed on the earnings when you take the money out."

"That doesn't seem like a very good deal," said Mike. "Why don't I just add more to my 401(k) plan?"

"That's certainly one strategy," I said, "but I recommend that couples even out their retirement savings as much as possible, rather than just loading it into one account. There's one more kind of IRA, called a Roth IRA, and I think it's the best of the bunch. Roth IRAs have only been around since 1998, so they're the newest form of IRA."

"And a new set of rules?" asked Cathy.

"As a matter of fact, Roth IRAs do have their own rules," I said, "but I think you'll like them. When you contribute to a Roth IRA, you don't get a tax break up front like you do with a deductible IRA or contributions to a 401(k). However, if you take the money out after age 59½, your withdrawals are tax free—not tax deferred. That's a huge advantage, especially for a young couple. You have lots of time to build a tax-free nest egg."

"Sounds good," said Mike, " but don't we need all the tax breaks we can get now, when we're young and not so rich?"

"You're thinking like a planner," I said. "I like that. It's true you could increase your contributions to your 401(k), Mike, or Cathy could step up her SEP contributions, and either one would give you an up-front tax break. You may decide you want to do that. However, the Roth has some special features that may ease Cathy's concern about tying up too much money for the long term. You can pull your original contributions out of a Roth IRA any time you like and pay no tax or penalty."

"Do we have to use the money for a particular purpose?" asked Cathy.

"There are no restrictions on how you use the money," I said. "When you withdraw your contributions, you're just getting your own money back. You have to leave your earnings in the Roth IRA until you're 59½ or you'll pay taxes and a penalty."

"So if I contribute $3000 to a Roth IRA and I make $200 on my investment, I can pull out $3000 any time I like," said Mike. "Is that right?"

"That's right," I said. "You'll have to leave the $200 earnings in the Roth to avoid taxes and a penalty. There are a few exceptions to these rules. You can tap up to $10,000 of earnings tax free if you've had the Roth for at least five years and you use the money for a first home."

"Sounds interesting," said Cathy, "although I hope we buy a house sooner than that. Any other tricks we should know about?"

"You can pull out money from a Roth IRA for educational expenses," I said. "You'll avoid a penalty, although you'll pay ordinary taxes. But the highlights of the Roth are tax-free withdrawals of earnings in retirement and the ability to pull out your contributions any time."

"I'm sold," said Cathy. "If I get panicky about money, I know I can get my contributions back."

"Yes, you can," I said, "but I hope you'd only pull money out of your Roth IRA as a last resort. When you withdraw your contributions, you remove the engine that drives those tax-free earnings."

"I promise I'll do my best not to touch it," said Cathy. "But knowing I can increases my comfort zone."

Investing in a Roth IRA

"The Roth IRA sounds great," said Mike, "I guess we should each set one up."

"Eventually I think you should do just that," I agreed. "But for now, you might consider setting up just one Roth IRA—in Cathy's name. Mike, you're contributing $4500 to your 401(k) and Cathy, you plan to contribute $1500 to your SEP-IRA, so putting the Roth IRA in Cathy's name evens things out a bit."

"I'd like to do that," said Cathy. "I know I'm not pulling my weight in the cash flow area yet, but I'd like to keep up my share of investing for retirement. When I finish my MBA, I'll make more money and contribute more to my SEP. Maybe Mike could start a Roth IRA and I could start a traditional IRA to add to my Roth. How much can we contribute to IRAs?"

"Whoa," I said. "Let's not get IRA-happy. The maximum amount you can each contribute to a traditional IRA or a Roth IRA or a combination of the two is $3000 in 2003. If you're eligible and you have the cash, you're better off fully funding a Roth IRA."

"What if Cathy decides to take a year off work?" asked Mike. "No earned income, so no IRA, right?"

"Great question," I said. "The general rule is you can only fund an IRA up to the amount you earned or $3,000, whichever is less. But the IRS is a little more generous than you might have guessed. Even if only one of you has earned income, the other can contribute to either a traditional or Roth IRA. It's called a spousal IRA. If Mike has earned income but Cathy doesn't and your total adjusted gross income is less than $150,000, Cathy can either fund a Roth IRA or a traditional IRA."

"The spousal IRA sounds like a good idea," said Cathy, "but who can remember all the rules?"

"And the rules keep changing," I said. "But, to be fair, many of the changes have been improvements. Roth IRAs are one of the best savings ideas Congress has passed in quite a while."

"There's one more Roth IRA strategy you might think about," I said. "As long as your combined income is under $100,000 and you file jointly, you can convert a traditional IRA to a Roth IRA. From then on all your earnings are tax free as long as you follow the Roth IRA rules. The catch is you have to pay taxes on the amount you convert."

"A friend of mine at work said he did that with his IRA," said Mike. "It sounded interesting, but we don't have any traditional IRAs."

"Cathy will have one when she rolls over her 403(b) plan," I said. "Let's see how the numbers would work. If you converted Cathy's IRA, you'd pay income taxes on the entire $6200 in her IRA. At your marginal tax bracket—we'll be talking about that in a future meeting—you'd owe about $1200 in federal and state taxes on the converted amount."

"Ouch," said Cathy. "That would severely dent our emergency fund. I'm not sure I want to do that."

"That may stretch your spending plan," I said, "but let's assume for the moment you are trying to decide between investing $1200 in a new Roth IRA or using the $1200 to pay the taxes on a Roth conversion. What a great financial planning dilemma. To convert or not to convert.

"After 33 years, your converted Roth IRA would be worth over $78,000. If you left your Traditional IRA as is and started a new Roth IRA, you'd only have about $68,000 after taxes. In this case, it looks like conversion wins.

"Of course, with any projection, the result depends on your assumptions. In this case, I assumed you would be in a higher tax bracket when you retired and you would cash out both your IRAs in 33 years. If those assumptions are accurate, you would be smart to convert your IRA into a Roth IRA, Cathy. What do you think?"

"I like the idea a lot, even if we can't do it this year," said Cathy. "My nest egg is smaller than Mike's, but at least mine will be in a Roth IRA. How do I convert?"

"As soon as you set up the rollover IRA, you can ask the mutual fund company for a Roth conversion form."

(Assumes 8% annual return. Future value in 33 years)		
	Converting to Roth IRA	Contributing to new Roth IRA
Current Value of Traditional IRA	$6,200	$6,200
Current Value of Converted Roth IRA	$6,200	$0
Current Value of New Roth IRA	$0	$1,200
Future Value of Traditional IRA	$0	$78,592
Taxes due on Traditional IRA	$0	$25,935
Net Future Value of Traditional IRA	$0	$52,657
Future Value of Converted Roth IRA	$78,592	$0
Future Value of New Roth IRA	$0	$15,211
Total Future Value of IRAs (after taxes)	$78,592	$67,868

FIGURE 8-4   **Converting to a Roth IRA versus Contributing to a New Roth IRA**

Funding a Roth IRA

It's very easy to set up and fund a Roth IRA. First you'll need to choose a custodian—a company or institution that agrees to keep track of your IRA. Typical custodians are banks, brokerage firms, and mutual fund companies.

Next you choose your investment. How much your Roth IRA earns depends on how you invest it. It might be helpful to think of an IRA as a box. You can choose which investments to put in the box: individual stocks, individual bonds, mutual funds, or CDs.

I recommend setting up a Roth IRA with a no-load mutual fund company. Some require a minimum contribution of $1000 to open an account, but others will let you open the Roth IRA with no minimum if you sign up for automatic withdrawals from your checking or savings account. When you set up your account, you choose which mutual fund you wish to invest in. If you change your mind, it's relatively easy to move your money to a different mutual fund or even to a different company. The best way to switch companies is to have the mutual fund company contact the old one and request a trustee-to-trustee transfer.

You won't touch the IRA money during the transfer, and you won't trigger any taxes.

Although tax-deferred or, in the case of Roth IRAs, tax-free retirement savings plans are great ways to save for the long term, the rules governing IRAs, 401(k)s, and other plans have become complex and confusing. The following table summarizes some—but not all—of the provisions of the main types of retirement plans under current law. The rules keep changing, though, and legislation has been proposed to streamline the plans. You can keep up with new rules by visiting the IRS Web site (*www.irs.gov*) or mutual fund companies' sites, such as *www.vanguard.com* and *www.troweprice.com*.

Changing Jobs? Roll Over

Sooner or later, you'll face the dilemma of what to do with your old 401(k) when you leave a job. You can cash it in, but unless you're teetering on the edge of bankruptcy, that's your worst option. Between ordinary income taxes (federal and state) and the 10-percent penalty, taxes can easily eat up 40 percent of your balance. Ouch.

To avoid taxes, you can leave your money in the old 401(k) plan (as long as your balance is more than $5,000), you can roll it over to a traditional IRA or you may be able to roll it over to a new plan.

If your old plan has great investment options, you might want to leave it where it is. You can't add to it, but it's your money and you can manage it. Plus, you can always roll it over to an IRA later if you like. The main disadvantage is keeping track of plans as you go from job to job.

You can usually roll over your balance to your new employer's plan. The rules for combining employer plans have become more liberal, so you may be able to mix 401(k) money with money from a 403(b) or 457 deferred compensation plan.

Your other choice is to roll the money over to a traditional IRA. You will have more control over your investments, and you can choose funds that complement the ones offered in your new plan. You may be eligible to convert your rollover IRA into a Roth IRA, but make sure you can handle the tax bite first.

It's fairly straightforward to roll over assets from an employer plan into an IRA. A no-load mutual fund company or discount brokerage firm will be happy to help you fill out the paperwork.

Summary of Retirement Plan Rules

	Am I eligible?	How much can I contribute?	How am I taxed?	Are there any special rules?
Traditional Deductible IRA	- You or spouse must have earned income. - Adjusted gross income for couple must be less than $70,000 if both are covered by retirement plans.	$3,000 in 2003 and 2004. $4,000 in 2005 and 2006. Higher limits if over 50.	Contributions are made before taxes (deducted from taxable income); Withdrawals after 59½ are taxed.	Withdrawals before 59½ generally subject to 10 percent penalty plus regular tax. Withdrawals for a first home (up to $10,000) or due to disability or death are exempt from taxes. Withdrawals for education are not penalized.
Traditional Non-Deductible IRA	- You or spouse must have earned income.	Same as Traditional Deductible IRA	Contributions not deductible. Earnings withdrawn after 59½ are taxed.	Same as Traditional Deductible IRA.
Roth IRA	- You or spouse must have earned income. - Must file jointly if married. - Adjusted gross income	Same as Traditional IRAs	Contributions are not deductible. Withdrawals of earnings after 59½ are tax free. Withdrawals of original contributions	Withdrawal of earnings before 59½ are generally taxable and subject to 10% penalty. Up to $10,000

Plan	Who Qualifies	Contribution Limits	Tax Treatment	Withdrawal Rules
	cannot be greater than $150,000-$160,000 (married) or $95,000-$115,000 (single).		at any time for any reason are not taxed.	in earnings may be withdrawn tax free for first home. Withdrawal of earnings for education expenses are exempt from 10% penalty.
401(k)/403(b)	- Your employer must sponsor a plan or approve sponsors. - Some employers require a waiting period of up to a year.	$12,000 in 2003 $13,000 in 2004 $14,000 in 2005 Higher limits if over 50.	Contributions are made by payroll deduction before taxes. Withdrawals are taxed as ordinary income.	Same as Traditional IRA. Withdrawals while still employed only permitted in case of hardship. Some plans allow loans.
SEP-IRA or Profit Sharing/Keogh Plan.	Self-employed (with or without employees).	Lesser of 25% of earned income or $40,000. (Owner's percentage slightly lower.)	Same as Traditional Deductible IRA.	Same as Traditional Deductible IRA. Loans may be allowed with Profit Sharing plan.
SIMPLE IRA	Self-employed or companies with fewer than 100 employees.	Lesser of 100% of earned income or $8,000, plus match.	Same as Traditional Deductible IRA.	25% penalty on withdrawals within 2 years of contribution.

What Cathy and Mike Have Learned

1. The way to fund their future is to live below their means.

2. The best way to save for retirement is to stash away money regularly in long-term investments. Automatic deductions from paychecks or bank accounts are best.

3. They have a great advantage—lots of time to grow their investments.

4. They should save in the most efficient way possible by taking advantage of free money first (like company matches) and tax breaks next (like IRAs).

5. Self-employed individuals can set up their own retirement plans.

6. Both spouses should contribute to their retirement. Even if one spouse isn't earning a paycheck, he or she may still be eligible to fund an IRA.

7. There are lots of ways to think about retirement. The goal is to become financially independent so they can live off their investments instead of depending on a paycheck.

Cathy's and Mike's Recommendations

1. Immediately set up a Traditional Rollover IRA and fund it with the $6200 withdrawn from the old 403(b) plan. (Cathy)

2. Once the Rollover IRA is set up and funded, convert it to a Roth IRA. (Cathy)

3. Maintain contributions to 401(k) plan. (Mike)

4. Set up a SEP-IRA, immediately fund it with $1000 and set up automatic contributions to reach $1500 goal this year. (Cathy)

Your Homework

1. Talk about your goals for financial independence with your partner.

2. Crunch some numbers to see if you are on track. Personal finance software, mutual fund Web sites and personal finance Web sites all have retirement calculators.

3. If you are self-employed, set up your own plan.

4. Consider funding Roth IRAs.

5. If you have a 403(b) plan at work and all the options are tax-deferred annuities, ask your employer to provide an option directly with a no-load mutual fund family like Vanguard, T. Rowe Price, or Fidelity.

Resources

1. *www.vanguard.com* and *www.troweprice.com* have retirement calculators. The T. Rowe Price calculator is more sophisticated. Be careful to read the assumptions behind the models so you'll know how to interpret the numbers.

2. *www.financialengines.com* is a Web site created by Nobel-Prize winning economist William Sharpe. The retirement planner calculates the probability of reaching your goals and allows you to tweak your inputs until you get to a scenario you feel comfortable with. The basic calculator is free to use; you can also sign up for a paid service that assists with asset allocation and investment choices. Some employers offer this service to their employees as a benefit.

CHAPTER 9

The Scoop on Investing

Investing has become way too complicated. At least that's the message many of the TV shows, magazines, and books offering investment advice seem to be sending us. We're bombarded with pie charts and graphs and ratings and performance numbers. We hear about the definitive investment formula only to discover that the next issue of the magazine or installment of the show is touting an even better system. After all, the media's business is getting us to watch and read and buy.

To add to the confusion, so-called advisors who are really just salespeople rely on jargon instead of clear, simple language to sell their wares. They would rather divert our attention from high commissions and so-so performance than educate us about our choices. I remember a stockbroker explaining why he used technical terms and complicated charts at his investment seminars. His goal was to leave his audience confused and overwhelmed so they would hire an expert—him—for help. No thanks.

That's not to say that all the investment advice out there is self-serving or unhelpful. There are lots of good resources for people who want to learn more about managing their investments. I've listed several at the end of this chapter. However, it's difficult for the individual investor to wade through the mass of information and pluck out the gems. So don't feel dense if you don't "get" investments. Much of what's out there is meant to confuse rather than enlighten.

What's a young couple to do? My advice is to keep it simple. A good investment plan takes some time up front to fashion a strategy and choose your investments, and a few hours a couple of times a year to review your portfolio and rebalance your holdings. You should also revisit your plan when changes in your life—like a new baby or career shift—affect the amount or type of investing you do. And don't worry if you and your partner don't see eye to eye on investment strategy. There's room for individual differences.

Unless you have a large portfolio, managing your investments does not have to take a lot of time. Maybe you have opened your IRA or 401(k) statement and thought that if only you had spent more time on your investments, you would have done better. It seems logical—more attention should yield better results. However, there's really no evidence that people who check their portfolio daily and move their investments around frequently do any better than those who don't. In fact, they typically do worse. Those movers and shakers who try to time the market are either looking at last period's performance— they're "shooting where the rabbit was"—or trying to conjure up a vision of the future. Neither strategy works well over time. History is valuable as an indicator of long-term trends, but it doesn't tell us what will happen next week, next month, or even next year. And even though we'd all love to have our very own crystal ball, we know there is no such thing.

Constantly switching around investments is more likely to damage than improve your long-term rate of return, not to mention your mental health. The ability to go on-line and rearrange your portfolio with a few keystrokes gives you the illusion of control even though you don't have power over the direction of the markets or the performance of individual companies. You do, however, have control over some very important variables, including how much you save and how well you diversify your investments.

It's important to be realistic about what your investments can and cannot do. Good investments will not make up for a low salary or extravagant spending habits or skimpy contributions to retirement plans. A good investment plan will simply speed you more swiftly along your path to your goals.

So let's stick to the basics. Here are the five steps every investor should take:

1. Determine your goals and investment time horizon.

2. Estimate how much risk you can comfortably take on.

3. Design your asset allocation "pie."

4. Choose your investments.

5. Monitor and rebalance your investment portfolio periodically.

Getting Started on Your Investment Plan

"We've come for our hot stock tips," said Mike with a grin as he sat down.

"Then I'm afraid you've come to the wrong place," I said. "There's no magic formula to get rich quick. But we can talk about getting rich slowly. Or, better still, how about focusing on investing to reach your goals?"

"It would be nice to hit that winning stock so we wouldn't have to work and save, work and save," said Cathy wistfully.

"And then the boom would be followed by a bust," said Mike, "and we'd be deeper in the hole than when we started."

"It's Mr. Doom and Gloom," said Cathy, smiling. "As you'll see, Mike and I don't always agree on our investments."

"I work hard and I hate it when my 401(k) statements have minus signs on them," said Mike. "It's depressing. Besides, what's wrong with a little safety? We don't always need to live on the wild side with our investments."

"It sounds like you two have different appetites for risk," I said. "That's not a problem; I'm sure we can come up with an investment plan that will allow you both to sleep at night. But before we get to that stage, we'll review some of the goals we talked about during our goal-setting and retirement meetings and talk about your time horizons."

"Why does the time frame matter?" asked Cathy.

"Different investment strategies are appropriate for different time horizons," I explained. "Let's take an extreme example. If you had ordered a new car to be delivered in two weeks and you had $20,000 in your savings account earmarked for the car, would you take that money out today and buy a bunch of stocks?"

"Who knows?" said Cathy. "I might get lucky and make some money while we're waiting for the car."

"Or you might lose a chunk of it," I said. "Then, when your car arrived, you'd either have to walk away and lose your deposit, or scramble to get a loan to make up the difference. Even if your stocks stayed even, you'd have to pay the transaction costs of buying and selling the stocks, so you'd be worse off."

"But everything I've read says investing in stocks is the best way to make money," said Cathy.

"That's right," I said, "as long as that sentence ends with the words *over the long run*. If you have enough time to ride out the ups and downs of the stock market, you'll generally do better if your investments are mostly in stocks. But the return on stocks is unreliable in the short term."

What's a Stock and What's a Bond?

"Before we go through the five steps of developing your investment strategy, let's take a few minutes and talk about the difference between stocks and bonds."

"Great," said Cathy. "I don't think I have a deep understanding of this subject. I remember my finance professor said stockholders are owners, and bondholders are creditors. If you hold a share of Walt Disney stock, for example, you own part of the Walt Disney company. That makes sense, but I think bonds are confusing."

"Your finance professor was right," I said. "When you're a stockholder, you're an owner. When you invest in a bond, you are loaning money to a company or, in the case of Treasuries and municipal bonds, to the government. Stocks outperform bonds on average, but stocks are also riskier than bonds.

"Let's use your consulting business, Cathy, as an example of investing in stocks and bonds," I said. "Imagine that the human resources director of a large corporation asked you to help with a major reorganization. You would be responsible for producing job descriptions, salary schedules, and bonus rates for dozens of different job categories. The job would need to completed in six months. What would you do?"

"Faint," said Cathy laughing. "There's no way I could tackle a job that big. My company is just me."

"This is not a one-person project," I agreed. "But it's a great opportunity, and you'd like to take on the job."

"Let me see," said Cathy. "I would have to upgrade my computer, purchase some software, hire consultants, book travel. I'd need to get paid up front."

"You would likely get a partial payment when you signed the contract," I said, "but you would have to wait until you had finished to get most of your fee. How would you finance the project?"

"I could go to a bank, I guess," said Cathy, "but I'd probably just ask my parents to float me a loan instead."

"Good idea," I said. "Let's say your parents agreed to loan you $20,000 and you promised to pay them $100 a month for the use of the money—that's equivalent to a 6-percent annual interest rate. You could agree to pay the $20,000 back to your parents in six months, when you are due to finish the project. It's as if you issued a $20,000 bond with a 6-percent coupon or interest rate and a six-month term."

"So a bond is really just a loan," said Mike. "Would that be a good deal for Cathy?"

"It might be," I said. "If Cathy felt she could make a profit of more than 6 percent on the project, offering a bond to her parents would be a smart move. Before companies issue bonds, they crunch the numbers to see if they are confident of making a higher rate of return than they will pay on the bond. Is it a good deal for Cathy's parents?"

"If I didn't complete the job and didn't get paid," said Cathy, "I wouldn't be able to pay my parents back. That wouldn't be good for business, and I would lose my status as favorite child."

"Leaving aside your place in the family," I said, "if you couldn't pay back the bond you would either default or try to refinance the debt. You might issue a new bond to pay for the old bond, but you would probably have to pay a higher interest rate because the new investment is riskier. Companies who receive low credit ratings because they are in precarious financial condition have to offer very high interest rates on their bonds in order to entice investors. These high-income or high-yield bonds are commonly known as junk bonds.

"If you're successful on the next few projects, your parents eventually would get their money back. In the meantime, you would try to continue making interest payments.

"There's another way your parents could help you finance the project," I continued. "You could sell them a piece of your company, Cathy."

"You mean my parents would be partners with me?" asked Cathy. "I'm not sure I like that idea."

"Forming a partnership is one alternative," I said, "but I don't think your parents are interested in getting involved in managing your company. You could form a corporation, issue stock, and sell some shares to your parents. You'd get the money, and they would own part of your company."

"How would Cathy know how much to charge for the stock?" asked Mike.

"First you would have to figure out how much your company is worth," I said. "If you were truly taking your company public—that is, issuing stock and offering shares for sale—you'd have to hire professionals to value your company. It's a tricky business, but we're going to keep it simple and assume your company is worth $100,000—the amount of fees you expect to bring in over the next 12 months, including your fee for the big project.

"If you issued 100 shares of stock at $1000 each, and your parents wished to invest $20,000, they could buy 20 shares or 20 percent of the company. You would still own the remaining 80 percent."

"Do you think your parents would go for that, Cathy?" asked Mike. "When would they get their money back?"

"Good question," said Cathy. "Plus, I wouldn't be paying them any interest."

"Now you're starting to see why stocks are riskier investments than bonds," I said. "Stocks don't earn interest, and there's no specific payback date.

"If you do well this year and make a nice profit, you might decide to distribute some of the profits to the shareholders in the form of dividends. If you paid a $5 dividend on each share of stock, your parents would get a check for $100, you would get a $400 check as the 80 percent owner. You could reinvest the rest of the profits right back in the company."

"Could I just plow all the profits right back into the company instead?" asked Cathy.

"Many companies do just that," I said. "Some fast-growing companies or newer companies reinvest the profits rather than pay dividends. Older, more traditional companies typically pay dividends."

"So if I buy stock in a company that doesn't pay dividends," said Mike, "I don't make any money until I sell the stock, right?"

"That's right," I said. "You make money in stocks either by earning dividends or by selling the stock for more than what you paid for it, or a combination of both. If your stock doesn't pay a dividend, you're hoping for a nice profit when you sell because you're not getting any income while you hold it. That's why non-dividend-paying stocks are riskier."

"Speaking of return," said Mike. "What happens when Cathy's parents want their money back?"

"If Cathy's parents had bought stock of a publicly traded company like Microsoft," I said, "they would contact a stockbroker or open an account at a discount brokerage firm. The firm would place the sell order and an intermediary would match a buyer with the seller—in this case Cathy's parents—and take a cut for the service. The brokerage firm would also make money on the transaction."

"My stock wouldn't be on the stock exchange," said Cathy. "How would we find a buyer for my parents' stock?"

"You'd probably have to find a buyer on your own," I said. "Maybe Mike would like to own part of Cathy, Inc.?"

"Sorry, Cathy," said Mike. "Too risky for me."

"I could ask an aunt or uncle, I suppose," said Cathy, "or a consultant I used to work with. But this company is my baby—I don't want just anyone owning a piece of it."

"You have another alternative," I said. "The corporation could buy the stock and hold it. The shares held by the corporation are called treasury stock."

"Why would a company want to do that?" asked Mike.

"A company might buy back its own stock to boost the price and show confidence in the company," I said.

"I'd have to come up with $20,000 to buy my parents' stock back," said Cathy.

"It depends," I said. "If you are doing well and have a few more big contracts lined up, your company may be worth more than when you first went public and issued stock. Your parents' 20-percent share of Cathy Inc. would be worth more than the $20,000 they paid. Aside from wanting to help their daughter, their motivation in buying the stock was to make money."

"That's the price of success, Cathy," said Mike. "You would have to pay your parents more than what they gave you just to get back 20 percent of your company."

"But isn't that how investing in the stock market is supposed to work?" I asked. "You buy shares of stock in a company you hope will grow and prosper. Your ownership slice is worth more when the whole pie gets bigger. It's just simple math—20 percent of a $200,000 company is worth twice as much as 20 percent of a $100,000 company."

"To be fair to my parents, they would have taken a big risk if they invested in my company," said Cathy. "They would have lost their money if I had gone out of business."

"You're right," I said. "Common stock shareholders are the last to get paid. The IRS, employees, and bondholders are in line to get their money before the stockholders even get a penny. If a company collapses, stockholders usually lose their investment."

"Let me see if I have this straight," said Mike. "If I own stock, I don't get any interest, I may not get any dividends, there's no set payback date like there is for bonds, and I'm low man on the totem pole for getting my money back if the company goes out of business. Doesn't exactly make me want to rush to my nearest brokerage house."

"On the upside, though, by owning stock you have an opportunity to share in the growth and prosperity of the company. That's why more than half of Americans own stock."

"I guess so," said Mike. "At least stocks are easier to understand than bonds. I have heard that when interest rates go up, bonds go down, and vice versa but I never understood that."

"Let's say you bought a $10,000 10-year corporate bond issued by Microsoft with a 6-percent coupon rate—that means Microsoft promises to pay you 6 percent interest each year for 10 years and then pays you back your original $10,000 investment. Now let's assume you want to sell your bond before the 10 years are up, and in the meantime the interest rate on similarly rated corporate bonds has increased to 8 percent. Cathy, would you buy Mike's 6-percent bond if you could get a brand-new bond paying 8-percent interest?"

"Sorry, Mike, but the answer's no," said Cathy. "I'm afraid you're stuck."

"Mike would have to offer you a deal to entice you to buy his bond. What if he offered to sell it to you for $9000? Remember, you'd get the full $10,000 when you redeemed it at maturity."

"That would make it more interesting," said Cathy. "I might go for that."

"You could calculate how much of a discount you'd have to get to make the deal equivalent to buying a new 8-percent bond," I said.

lternatively, if interest rates had sunk to 4 percent, you'd have a mmodity, Mike, and you could charge a premium for your bond. Or ourse, you could always hold on to your bond until it matured, and then you could get the full $10,000 back."

"So changes in interest rates affect what I would get for my bond if I sold it before it matured," said Mike. "I've noticed the share prices in the bond fund in my 401(k) plan bounce around. Doesn't the fund just hang on to the bonds and cash them in when they mature?"

"Managers of bond mutual funds are typically buying and selling constantly," I said. "Plus, they have to revalue the fund each day to reflect the market price of their bonds even if they don't intend to sell them.

"As long as we're on the topic of bonds, let's talk about the different kinds you can buy. There are four main categories. Corporate bonds are, of course, issued by corporations. The interest earned is taxed by the federal and state governments. Municipal bonds are issued by state and local governments to finance projects like schools and hospitals and public buildings. The interest they pay is generally exempt from federal income taxes. If you buy municipal bonds issued by your state of residence, the interest is exempt from state tax as well."

"So municipal bonds are a better deal because you don't pay tax on the interest, right?" asked Cathy.

"Actually, it depends," I said. "Muni—short for municipal—bonds generally pay a lower rate of interest. You can calculate how much a taxable bond would have to pay to be equivalent to a muni bond by dividing the interest rate on the muni bond by one minus your tax rate. For example, if a muni bond is paying 5 percent and you're in the 25-percent tax bracket, you'd have to earn 6.67 percent—that's .05 divided by .75—on a taxable corporate bond to get the same after-tax return.

"Then there are U.S. Treasury securities—bills, notes, and bonds as well as savings bonds. The interest is taxed by the IRS but exempt from state income tax. When you cash in your EE bonds, Cathy, you'll owe federal tax on the interest but no state tax.

"Finally, there are bonds issued by U.S. government agencies. Mortgage bonds issued by the Government National Mortgage Association are called Ginnie Maes—that comes from the initials GNMA. The interest is taxable by the federal government and sometimes by states. The interest rate is generally higher than U.S. Treasury securities. On a safety scale, they fall in between U.S. Treasuries and corporate bonds."

"So U.S. Treasuries are the safest kinds of bonds?" asked Mike.

"By far," I said. "They're backed by the full faith and credit of the U.S. government. "

Risk and Return

When choosing long-term investments, it's important to have a long view of the markets. If you made your decisions on what happened yesterday or last week in the stock market, you'd either put every dollar in stocks—if it had been a good run—or shy away from stocks altogether if the market had tumbled. Neither is a wise decision. (See Figure 9-1.)

If you compare the rates of return over the past 76 years, stocks win hands down with an average annual return of over 12 percent for small-company stocks and over 10 percent for large-company stocks. Government bonds have returned just 5.5 percent per year, on average, barely keeping ahead of inflation. When you add in the tax bite on the interest you earn, you're lucky just to tread water in bonds.

In any particular year, however, stocks can lag way behind other investments. The booming bull market of the late 1990s was followed by several dismal years. Many investors became disillusioned with stocks and pulled their money out of the market. Although that move might have proven profitable in the short term, unless those investors

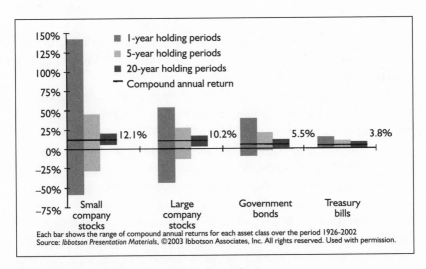

Each bar shows the range of compound annual returns for each asset class over the period 1926-2002
Source: *Ibbotson Presentation Materials,* ©2003 Ibbotson Associates, Inc. All rights reserved. Used with permission.

FIGURE 9-1   Reduction of risk over time

start putting money back into stocks, they'll miss out of years—and thousands of dollars—of growth.

When you invest, you balance risk and reward—two variables that tend to move in the same direction. If you invest in riskier investments, like stocks, over time your return—or reward—should be greater. If you stick to conservative investments like CDs or savings accounts, your risk will be minimal, but so will your return.

Large-company stocks ("blue chips") have fallen more than 40 percent in a single year, and small-company stocks tumbled almost 60 percent one year. If you're investing your money for a single year, stocks are much too risky. However, there has never been a 20-year period over the past 75 years when stocks lost money. So the trick is to match your investment with your time horizon. If you can keep your money invested for a longer period of time, you can ride the ups and downs of the stock market and reap the returns. You'll be rewarded for the risk you take on.

The riskiness of an investment depends on the volatility or unpredictability of the return. Savings accounts are very low-risk investments; stocks are more volatile and less predictable. When it comes to investing, risk simply means you don't know if you'll win or lose. Next year, stocks may go way up or way down or stay about even. Of course, most people focus on the losing side of the equation—they consider the possibility of making money a happy prospect, not a risk.

Investing isn't the only time you take risk in your life. Sometimes the risks are relatively small—like the risk you take when you leave your umbrella at home even though it looks like rain. Other risks, like starting your own business, can significantly affect your financial situation—and your life.

There are two fundamental kinds of investment risk—the danger that you'll lose the money you invested and the risk that your investments will not keep up with inflation. Which is more tolerable depends on your time horizon. The stock market is no place for money you'll need in the next few months or even few years. You won't have time to ride out a market decline. On the other hand, if you're timid and keep your retirement money in savings or money market accounts, inflation will keep nibbling at your investments. It's very difficult to build a nest egg when your investments don't grow any faster than inflation. That's why figuring out your time horizon is your first step to putting together an investment strategy that will work for you.

Your Investment Horizon

First, divide up your goals into three categories: short-term goals—those with a two-year time horizon or less, medium-term goals that you wish to accomplish in three to five years, and long-term goals that are at least five years out in the future.

Your short-term goals might be building an emergency fund or saving for a home or car purchase in a year or two. The best place for short-term money is a credit union or bank account, or a money market account you set up with a no-load mutual fund company like Vanguard or Fidelity. Short-term CDs can work as well if they mature before you need the cash.

EE savings bonds are very safe because they are obligations of the U.S. government. You can buy them at your local bank or on line at *www.savingsbonds.gov*. They are issued at half the face value, so if you purchase a $100 bond, you pay $50. The interest is paid out every six months and is added to the value of the bond, and taxes on the interest are deferred until you cash in the bond.

EE Savings Bonds pay interest for 30 years, so if you've held them a long time, they may be worth more than their face value. The interest rate on EE bonds is 85 percent of the rate on five-year Treasuries. For the past several years, that has ranged between 3 and 5 percent. Remember, savings bonds are good for safety—not for growth—so you're not going to make a fortune on them.

If you're thinking of buying more savings bonds, I recommend looking at the new version called I-bonds. The *I* stands for inflation. These bonds pay a base rate of interest, and then the value of the bond is adjusted every six months to compensate for inflation. If you owned I-bonds with a base rate of 2 percent and the inflation rate was 4 percent, the bonds' total rate of return for that year would be 6 percent.

You can take a bit more risk with money earmarked for medium-term goals—purchases you'll make in three to five years. Short- or medium-term bond funds have a higher return, on average, than bank accounts, with only slightly more risk. Bond funds are more convenient than individual bonds because you can add to or withdraw from your account more easily.

If you're willing to take on a bit more risk, you could invest part of your stash in a mutual fund that invests in both stocks and bonds. These are called balanced funds, and my favorites are Dodge & Cox

Balanced fund, Vanguard Wellington, and Vanguard Wellesley Income. They're all no-load mutual funds—no cost to get in or out—with low operating expenses and strong long-term track records.

Finally, you have to decide how to invest your long-term money—investments stashed away for financial independence or a college fund for a young child. Stocks or stock mutual funds should be the core holding in your long-term portfolio. Your time horizon is long enough to wait out the ups and downs of the market, so you can be more aggressive. That doesn't mean every penny should be in the stock market. The way you split your investments between stocks and bonds or cash also depends on your appetite for risk.

How Much Risk Can You Stand?

Your risk tolerance cannot be measured precisely like your weight or the temperature in this room. In fact, it's a pretty slippery thing to quantify. When the stock market is going strong, investors feel confident that they can stomach the ups and downs of the market, and they pour money into stocks. Then when the market collapses, those same investors may turn timid and shy away from stocks.

Many financial advisors ask clients to fill out long questionnaires so they can assign a number to your appetite for risk. I'm not sure those are very helpful. If you're interested, however, many of the large mutual fund families, like Vanguard, have risk tolerance quizzes on their Web sites.

"Cathy would probably feel comfortable sticking to stocks for all her retirement money," said Mike. "I just don't have as much faith in the market as she does. I understand what you've said about the dangers of being too conservative with our long-term money, but I don't like the idea of dumping all my money in stocks."

"You've put your finger on the fundamental investing dilemma," I said. "It's sometimes called the choice between sleeping well and eating well. If you keep all your investments in safe places like savings accounts, you'll sleep well because the volatility of the market isn't keeping you up at night. You may not eat well in retirement, however, because your nest egg won't grow much."

"How do we agree on how to invest our retirement money when we think differently about risk?" asked Cathy.

"If you have different comfort levels, you don't have to agree," I said. "You can load up on stock mutual funds in your IRA, Cathy, and Mike can play it a bit safer with his 401(k) money. You can complement rather than match each other.

"If you use a tool called dollar-cost averaging, Mike, you might feel more comfortable investing in the stock market."

"I think I'm already doing that by investing regularly in my 401(k) plan," said Mike.

"That's right," I said. "By investing the same dollar amount each paycheck, you buy fewer shares of stock when prices are high and you buy more shares when stock prices are low. Since the general direction of the stock market is upward, all those shares you bought low will tend to float up in value. It's a less risky strategy than dumping in a big chunk of money at one time."

Let's assume that you contribute $400 a month in your 401(k) plan, and you invest in a fund that mirrors the U.S. stock market. If in the first month you invest, shares of the fund are selling at $20 each, your $400 will buy 20 shares. Then let's assume the next month, the fund drops in value and shares are worth $16 each. Your $400 will buy 25 shares that month.

If the shares dropped, you might not be eager to keep investing. That's the beauty of dollar-cost-averaging. You don't decide each month how many shares to buy, you just stick to your plan of investing a fixed amount of money. When the share price drops, you load up on cheap shares. Let's say that six months from now, the share price increases to $22. The 45 shares you purchased for $800 are now worth $990, a profit of $190. Your profit is enhanced by all those cheap shares you bought when the price was down.

Asset Allocation

"We're ready for step number three—picking an asset allocation," I said. "That's just a term for splitting up your portfolio among different investments. I don't think you're a candidate for a 100-percent stock portfolio, Mike. To make it easier to live with your portfolio, you might invest part in a bond fund or stable value fund. That will soften the roller-coaster effect stocks can produce. Cathy, it sounds like you're leaning toward choosing stock mutual funds for most or all of your IRA. You and Mike don't need to have identical asset allocations. You two will have to agree on several pieces of your financial plan, but you can split up your investments differently and still have a coherent plan. As long as you agree that all your short-term money and most of your medium-term money should stay out of the stock market.

"Let's start with the three main categories of financial investments: cash or cash equivalents, bonds, and stocks. Each one has a different role to play in your investment portfolio. Cash adds stability because the amount you invest—the principal—doesn't fluctuate, although the interest rate usually varies. Bonds generate more income than cash, but the principal can bounce around somewhat. Stocks are the growth engine in your portfolio. They're the riskiest piece of the pie but are the most likely to produce real growth."

"Before you go on," said Mike, "what do you mean by real growth? Is other growth fake?"

"It sounds like that," I said. "But *real* simply means adjusted for inflation. If you look back at the performance chart, you'll see that the rate of return for large stocks over the past 76 years has averaged 10.2 percent—that's the nominal rate. The real rate of just over 7 percent is calculated by subtracting the average rate of inflation—3 percent—from the nominal rate. Taxes take another bite out of the return—around 3 percent—so the real rate of return adjusted for taxes is about 4 percent."

"You didn't mention real estate," said Cathy. "Isn't that an investment?"

"It certainly is," I said. "Real estate is not a financial security like a stock or bond, but it plays an important role in your total portfolio. It's an inflation hedge because when the general price level rises, real estate tends to outperform stocks and bonds. The market price of your house should represent between 25 and 40 percent of your marketable assets.

"Are you ready to split up your investment pie?"

"I feel comfortable investing my IRAs in stock mutual funds," said Cathy. "What do you think?"

"Let's look at the pros and cons of that strategy," I said. "If, over the next 50 years or so the average rate of return on stocks is about what it was over the past 50 years, you'll make more money investing 100 percent in stocks than if you had put some money in stocks and some in bonds and cash. We don't know if the future will look like the past, but that's a very reasonable scenario.

"The disadvantage is you will have a much bumpier ride because you won't have any stable investments to cushion the blow when the stock market tumbles. If you were to lose your nerve and bail out of stocks at the bottom, your strategy would be wrecked. In that case, you would have been better off playing it safer. Additionally, if you misjudged your time horizon and needed to dip into your long-term investments sooner than you had anticipated, you wouldn't have any stable piece you could draw from. You'd just have to cross your fingers that your need for cash would coincide with a good period in the market."

"Those are risks, I'll admit," said Cathy, "but I'm willing to accept them, especially when I'm young."

"Of course, you still need to have adequate liquidity for day-to-day transactions as well as for an emergency fund. At our last meeting, you mentioned you liked the fact that you can pull contributions out of a Roth IRA any time tax free. You might want to invest part of your converted Roth IRA in a more stable mutual fund, like a bond fund, in case you need to tap into it while you build up your emergency stash."

"I like that idea a lot," said Cathy. "Okay, I'm going to invest one-third of my Roth IRA in a bond fund, and the rest, plus my SEP-IRA, in stock funds."

"There's a decisive statement," I said. "What about your 401(k), Mike?"

"I definitely don't want to put the whole thing in the stock market," said Mike. "What do you suggest?"

"Let me give you a starting point," I said. "When advisors refer to a balanced portfolio, they typically mean a portfolio that's invested 60 percent in stocks and 40 percent in bonds and cash. Institutional investors who manage big pension funds often stick close to a balanced portfolio because it provides enough stability to accommodate payouts from the fund but enough growth for the long term. If you put a larger percentage in stocks, your investments will be more aggressive than a balanced portfolio."

"Thanks, that helped," said Mike. "I guess I'd feel comfortable going slightly more aggressive because I won't need to pull money out of my 401(k) for many years. I'd like to invest 75 percent in stock mutual funds and 25 percent in safer stuff."

"Great," I said. "Now we have the basic allocations in place. Next we need to subdivide the stock portion and the bonds and cash portion into more categories. Let's start with bonds and cash. You have three main choices: cash and equivalents, short-term bonds, and intermediate-term bonds."

"What about long-term bonds?" asked Mike.

"Long-term bonds add more risk to a portfolio without significantly increasing the rate of return," I said, "so I recommend skipping those. I suggest you split the bond section of your portfolio about equally between short-term and intermediate-term bonds. Short-term bonds mature in less than 4 years; intermediate-term bonds mature in about 4 to 10 years."

"Should we also split our bonds between corporate and muni bonds?" asked Mike.

"Municipal bonds don't belong in IRAs, 401(k) plans, or other tax-deferred investments. Munis pay a lower rate of interest and you lose the tax-free feature when they're in a tax-deferred account. Every dollar that comes out of a traditional IRA or 401(k) plan is taxed as ordinary income whether it came from a municipal bond or a corporate bond or a stock dividend or an increase in the value of a stock. It's okay to hold U.S. Treasury and agency bonds because losing the state tax exclusion doesn't hit your return very hard."

"I hadn't thought of that. So we'll stick to short- and intermediate-term corporate and U.S. government bonds," said Mike.

"That's my recommendation," I said. "Now let's divvy up your stock holdings. There are four main categories of stocks: large-cap stocks, mid-cap stocks, small-cap stocks and foreign stocks."

"What exactly does cap mean?" asked Cathy. "I know large-cap means big company stocks."

"Cap is short for capitalization," I said. "The capitalization of a company is simply the number of shares outstanding times the price per share. If there are a million shares of ABC Company's stock held by shareholders and the price per share is $20, ABC's market capitalization is $20 million. You can think of that as the value the shareholders place on the company.

"Definitions vary but small-cap companies have a market capitalization of about $1.5 billion or less; mid-cap companies range from about $1.5 to 8 billion, and large caps are over $8 billion. So ABC would be a small-cap company."

"I think I know the answer to this," said Cathy, "but let me ask anyway. Why is it necessary to slice up our portfolio among large, medium, small, and foreign companies? Are you going to say diversification?"

"You're right," I said. "But diversification goes beyond just splitting up your eggs in several baskets. You want to combine investments that react differently to different market conditions. If you had 10 different stocks but they all went up together and then all went down together, you wouldn't be diversified. Stocks and bonds often perform differently. For example, between 1998 and 1999, the Vanguard Total Stock Market Index—which mirrors the total U.S. stock market—gained about 23.5 percent per year. Bonds, measured by the Vanguard Total Bond Market Index, averaged less than 4 percent per year. However, for the next two years—2000 and 2001—the tables turned and the Total Stock Market Index fund lost over 14 percent per year and the Total Bond Market Index gained over 9 percent per year. Stocks and bonds don't always move in this teeter-totter fashion, but they don't move in lockstep either."

"I thought the objective was to make money," said Mike. "Don't you want all your investments to do well?"

"Over time, yes," I said. "However, in any given year, if all of your investments are doing fabulously well, you can bet that when market conditions change they'll all plummet. Ask anyone who owned nothing but technology stock funds in the late 1990s. They had some fabulous years, but if they didn't diversify, they're still trying to dig themselves out of the hole that the market shift in the early 2000s caused.

"Different size companies tend to perform differently as well. From 1994 to 1998, large-company stocks trounced small-company stocks, and then for the next four years, small-company stocks outperformed big-company stocks. If I could see into the future, I could tell you exactly which sector of the market would be hot next year, but nobody has that power. The smartest strategy is to diversify."

"What about all those analysts and brokers we hear on TV," said Mike, "who talk about what's going to happen in the market. Aren't there some pretty smart people looking at this stuff?"

"Some of them are smart, but they're not clairvoyant," I said. "The stock market is unpredictable in the short term. I feel very comfortable predicting that the stock market will be higher in 20 years than it is today, but I have no idea what the market will do tomorrow or next week or even next year. Anyone who claims to be able to predict accurately short-term movements of the stock market is just plain wrong.

"It's very tempting to try to time the market, and we've all heard stories about someone who got out just in time. You might hit it lucky occasionally. But no one has consistently been able to sell at exactly the right time and get back in at the right time. No one rings a bell to announce when the market has hit a low or a high. We only know that in hindsight. When the market starts to advance, it often goes up very swiftly, and the market timers are left on the sidelines. If you miss out on only a few good days in the market over several years, your average return is much lower."

"I'm convinced," said Cathy. "How should we divvy up our stock investments?"

"In general, foreign stocks and small-cap stocks are the riskiest, large-cap stocks are the least risky, and mid-cap stocks are somewhere in between, so how you divide up your stocks will depend on your risk tolerance," I said. "Having said that, I'll give you my rules of thumb and you can tweak it from there. I usually recommend keeping 10 to15 percent of your stocks in small-company stocks, 10 to 15 percent in foreign, 20 to 25 percent in mid-cap stocks and the rest—45 to 60 percent in large-company stocks.

"Many advisors also divvy up investments between growth and value—two different investment styles. In general, managers who invest for growth choose stocks of companies they think will grow faster than the stock market as a whole. Value managers look for bargains—stocks that are selling for less than the manager thinks they're worth. When growth stocks are hot—as they were in the late 1990s—value stocks lag. When value stocks do well—as in 2000 and 2001—growth stocks tend to fall behind."

"So we should hold some of each, right?" asked Cathy.

"That's right. You want to have both bases covered," I said.

"Let's put it all together. I combined the split between stocks and bonds that you each came up with and my rules of thumb for splitting up stocks and prepared an asset allocation pie for each of you. This is only a starting point, and you'll probably modify it as you go along. Your portfolio, Cathy, is fairly aggressive, and you'll have to gauge how comfortable you feel investing such a big chunk in the stock market." (See Figure 9-2.)

"I realize that my portfolio is pretty risky, and if I weren't so young, I'd be a lot more nervous," said Cathy. "I'll see how I feel in the coming months and years."

Choosing Your Investments

Let's use Mike's 401(k) plan as an example of how to choose investments to match up to your asset allocation. His choices are the Vanguard

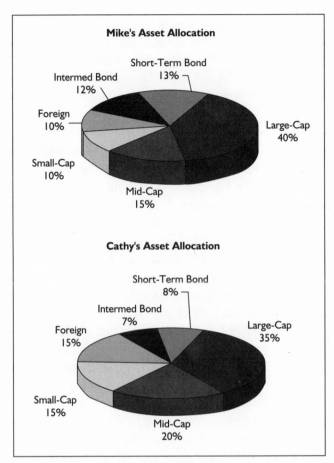

FIGURE 9-2   **Mike's and Cathy's Asset Allocation Pies**

500 Index, Vanguard Windsor II, Vanguard Mid-Cap Index, Vanguard Small-Cap Index, Vanguard Wellington, Vanguard International Growth, Vanguard Total Bond Market Index, and a Stable Value fund.

Two of the funds—the Vanguard 500 Index and Vanguard Windsor II—invest in large companies. The first is an index fund—the kind of mutual fund that mirrors a particular stock of the stock or bond market. Index funds are also called passive funds because the stocks or bonds in the fund are not actively chosen by a manager. Instead the fund contains all the stocks or bonds—or a representative sample of stocks or bonds—in the particular index. An S&P 500 index is composed of the 500 largest companies in the U.S. stock market, so an S&P 500 index fund holds the stocks of the largest 500 companies. Although the most famous index funds are those that mirror the S&P 500, there are dozens of index funds that track different stock and bond market indexes such as the Russell 2000 Small-Cap Index or the S&P 400 Mid-Cap Index.

Index funds have a significant advantage over actively run funds because they are very inexpensive to manage. More of the money earned by the fund goes into investor's pockets and less goes to pay the operating expenses. The average operating expenses of a stock mutual fund add up to about 1.4 percent of the value of the fund; the operating expense of the Vanguard 500 Index fund is .18 percent. That means an actively managed fund has almost a 1.25 percent disadvantage right out of the gate. Since stocks have earned an average of about 10 percent per year over the past several decades, an investor in an average actively managed stock mutual fund gives up over 12 percent of the return in expenses.

It might seem like a good mutual fund manager could overcome that hurdle by making smart investment choices, and every year some managers beat the S&P 500. But it's a different group each year. Fewer than a dozen managers who invest in large-company stocks have 10-year records that matched or beat the Vanguard 500 Index fund.

It's very difficult to beat the large-cap stock market—that is, the S&P 500. To do so, you would have to find the diamonds in the rough that the other managers are missing. But the big companies have lots of analysts assigned to them and pounds of research are generated on each company, so discovering that overlooked gem is a Herculean task.

The proof is in the statistics. The Vanguard Index 500 fund's 10-year performance was better than that of 89 percent of its peers, according to Morningstar data. So the case for investing in S&P 500 index funds is pretty compelling. The data are not quite so impressive for small-cap and foreign stock index funds. There is evidence that active managers can add value in these areas because there are so many stocks and the research on each company is much skimpier.

Mike's lucky because he can build a diversified portfolio with the choices in his 401(k) plan. He can invest in large-company stocks by contributing to the Index 500 or Windsor II fund. The Small-Cap and Mid-Cap Index funds will give him broad exposure to those segments of the market. The International Growth fund invests in foreign stocks. The Total Bond Market Index invests in a broad array of government and corporate bonds, and the Stable Value fund is a good substitute for the short-term bond piece of his portfolio. Mike just needs to match the percentages he invests in the funds to his asset allocation pie, and he will have a diversified portfolio that matches his investment horizon and his tolerance for risk.

Not all 401(k) plans offer such a diversified menu of mutual funds. Even though you may have a long list to choose from, there's no guarantee the funds invest in different segments of the market. If your plan offers six large-company funds and a few bond funds, you'll have to fill in the gaps by investing your IRA in a small-company or foreign fund, for example.

Cathy has had some experience investing in individual stocks, but it's very difficult to put together a diversified portfolio of individual stocks unless you have hundreds of thousands of dollars to invest. Even then, investing in individual stocks requires more attention than most investors are willing to devote. Your best bet is to invest in no-load mutual funds. By pooling money from many investors, mutual funds can hold a broad variety of stocks or bonds or both so you get instant diversification.

Mutual funds are also very convenient. You don't have to worry about buying lots of stocks—100 shares at a time. Once you have met the minimum investment in the fund, you can add and withdraw small amounts as you wish. You can mirror a piece of the market—in the case of index funds—or get professional active management—in the case of active funds—for a relatively low price.

That doesn't mean all mutual funds are good investments. You have to choose carefully because some funds have very high expenses or uneven investment styles. If you are investing in a regular account—and not in an IRA or a retirement plan—you should watch the turnover of a fund. If the manager buys and sells frequently, you are more likely to end up with hefty capital gains distributions and a big tax bill.

You also need to check if you'll pay extra to invest in the fund. Load funds carry commissions or loads and are sold by banks, brokers, and commissioned planners. No-load funds are purchased directly from the mutual fund company. There's no evidence that load funds perform better than no-load funds. In fact, when you take the load into account, load funds' performance is typically worse.

Load funds are usually—but not always—identified by a letter after their name. There is an alphabet soup of loads, but generally a fund with an A after its name carries a front-end load—a commission you pay when you purchase the fund—and B shares carry both a back-end charge and an ongoing charge. C shares have an extra annual charge for as long as you own the fund.

Front-end fees are typically 5 to 6 percent; back-end charges start at about 6 percent and decline over five or six years, and level charges are about 1 percent of the value of the fund each year.

Several mutual fund families, like Vanguard, offer no-load funds exclusively. Others, like Fidelity, offer both load and no-load funds. The fund companies publish prospectuses—informational brochures—for their funds, and you should always get one and read it before you invest.

The best resource for researching mutual funds is Morningstar. There are thousands of mutual funds, but you can use the tools on the Web site (*www.morningstar.com*) to carve out a manageable list of funds.

Splitting up Your Pie

Psst. Here's a hot investment tip. The most important investment decision you make is how to divvy up your portfolio among the main types of investments: cash, bonds, stocks, and real estate. In fact, studies have shown that single decision plays a much greater role in your rate of return than your choice of specific stocks or bonds or mutual funds. That may sound wrong —it did to me the first time I read about it. But the more I thought about it, the more sense it made. Let's say you were a brilliant judge of intermediate-term bond funds, and 15 years ago you dumped all of your money into the fund that turned out to be one of the very best intermediate-term bond funds. Your money would have grown by an average 9.14 percent per year over those 15 years, and a $10,000 investment would have grown to just over $37,000. Not bad for a bond fund. And that's the point. Compared to other investors who split up their investments among bonds and stocks, for example, your performance was only so-so. Your investment-picking skill was extraordinary, but your asset allocation talent was only mediocre. If you had split your $10,000 and invested one-third in a bond index fund and two-thirds in an S&P 500 index fund, you would have made an average of 9.93 percent per year. That $10,000 investment would be worth more than $41,000 15 years later, about 11 percent more than your bond-only portfolio.

How to Get Started

Mike and Cathy have already had some investing experience, but what do you do if you're new to investing? The biggest obstacles are

Start by eliminating all the load mutual funds. If you're doing the research yourself, there's no need to pay a commission to someone else. Next, I would decide which type of fund you are searching for—a large-cap stock fund or a foreign stock fund, for example. Then, if you are looking for an actively managed fund, I would limit my search to funds with managers who have been at the helm for at least five years. Because high operating expenses eat into your return, I recommend looking for funds with lower than average expenses—1 percent or lower is a good start. With the Morningstar tools, you can specify the type of past performance and risk you are looking for in a variety of ways, such as a five-year return that beats the category average with low or below average risk.

choosing an investment, scraping together enough money, and setting up an account, but you can knock those down one by one by following these guidelines:

1. A great first mutual fund is a balanced fund that automatically splits your investment into about 60 percent stocks and 40 percent bonds. You get instant diversification and don't have to worry about rebalancing—the fund manager does it for you. Another good choice is a "fund of funds"—a mutual fund that spreads your investment among several funds in the same family. Skip the pricey commissions and pick a no-load mutual fund.

2. Many no-load mutual funds allow you to get started for $1000 or less. Others require no initial minimums as long as you sign up for automatic monthly investments, and others have lower minimums for IRAs.

3. Setting up an account is easy. Just download an application from the fund family's Web site or call their 800 number. If you need help, a company representative can walk you through the questions.

Here are a few good starter funds:

Vanguard STAR—a fund of funds that spreads your investment over about 11 Vanguard funds. $1000 minimum. 800-662-7447 www.vanguard.com

Dodge & Cox Balanced—one of the oldest, best-performing balanced funds around. $1000 minimum for IRAs. 800-621-3979 www.dodgeandcox.com

Pax World Balanced—a balanced fund that invests in companies that pass its socially responsible screens. $250 minimum. 800-767-1729 *www.paxfund.com*

T. Rowe Price Balanced—classic balanced fund. No initial minimum if you set up $100 a month automatic investments. (Some T. Rowe Price funds have $50-a-month minimums.) 800-638-5660 *www.troweprice.com*

What Mike and Cathy Have Learned

1. Stocks and bonds have different risk-reward characteristics.

2. The riskiness of an investment depends on the volatility or unpredictability of its return.

3. It's important to match your time horizon with the appropriate investment. Stocks are good investments for long time horizons, but too volatile for short-term investments. CDs, money market funds, and other stable investments are great choices for money you'll need in a year or two, but the return is too low to make them good candidates for long-term investing.

4. How you divvy up your investment "pie" is one of your most important decisions.

5. Mutual funds are more appropriate than individual stocks unless you have a very large portfolio and the time or expertise to manage it. Morningstar is a great resource for researching mutual funds.

Your Homework

1. Gather all your investment statements and figure out your current asset allocation.

2. Divide your goals according to the time horizons—short-term, medium-term, and long-term—and list appropriate types of investments for each group of goals.

3. Modify your current asset allocation if necessary to reflect your goals and your risk comfort level. If you haven't started investing, you can start with a balanced allocation (60 percent stocks and 40 percent bonds and cash) and modify it as appropriate.

4. Choose investments for each slice of your asset allocation pie.

5. Mark your calendar to review and rebalance your investments once a year.

Resources

1. Malkiel, Burton G. *A Random Walk Down Wall Street*. 2003. W. W. Norton & Company.

2. Bogle, John C. *Common Sense on Mutual Funds*. 1999. John Wiley & Sons.

3. Rowland, Mary. *A Commonsense Guide to Mutual Funds*. 1998. Bloomberg Press.

4. *www.vanguard.com*

5. *www.troweprice.com*

6. *www.morningstar.com*

CHAPTER 10

And Baby Makes Three

They're small and cuddly and can cost a fortune. Babies have a huge impact on your financial picture. Priorities get shifted, and carefully thought-out spending and savings plans become obsolete.

Cathy and Mike had planned to start a family in a year or two, but they found out that babies don't always follow their parents' timeline. Cathy's expecting a baby, and the due date is just about the time she planned to finish her MBA. Cathy and Mike have about seven-and-a-half months to prepare for their son or daughter, and they have already begun to think about how their finances will change. We had planned to talk about taxes at this meeting, but we all agreed that planning for baby should come first.

"I'm really anxious to talk about the things we should be doing now to get ready for our baby," said Cathy. "And I'd like to open a college fund. The sooner we get started saving, the better."

"Saving for college will be a new piece of your financial plan," I agreed. "There are several other topics on the baby checklist that we should talk about as well, including child care and taxes.

"This is such an exciting time for you both. You're smart to start thinking now about how a baby will change your financial picture. Once the baby arrives, it will be hard to carve out time for planning and reflecting.

"Let's start by reviewing your insurance coverage."

Insurance

Cathy is covered by Mike's health insurance, and they checked that pregnancy and birth were covered by the policy. Cathy's doctors and the hospital where they plan to have the baby are in the policy's network, so they'll just need to cover the $15 copayment for doctor visits and the $7 copayment for prescriptions. If they decide to consult a doctor who is not in the network, they'll have to pay a $250 deductible, and then 30 percent of costs.

Once the baby is born, they'll need to register him or her with the insurance company. Most policies cover a newborn for up to 30 days automatically, but it's best to check with your company.

Cathy signed up for a long-term disability insurance policy two months ago. Her policy covers complications due to pregnancy, but only after a 60-day waiting period. Since she is self-employed, Cathy would have to tap into their emergency fund to cover living expenses during the waiting period if she were disabled. Employees can often accumulate sick and vacation days to cover time off during a pregnancy or after the baby is born.

One of the most immediate changes you'll experience when you have a child is your need for life insurance. When it was just the two of you, the need wasn't so urgent as long as you both had the ability to earn a salary. Unless your baby becomes a highly paid TV or movie star, he or she will rely on you for living expenses for many years. Many parents increase their life insurance coverage to make sure their salaries would be replaced while the child remains dependent on them—often right through college. Now more than ever, you'll need to get the most coverage for the lowest price, and term insurance fits the bill. If you opt for costly permanent insurance—whole life, universal, or variable—you'll either wind up getting skimpy coverage or gutting your spending plan.

Both of you need life insurance, even if one of you decides to stay home with the baby. Just because you're not earning a paycheck doesn't mean you can forego life insurance. Calculate what it would cost to hire a nanny or housekeeper to take care of your child if something happened to you. That's the "salary" you'd have to replace with life insurance. Depending on what part of the country you live in, $25,000 to $40,000 a year is a good rule of thumb.

Child Care

"Speaking of nannies and child care, have you thought about what you'll do when the baby arrives, Cathy?" I asked.

"Mike and I talked things over last night and I decided to postpone my plan for expanding my business for the time being," said Cathy. "I'll continue working on my MBA because I'm so close to graduating, but I'll just stick to my current client base so I can work part time when the baby arrives. I'll need some child care—just not a full-time sitter or nanny."

"How many hours a week will you need child care?" I asked.

"Cathy and I figured three mornings a week should be enough at the beginning," said Mike. "Cathy can schedule meetings for the mornings when she has child care. In the afternoons, while the baby is napping, she can do some more work. When I come home at night, I can take over with some child duties."

"You two have really thought things out," I said. "I'm glad you plan to finish your MBA, Cathy. It's so hard to start that up again after an interruption. Let's see—your due date is just a few weeks after your graduation date. You're going to have a busy pregnancy, but at least you won't have to study and write papers while you're taking care of a newborn. As far as your post-baby work schedule, I hope you're right and you'll get some work done in the afternoons—you may have to play that one by ear. Have you looked into how much you'll have to pay a babysitter?"

"We decided we want to hire someone who will come to our home," said Cathy. "My friend, Cindy, has a wonderful babysitter who charges $50 for a half-day or $90 for a full day. Cindy only needs child care for two days a week, so I'm hoping I can hire her babysitter for three mornings a week—say, Monday, Wednesday, and Friday."

"So $50 three times a week would be $150 a week or about $7200 a year, if you take vacation time into account," I said. "And, because the babysitter is working in your home, she is your employee. That means you'll be responsible for withholding income taxes and the employee's share of social security taxes, plus you'll have to pay the employer's share of social security taxes. I strongly recommend that you get worker's compensation coverage on any babysitter who regularly works in your home. Throw in unemployment insurance and your total annual child care cost will be close to $8000 a year."

"Yikes," said Mike. "Does it even make sense for you to keep working, Cathy?"

"That depends," said Cathy. "From a professional and emotional point of view, I definitely want to keep working. I need to keep my skills fresh, and as much as I'm looking forward to parenthood, I think I would go stir crazy if I stayed home all day and didn't have a career. Besides, this is what we had planned for all along even if it's a wash financially for a while."

Spending Plan

Child care is the biggest addition to Mike's and Cathy's spending plan, but new babies mean other expenses as well. Health insurance premiums often increase if you move from single or couple's coverage to family coverage. You might also decide to switch your type of coverage. If you currently have a traditional 20-80 plan, you might save by moving to a PPO or even an HMO. Under these plans, copayments are often low, and you don't need to meet a deductible if you stick to in-network doctors.

Your grocery bill will increase as you start to buy diapers, formula, and other baby products. Mike and Cathy figured they'll spend another $100 a month on groceries. They plan to keep baby clothes, toys, and miscellaneous expenses to $50 a month, and they're counting on gifts and hand-me-downs from relatives to fill the gap.

Depending on your family situation and your lifestyle, your vacation budget could increase or decrease. If your families live out of town, you may spend more on travel when your child is young, as you make the rounds visiting relatives.

Cathy and Mike calculated baby expenses will add about $10,000 to their spending plan the first year or two—$8000 for child care and $2000 for other expenses. They're hoping they'll get some tax breaks to offset the extra costs.

Taxes

"It seems like a lot of the tax breaks I've heard about in the last few years were aimed at couples with children," said Mike. "We'll finally be able to take advantage of those."

"There are some tax benefits associated with parenthood," I agreed, "but babies are still pretty expensive little creatures. The U.S. Department of Agriculture estimated that a middle-income family will spend almost $250,000 to raise a child—not including college costs."

"That was a number I probably didn't need to hear," said Cathy. "I had no idea it was so much. But if other parents can do it, we can, too."

"If money were the only consideration, population growth would come skidding to a halt in this country," I said. "But back to taxes. First, you get to take an extra exemption. In 2003, that's an additional $3050 you can deduct from your taxable income, which, in your tax bracket, will save you $457.50 in taxes."

"The baby isn't due until the end of the year," said Cathy. "Do we still get a full exemption?"

"As long as the baby is born by midnight on December 31st, you'll get the full exemption," I said. "Parents also get a child tax credit for each child under 17 years old. The credit is currently $1000 per child, and it starts to phase out for high-income taxpayers—those who make more than $110,000. A credit reduces your tax bill by the amount of the credit, so the child credit saves you $1000."

"Don't we also get a tax break for our babysitting expenses?" asked Cathy.

"That's right," I said. "You get a choice—you can either take a tax credit or participate in Mike's dependent care program at work. The tax credit is equal to 20 percent of the first $3000 you spend on child care, so your credit would be $600. The tax credit is calculated on a sliding scale—lower-income parents can take a larger percentage of their expenses off their tax bill. If you have two or more children, you calculate the credit on the first $6000 of child care costs.

"If you take advantage of Mike's dependent care program you can exclude child care expenses—up to $5,000 a year—from your income."

"They probably told me something about the program when I was first hired," said Mike. "I heard it's kind of a hassle."

"There's some paperwork involved," I said, "but you can save a lot of taxes if you participate."

If your employer offers a dependent care plan, I recommend that you consider signing up. Here's how they work. You estimate how much you'll spend on child care expenses during the year and ask your employer to withhold that amount from your paycheck. The maximum you can withhold is $5000 each year, so if you're paid every other week or 26 times a year, your employer can withhold $192 from each paycheck. When you present proof that you paid a babysitter or other child care provider, your employer will reimburse you for your expenses, up to the amount you had withheld.

So far, it just seems like a one-for-one swap, but it's much better than that. The money withheld from your paycheck is exempt from federal, state, and Social Security taxes. If you're in the 15 percent federal and 5 percent state bracket, that adds up to a savings of over 27 percent, counting the 7.65 percent Social Security taxes. For every $192 you have withheld, you save $52 in taxes. Because money doesn't have to come out of your paycheck to pay taxes, your paycheck is only reduced by $140 ($192 minus $52), even though a full $192 goes into your flexible spending account.

Over the course of the year, you can save about $1350 if you're in the 15 percent federal and 5 percent state tax brackets—more if you're in higher brackets. You'll get a full $5000 back when you present your receipts, but your paychecks will only be reduced by a total of $3650. The difference is your tax saving. (Married taxpayers who file separately are each only eligible to exclude $2500 of expenses from their income.)

If you choose not to participate in a dependent care plan or your employer doesn't offer one, you may still be eligible to take a tax credit for dependent care expenses. The credit is equal to between 20 percent and 35 percent of up to $3000 in child care expenses ($6000 if you have to pay for care for two or more children). The exact percentage depends on your income. Cathy and Mike would save $600 by taking the credit—considerably less than they would get by participating in a dependent care plan at work.

In order to qualify for either plan, both spouses must have earned income. If only one spouse works, you can still qualify if the nonworking spouse is a full-time student or is disabled.

Saving for Baby

"We had hoped to be in a house before the baby was born," said Cathy, "but that's not going to happen, so we'll make the spare bedroom in our apartment into the baby's room. What's the best way to set aside some money for extra baby expenses?"

"How about approaching it as a mini spending plan?" I asked. "Make a list of the things you'd like to buy, research the prices, and figure how much you'd like to have saved by the time the baby arrives. It's such a short period of time, we don't need to account for any interest, so just divide your target savings amount by the seven months remaining in your pregnancy. I recommend setting up automatic contributions to a savings account."

"So if I come up with a $700 spending plan, I should save $100 a month," said Cathy. "It's going to be tough to carve that much out, but we should probably get used to it. Child care is going to cost more than that. I can have the money deposited in my credit union account each month."

"That's a good place for it," I said. "You'll want to keep that money safe and available. When you're making out your spending list, don't forget to add the $250 deductible on your health insurance. And you'll need to set aside some money for maternity clothes, I imagine."

"Cindy has promised to lend me a bunch of her clothes," said Cathy, "but I'll have to buy a few things. I think we can spare $100 a month, Mike, for our baby budget. It'll be nice to have the money already saved when the baby comes instead of running up the charge cards."

"It's easy to overspend when outfitting a nursery," I said. "You may consider stretching your money by searching for a few gently used items. Just be careful they meet current safety standards, of course.

"Before we tackle saving for college, let me mention one more thing new parents need to think about—estate planning. You won't just have each other to plan for—you'll have to make provisions for your child, so there will be lots to talk about when we have our estate planning meeting."

Saving for College

"At the beginning of the meeting, Cathy, you mentioned setting up a college fund," I said. "I realize you're just getting used to the idea of having a baby, but have you two talked about how you want to handle college expenses? During our goal-setting meeting, you both talked about how your own parents dealt with college costs."

"That's right," said Cathy. "I was lucky. My parents covered all the big costs—I just had to pay for books and incidentals."

"I had to take out some loans to cover my college costs," said Mike. "My grandparents helped me pay the loans off early. I always got the feeling college kind of took my parents by surprise."

"You grew up with different models of paying for college. Any thoughts about what you two would like to do?" I asked.

"I would like to pay for as much as we can," said Cathy.

"I'm not so sure about that," said Mike. "I'm not saying that you don't value your education, Cathy, but I think children appreciate things more if they have to work for them. Just dropping college education in their laps may send the wrong message."

"It wasn't dropped in my lap," said Cathy. "I still had to work summers and part-time during a few semesters to pay my share. I contributed even though I didn't have to worry about tuition and room and board. I think it depends on the parents' attitude—if they value education, the children are likely to do the same."

"I guess," said Mike slowly. "It's just a little shocking how much college will cost by the time our baby is ready to start. I was on the Web last night, and I found some information on projected college costs. Four years at a decent private college could easily cost $350,000 in 18 years. And I'm not talking Harvard or Princeton."

"Those numbers always look scary," said Cathy. "The point is if we start saving now, we can get a head start. Isn't that right?"

"You're right," I said, "but my next suggestion may surprise you. I recommend you don't place saving for college high on your priority list."

The fact is, there are lots of ways to finance education costs. Your children will be able to go to college even if you haven't saved the whole amount up front. On the other hand, there's only one way to finance your retirement, and that's to save for it. You can borrow for college, but you can't ask your friendly banker for a loan to cover a shortfall in your nest egg.

Too often, parents shift their focus away from retirement to college funding. For most of us, college will come up before retirement, so it seems logical to fund college first. Couples end up jeopardizing their own retirement because they neglect their nest egg while they conscientiously plow money into college savings. When their children finish college, they turn back to retirement planning, but by then it's hard to make up for lost time.

If you're already fully funding your retirement accounts, paid off your credit cards, own a house, and have an emergency account, by all means start a college fund. But if your situation is like Mike's and Cathy's, the only way to save for college would be to cut back on retirement contributions or additions to the house fund or to reduce some expenses in an already pared down spending plan.

If you feel guilty if you don't start a college fund, set up a Roth IRA. This can be a "dual use" account. If you contribute $3000 a year, by the time your child is 18, you'll have $54,000 in the account that you can pull out tax free for college (or anything else). If you leave the earnings in the account until you're 59½, you can withdraw them tax free for retirement expenses.

Most couples end up financing college through a patchwork of investments, loans, and current income. By the time your child enters college, you will probably have built up a chunk of equity in your home that can be tapped for college. Children can work summers or during the school year to help out, and they may be eligible for some scholarship money.

If you decide you can afford to earmark some money specifically for college, or if a grandparent or other relative would like to help out with college costs, you have a few options.

The college-saving tool that has received the most publicity over the past few years is the 529 plan—named after a section of the IRS code. The plans vary from state to state, but the basic rules are the same. The parent or grandparent sets up a plan and names a beneficiary—the college-bound child. The owner of the plan can make substantial contributions—as much as $55,000 the first year. The plan owner generally gets a break on state income taxes if they invest in the plan sponsored by their home state. There is no up-front tax break from the federal government, but distributions from the plan are tax free if the money is used for college costs—including tuition and room and board. The law guaranteeing tax-free distributions expires in 2010, and if Congress doesn't extend the provision, beginning in 2011 distributions will be taxed at the child's rate. That's still a tax break, but not nearly as good as tax free.

Distributions from a 529 plan can be used at any accredited school of higher education in the country, including junior colleges. Most plans offer a variety of investment choices, including an age-based option that keeps most of the money in stock mutual funds when the child is young and gradually moves the money to more conservative investments—bonds and cash—as the child approaches college. If you don't want to keep monitoring and rebalancing your investments, the age-based option may be a good choice.

You can usually set up a 529 plan with a very small initial invest-ment—around $15 in some states. Grandparents often like that feature because they can add to it gradually, as birthday and holiday gifts, for example.

Only one child can be named for each account, but the plan owner can change beneficiaries, with some restrictions. For example, if your child got a full scholarship and didn't need college money, your parents could change the beneficiary to another grandchild.

You can get information about 529 plans, plus links to specific state plans, at *www.savingforcollege.com*. If you decide to invest in one, get the application directly from the state sponsor and skip the middleman—or woman. If you open your account with a broker or commissioned planner, or even your local bank, you'll pay an extra charge.

Coverdell Education Savings accounts work in much the same way as 529 plans except that there is a $2000 maximum contribution per year per child, and you can pick your investments just like you do with an IRA. In a 529 account, your investment choices are limited to the ones offered in the plan. Eligibility to contribute to a Coverdell account phases out for married taxpayers whose income is over $190,000 ($95,000 for singles). There are no income limits for contributions to 529 plans.

Coverdell accounts are more flexible than 529 plans because distrib-utions can be used for private elementary and high-school tuition as well as college, or for the purchase of a computer for a school-age child.

If you open a Coverdell account with a no-load mutual fund com-pany, you'll skip the commissions. Check the minimum amount needed to open an account—it varies by fund company.

Some families build a college fund by investing in the child's name. Minors (children under the age of 18 or 21, depending on the state) can't own investments directly, so UTMA or UGMA accounts must be set up to hold the stocks or mutual funds. The initials stand for Uniform Transfer to Minors or Gift to Minors Act. A custodian, typi-cally a parent, is named to manage the investments. Because the child is usually in a lower tax bracket than the parent or grandparent, he or she pays less tax on dividends, interest, or capital gains. The first $750 of income is tax free, and the next $750 is taxed at the lowest tax rate. If the child is under 14, the "kiddie tax" kicks in after those amounts, and any additional income will be taxed at the parent's tax rate.

There are a few problems with custodial accounts. The money ultimately belongs to the child and can't usually be shifted to another child's account or back to the parents. When the child turns 18 (21 in some states), he or she controls the account—not the custodian. Even if the parent set up the account as a college fund, the child may decide to buy a sports car instead.

A well-funded custodial account can hamper the child's ability to qualify for college financial aid. Under current rules, money in the child's name reduces aid more than money in a parent's name. If a child has $10,000 in investments when he applies to college, the financial aid award is reduced by $3500. If $10,000 were in a parent's name, the child would lose less than $600 in aid. Of course, financial aid may not even be an option if your income and assets are too high by the time your child enters college.

A better strategy is to invest in tax-efficient mutual funds—the kind that distribute very little in dividends and capital gains each year—in your own name. You'll pay almost no taxes while you hold the fund. When your child is ready for college, if he or she isn't eligible for financial aid, you can gift the shares to your child and cash them in at the child's lower tax rate. You maintain control of the investments while the child is growing up and shift them to a lower tax rate when it's time for college. If the child gets a scholarship or doesn't go to college, you can add the investments to your own nest egg.

U.S. savings bonds can also be used to fund college. If you purchase the bonds in your own name, you won't pay taxes on the interest earned if the money is used for college and your income is below a certain level—currently $86,400 for a married couple.

If you're unable to save for college right away, you can still start building a fund for your children. Certain companies will contribute cash to your child's college fund if you buy products from them or shop at their stores. Two such programs are Upromise and BabyMint. Check out their Web sites—*www.upromise.com* and *www.babymint.com*—for details. You won't accumulate a ton of money, but every little bit counts.

What Cathy and Mike Have Learned

Good planning can make the financial impact of having a baby easier to absorb.

Recommendations for Cathy and Mike

1. Check out health and disability insurance coverage.

2. Explore your child care options.

3. Prepare a spending plan for expenses you'll incur, such as decorating and outfitting the nursery, and put aside money each month.

4. Redo your overall spending plan to incorporate ongoing baby-related expenses such as child care and added groceries and clothes expenses.

5. Fund your retirement before you earmark money specifically for college. Consider dual-use vehicles like Roth IRAs.

6. Change your estate planning documents and beneficiary designations as appropriate.

Your Homework

1. If you're planning to have a baby, develop your own checklist, using Cathy's and Mike's as a model.

2. If you're considering adopting, consult IRS Publication 963 for details on special tax benefits for adoptive parents.

Resources

1. *www.savingforcollege.com* for information on tax-advantaged college savings programs.

2. *www.upromise.co*m and *www.babymint.com* for details on how to sign up for programs that allow companies and stores to contribute money to your child's college plan.

3. *www.irs.gov* to obtain Publications 503 and 972 containing details on dependent care tax benefits and the child tax credit.

CHAPTER 11

Tax Saving for Couples

F or most of us, April 15th is like Halloween without the candy. It comes around once a year, scares us, and then drops off our radar screen. We scramble to gather our W-2s and 1099s and pull receipts from drawers, wallets, and shoeboxes. Then we hand our pile of information over to a tax professional or struggle with forms and software ourselves. Finally, we sign the return and drop it into the mailbox with a sigh of relief. Done! And we barely give it a thought until next year.

Many of us could profit by paying a little more attention to taxes. After all, if we add up all the taxes we pay—income, payroll, property, and sales—they're the biggest bills we face. Although the tax code is complicated, you don't have to be a CPA to save money on your taxes. A small amount of knowledge can go a long way.

As Mike and Cathy are about to find out, couples have special issues when it comes to taxes. Because Cathy is self-employed, we'll explore opportunities for saving taxes on her earnings. We'll also talk about how to estimate income taxes and adjust paycheck withholdings.

Getting Started on Taxes

"I agree with the philosophy of planning for taxes," said Mike, "but it seems to me that this is one part of our financial plan we can just delegate to a tax preparer and be done with it. That worked okay last year and we have plenty of other things to occupy our time."

"It might seem that way," I said, "but I hope I can convince you that this is an area where some time and knowledge can yield big returns. Remember when we set up your spending plan? Taxes were a big wedge of your expense pie. At your current income, you are paying about $7500 per year in federal income taxes, more than $3300 in pay-roll taxes, and $2700 in state and local taxes. That's about 23 percent of your gross income.

"Plus," I continued, "every dollar you save in taxes is equivalent to earning another $1.30 of income."

"How's that?" asked Mike.

"Well, if you save $1 in taxes, that's another dollar in your pocket," I explained. "When you earn money, you have to pay taxes before you can put that dollar in your pocket. You would have to earn $1.30 to pay your taxes and wind up with $1. Learning how to save on your tax bill can be very profitable."

"Okay," said Mike, "but I still think the tax code is way too com-plicated. And every time Congress simplifies the code, it gets worse. More rules and more regulations."

"You make two good points, Mike," I said. "The tax code is quite complex, and a good tax professional can be well worth the fee. Cathy is self-employed, so that makes your return a little trickier. You may find working with a CPA useful to make sure you catch all the allow-able business expenses. But, remember, tax preparers only see your information after the year has ended and by then there are very few tax-savings strategies available for that year. Plus, tax preparers are under very tight deadlines, and they're focused on completing your return, not scouring your records for tax savings opportunities.

"The bottom line is, the person who prepares your taxes isn't going to be looking over your shoulder during the year making sure you con-sider the tax consequences of each financial decision. That's your responsibility."

"I know decisions like buying a house and having a baby can affect your tax situation," said Cathy. "But can we really save money on taxes in other areas?"

"You bet," I said. "Going back to school to get your MBA, having your office in your home, contributing to Mike's 401(k), investing extra cash in a stock index mutual fund—even giving used clothing to charity instead of having a garage sale—all affect your taxes."

The Nitty-Gritty on Our Tax System

"Let's start with a few facts about the U.S. income tax system. And, no, this will not be on the exam," I said when I saw Mike's worried look. "Remember, the more you know, the more you can save."

President Lincoln instituted an income tax during the Civil War, and the tax was repealed 10 years later. It took an amendment to the Constitution in 1913 to set up the income tax system that is still in effect today, although it has gone through many changes. The impetus for an income tax was the need to finance government expenses, mainly the costs of war. But the tax system has also been used to encourage certain kinds of spending. Congress decided home ownership was good for families and good for the economy, so several tax breaks for homeowners have become part of the IRS code. It's the American dream, after all.

We get a tax break for contributing to 401(k) plans, which is evidence that Congress encourages saving. You postpone paying taxes on the income you contribute to your retirement nest egg. If individuals have an incentive to stash away money, Congress reasoned, they will save more for their retirement. And that's what has happened. Millions of Americans participate in 401(k) plans.

You may already know that the U.S. income tax is progressive, which means it has a Robin Hood slant to it. Wealthier Americans pay more income taxes—not just in absolute dollars but proportionally as well. The wealthiest 5 percent pay over half of all income taxes. Some of the taxes collected go to less well-off individuals through programs like Medicaid and the Earned Income Credit. So income redistribution is a powerful force behind our tax structure.

Our tax system is set up with a series of tax brackets, and each bracket has its own tax rate. Because it's a progressive system, the higher your income, the higher your tax bracket.

"I remember when my Aunt Karen went back to work after my cousins were grown," said Mike. "My Uncle Ed grumbled that Aunt Karen's salary pushed them into a higher tax bracket and, after taxes, they were worse off then before she started working. How unfair is that?"

"Your Uncle Ed's math wasn't quite on target. Even though they paid more taxes when they were both working, they didn't end up with less money, " I said.

"Aunt Karen's paycheck may have pushed them into a higher *marginal* tax bracket, but Uncle Ed's salary is still taxed the way it was before. Only the part of the new money that is in the higher tax bracket is taxed more heavily. Here's an example.

"Let's say Uncle Ed earns $50,000, and after deductions and exemptions, his taxable income is $35,000. That puts Uncle Ed and Aunt Karen in the 15-percent tax bracket. The first $14,000 is taxed at 10 percent, and the next $21,000 is taxed at 15 percent. Their tax liability equals 10 percent of $14,000 plus 15 percent of $21,000 or $4550. After paying federal taxes, they're left with $30,450.

"Now, let's assume Aunt Karen gets a job paying $75,000 a year. After deductions, let's say that adds $65,000 of taxable income to their return. Their total taxable income is now $100,000. The first $14,000 of their combined income is still taxed at 10 percent and the next $21,000 is taxed at 15 percent same as before. So all of Uncle Ed's salary is taxed the same. The first $21,800 of Aunt Karen's salary fills up the 15-percent bracket, and the remaining $43,200 is taxed at the 25-percent bracket. Their total federal tax bill is $18,620. The 2003 tax brackets for married couples are shown in Table 11-1.

"So even though Aunt Karen's new salary moved them into the 25-percent tax bracket, their whole income isn't taxed at that rate—only the last chunk. Their marginal tax rate is 25 percent, but their average tax rate is just over 18 percent. After paying their federal income taxes, their income is $81,380 —a lot higher than when Uncle Ed was the only wage earner.

Table 11-1   2003 Tax Rate Schedule

Tax Rate	Married Filing Jointly	Married Filing Separately
10%	$0 to $14,000	$0 to $7,000
15%	$14,000 to $56,800	$7,000 to $28,400
25%	$56,800 to $114,650	$28,400 to $57,325
28%	$114,650 to $174,700	$57,325 to $87,350
33%	$174,700 to $311,950	$87,350 to $155,975
35%	Over $311,950	Over $155,975

"Think of the tax brackets as a series of buckets. Each bucket is taxed at a different rate, and when your income fills up one bucket, you move to the next bucket, fill it up, and so on. All of your income doesn't end up in the top bucket.

"Wait till I tell Uncle Ed," said Mike grinning. "So do I really care what my tax bracket is?"

"Good question," I said.

"It's important to know your tax bracket because it's the rate at which the last dollar of income was taxed. Your tax bracket is also the rate at which the next dollar is taxed (unless that next dollar moves you into a higher bracket). As you consider the tax consequences of a particular saving or spending decision, you want to know how that last chunk of money will be taxed. For example, if Cathy is considering contributing $1000 to her SEP-IRA and she knows her tax bracket is 15 percent, she can calculate exactly how much she would save in federal income taxes if she makes the contribution—$150."

"Wow," said Cathy. "I never really got that before. I figured if I was in the 15-percent tax bracket, then 15 percent of all my income was taxed. It's really just the last chunk of income. That makes me feel a little better."

"Keep that happy feeling," I said. "I'm going to talk about how self-employed people, like you, are taxed, and the news isn't good."

Self-Employed? Uncle Sam Wants His Share

"We're going to talk about Cathy's income next, and I have good news and bad news," I said. "Let's start with the bad news. Cathy, what does a typical paycheck look like for you?"

"Well," said Cathy slowly, "I don't really have a typical paycheck. At the end of each month, I add up the money that has come in, subtract out my expenses, and I figure what's left over is mine to keep."

"Except for taxes, of course," I said. "Sole proprietors—self-employed individuals who have not incorporated or formed a partnership—are responsible for paying their own taxes. Federal, state, and local taxes are not automatically withheld, so you are required to estimate your tax liability for the year and then make quarterly tax payments. If you wait until April 15 to pay all your taxes from the previous year, you'll likely owe a penalty. It takes extra tracking and discipline to make sure you're up to date with tax payments.

"That's not all. On Mike's pay stub you can see the deduction for Social Security and Medicare taxes. What you don't see is that Mike's employer paid in an identical amount on Mike's behalf. When you're self-employed you wear two hats—employer and employee—and you have to pay both shares of Social Security and Medicare taxes."

"Is that a big deal?" asked Cathy.

"It is when you add it to all the other taxes you pay. Cathy, if you grab that calculator, you can total it all up as we go along. If we assume that Mike's salary fills up the 10-percent and part of the 15-percent tax bracket, then Cathy's income is taxed at the 15-percent rate. We'll also assume that you are in the 3-percent tax bracket for state taxes and you pay 2 percent local taxes. What are we up to so far?

"Let's see—20 percent," said Cathy.

"Now we need to add the employee's share of Social Security taxes, 6.45 percent, and the employee's share of Medicare taxes, 1.2 percent. Finally, we need to add the employer's share of Social Security and Medicare so that 's another 6.45 percent and 1.2 percent. What's the grand total, Cathy?"

"I hope I added wrong," said Cathy. "I get 35.3 percent. That's a big number."

"Especially since you're in the 15-percent tax bracket," I said. "I'm afraid that means for every dollar of profit you make, 35.3 cents goes to taxes. The double hit of Social Security and Medicare taxes really pushes up your marginal tax rate. You pay Social Security taxes on the first $87,000 (in 2003) you earn. Medicare taxes are charged on all of your earnings.

"There is one bright spot. The IRS allows you to deduct one-half of your Social Security and Medicare taxes from your income in the Adjustments section on your tax return. But before you decide to dump your business, there's a flip side to your high marginal tax rate. Every dollar of business expenses you deduct *saves* you 35.3 percent of taxes."

"How does that work?" asked Mike.

"Let's take an extreme case," I said. "If you collected $10,000 in consulting fees, Cathy, and you had no business expenses, your total tax bill would be $3530—35.3 percent of $10,000, right? On the other hand, if you had $10,000 of business expenses, you would have no profit and owe no taxes. So $10,000 of deductible expenses would save $3530 of taxes."

"I haven't had to face my high tax bracket yet," said Cathy, "because last year was my first year as a consultant, and I had a loss. Our tax preparer said we were able to deduct my loss from Mike's earnings on our tax return. I didn't owe any taxes, and my loss reduced our total tax bill. Things are better this year, and I expect to show a profit of $15,000, so I guess I'll owe some money."

"I'm afraid so," I said. "At the end of the meeting I'll show you how to project your taxes so you'll know how much to pay in estimated taxes throughout the year. But first, I want to make sure you're deducting all your business expenses."

"I think I do a pretty good job," said Cathy. "I deduct my supplies, reference books, professional memberships, postage, the ad I placed in the Yellow Pages, and the cost of the extra phone line I use for business. I also keep track of mileage when I go to meet with a client."

"Good work," I said. "What about expenses for a business in your home?"

"I've always heard you'll get audited if you take the home office deduction," said Cathy.

"The IRS tends to take a closer look at self-employed individuals," I said, "but you shouldn't shy away from taking legitimate business deductions. If you are eligible to deduct home office expenses, I recommend that you do it. Do you have a space in your home that is used exclusively and regularly for business?"

More Tax Tips for the Self-Employed

- If you pay your own health insurance premiums, you can deduct the cost under the "Adjustments" section of your tax return.

- Consider hiring your spouse so you each have self-employment income, and you can each contribute to a retirement plan. If your spouse makes more than the Social Security limit ($87,000 in 2003) at his or her regular job, he or she won't pay Social Security taxes on self-employment income.

- If you have school-age children, consider hiring them to do jobs around the office. They won't pay Social Security or Medicare

"I use the extra bedroom as my office and it's only used as an office, so the answer is yes. If we have overnight guests, they get the sofa in the living room."

"Then you are eligible to take a proportional amount of your rent, utilities, and upkeep as a business expense," I said. "Figure out the percentage of square footage occupied by your office compared to the total square footage in your apartment. That's the percentage of apartment expenses you can deduct. If you owned your apartment or home, you could also take a deduction for depreciation.

"You mentioned tracking mileage to client meetings. You can also deduct business trips to the bank, post office, supply stores, and professional meetings."

"I thought of another deduction we can take," said Cathy. "I plan to buy a new laptop this year. I seem to remember from corporate accounting that big-ticket items like computers have to be depreciated."

"Ordinarily that's right," I said, "but small business owners can deduct the full cost of equipment and furniture in the year they acquire it, up to $100,000. If you use the computer for personal work as well as for business, you won't be able to deduct the full cost—just the percentage you used it for business."

"Is there anything else we might have forgotten?" asked Cathy.

"You'll get a tax break when you set up your retirement plan," I said. "Contributions to your SEP-IRA are still subject to Social Security and Medicare and local taxes, but you won't have to pay federal

taxes on their earnings if they're under 18 (and you're a sole proprietor). They're probably in a lower tax bracket than you are, and you can stash away their earnings (up to $3000 in 2003) in a Roth IRA to start a college fund for them. Just make sure they're doing real work and the wage you pay is reasonable.

- Self-employed people sometimes mix business and personal travel. If the main reason for your travel is business, you can generally deduct the full cost of transportation plus any expenses associated with business. If the travel is a vacation but you take some time for business, you can only deduct the business-related expenses.

and state taxes until you pull the money out when you retire. Based on your 15-percent tax bracket, you'll save $225 in federal income taxes if you contribute $1500 to your SEP-IRA. You'll also save about $45 in state taxes. The full $1500 gets invested, but your after-tax cost is $1500 minus $270 or $1230. It's a nice incentive to put away money for the long term."

"So, knowing the rules and having a good system to track my income and expenses can really help save taxes," said Cathy.

Education Tax Breaks

In order to lighten the burden of taxpayers who are paying educational expenses for themselves or for their children, Congress has passed an array of tax deductions and credits. The rules are tricky and you may have to choose between tax breaks, but the bottom line can be a nice reduction on your tax bill to offset part of your tuition cost. Some of the tax breaks are credits and some are deductions, so in order to evaluate which is right for you, it's important to know how these two types of benefits work.

Tax credits reduce your tax bill by the amount of the credit, dollar for dollar. Deductions reduce your taxes because the allowable expense is subtracted from your income before your taxes are calculated. How much you save depends on your tax bracket. If you're in the 25-percent bracket, a $1000 deduction will save you $250 in federal income taxes. A $1000 tax credit, on the other hand, will save you $1000 on your tax bill.

The Hope Credit provides a tax credit of up to $1500 for tuition paid for higher education, but it's limited to coursework in a degree program during the first two years after high school. The Lifetime Learning Credit is available to taxpayers enrolled in a degree program—undergraduate, graduate, or professional—or taking courses to acquire or improve job skills, even if only as part-time or nondegree students. To be eligible for the full credit, you must file a joint return if you're married, and your adjusted gross income must not be higher than $41,000 if you're single or $82,000 if you're married. (The credit phases out completely if you make more than $51,000 if you're single or $102,000 if you're married.) If you're eligible for the Lifetime Learning Credit, you can take a credit of up to 20 percent of the first $10,000 you spend on tuition and fees. It is a "per household" credit, so if Mike and Cathy both take courses, their maximum total credit is $2000.

If you earn too much money to be eligible for the tax credits, you may still be able to use the higher education tax deduction. As long as your adjusted gross income is below $65,000 (for singles) or $130,000 (for married couples), you may be eligible to deduct up to $3000 of tuition paid for college courses. You don't need to itemize your deductions to get the break.

There is another way to get a tax break from going to school. You may be able to deduct education costs as unreimbursed employee expenses or, if you're self-employed, as a regular business expense. The rules are a bit stickier. You can't deduct the expenses if you're taking classes to qualify for a new job or profession, return to a job or profession, or meet the minimum requirements for a trade or business. Cathy can deduct her MBA expenses because she is enhancing her skills in her current profession. If she switched gears and decided to go to dental school, her costs would not be deductible.

In addition to tuition, other education expenses including fees, books, supplies, transportation, and even meals and lodging for out-of-town coursework are deductible. If you're an employee, the expenses are lumped in with other miscellaneous expenses and deducted on Schedule A (you must itemize) and are deductible only if greater than 2 percent of your adjusted gross income. If you're self-employed, you can deduct the expenses on your Schedule C.

If you're paying educational expenses, first check your eligibility for the different tax breaks and then decide which saves you the most taxes. No double-dipping is allowed.

Let's use Cathy's case as an example because she has three choices: She could take either the Lifetime Learning credit or the higher education tax deduction, or she could deduct her educational costs as business expenses. If she has $3500 of tuition expenses plus $1500 of books, fees, and transportation costs, here are how the three tax breaks stack up. The Lifetime Learning Credit would save $700 in taxes (20 percent of $3500, the higher education deduction would save $525 because she is in the 15-percent tax bracket (15 percent of $3500 is $525). If she took the third alternative and deducted her educational expenses as business expenses, she could deduct the full $5000, and she would save 15 percent or $750, plus the 15.3 percent or $765 she would save in payroll taxes for a total benefit of $1515. We have a winner—Cathy's best option is to deduct her school costs as a business expense.

If Mike spent $3500 on tuition, he would save $700 by taking the Lifetime Learning credit compared with $525 for the higher education tuition deduction. He doesn't have his own business, and he doesn't itemize expenses, so deducting his costs as business expenses isn't an option.

By the way, Cathy can't get a tax benefit for tuition paid by a scholarship or grant, but she keeps the tax break for tuition paid by a student loan. The scholarship is free money; Cathy will eventually have to pay back the loan.

Speaking of loans, up to $2500 of student loan interest is deductible as long as your income is below $50,000 if you're single and $100,000 if you're married filing jointly. The deduction is known as an "above-the-line" deduction, which means you don't have to itemize to get the break. If your income is below $65,000 (single) or $130,000 (married), you are eligible for part of the deduction, but you don't get any deduction if you're married and file separately.

If you already filed your taxes and missed out on a tax benefit, you have up to three years to amend your tax return. If you filed separately, however, you can't go back and file a joint return.

Investments and Taxes

So far we have only talked about taxes on earned income. The government taxes unearned income as well. Interest on bank accounts and dividends paid on individual stocks and mutual funds are taxed in the year received, even if you reinvest every penny. As far as the IRS is concerned, you could have received that money in cash, so it's taxable income.

A different rule applies if the shares of your mutual fund or stock increase in value because the stock market has gone up. Even though your investment is worth more now than what you paid for it, you don't pay taxes on the gain until you sell the shares. When you sell, you realize your gain. The rate of taxes you pay depends on your tax bracket and how long you've owned the asset.

If you've held on to your investment for at least one year and a day before selling, your profit or gain will be taxed at the capital gains rate. This rate is lower than the ordinary income rate at which other income, like your salary, is taxed. If you're in the 25-percent tax bracket or higher, your capital gains rate is 15 percent; if you're in a lower tax bracket, your capital gains rate is 5 percent. On the other hand, if you bought a stock and held it for a year or less, you'd realize a short-term capital gain when you sold it, and you'd owe taxes at your regular tax rate. Let's say you made a $1000 profit on a stock and you're in the 25-percent income tax bracket and the 15-percent capital gains bracket. Your federal taxes would be $250 if you sold within a year, or $150 if you had waited more than a year. That's a significant difference and for larger gains or for people in higher tax brackets, it can be a very big deal. It's another way the tax laws encourage certain financial behavior. You can imagine Congress looking over your shoulder whispering "Don't be a speculator, trading in and out. Be a long-term investor." I have to agree with Congress on this one.

When you sell shares of a mutual fund, it's not as simple as just keeping track of how long you've owned your investment. In order to figure out your taxes, you also have to calculate the difference between the shares you've already paid taxes on—called your cost basis—and the shares that haven't been taxed yet—your gain. Your cost basis is made up of the money you originally invested plus the dividends and other distributions you reinvested. If you neglect to add your reinvested income, you'll end up paying taxes twice on those shares—once when they were distributed and once when you sell them.

Consider this example. Let's say you took $2000 from your savings account in June 2001 and bought 100 shares of a mutual fund we'll call the Deep Value Fund at $20 per share. In December 2001, the fund distributed $200 of capital gains and dividends that you reinvested back into the fund. Your cost basis is now $2200: the original $2000 plus the $200 distribution. It's as if you earned that $200, paid taxes on it, and used the money to buy more shares in the Deep Value Fund. Then, in 2002, the Fund distributes an additional $150. Your cost basis is now up to $2350. If you sell all your shares in the fund in 2003 for $2500, your taxable gain is $150—the difference between $2500 and your cost basis of $2350. If you reported your taxable gain to be $500—the difference between how much you invested and how much you sold—you'd end up paying taxes twice on $350 of distributed capital gains and dividends.

Luckily, most mutual fund companies keep track of cost basis for us, and many report it right on your statements each quarter. But if you sold shares of a fund and the fund company didn't keep track, you'll need to go back to all of your old year-end fund statements and figure out the total of reinvested dividends and capital gains over the years.

Now, you may ask, why do mutual funds make distributions at all? Why not just keep everything in the fund so you only pay taxes when you sell? It would be more convenient, but it wouldn't be legal. Each year mutual funds are required to distribute to their shareholders at least 98 percent of the gains they realize by buying and selling securities in the fund. Shareholders are required to pay taxes on those distributions unless the mutual fund is held in a tax-protected place like an IRA or a 401(k) plan. In that case, taxes are paid when the money is taken out of the retirement plan.

A mutual fund manager who buys and sells frequently can generate big tax bills for shareholders because the gains from stocks sold within the fund are passed on each year. Buying and selling is kept to a minimum in index funds—mutual funds that mimic a particular slice of the market—and as a result distributions are kept to a minimum. If you're searching for tax-efficient investments, index funds are good choices.

Gifts

You might think a gift is a gift is a gift, but not where taxes are concerned. Let's say your Great Aunt Bessie was an astute investor and bought 100 shares of Pie Plates, Inc. four years ago at $10 a share—a total purchase of $1000. The stock split, and as the company made money, the share price increased, so she now has 200 shares worth $50 a share, or $10,000. The stock never paid dividends, so there are no reinvested shares.

You are Bessie's favorite niece because you bake pies from her recipes. She would like to give you either her Pie Plates shares or the money she'll make after taxes when she sells the shares. Does it matter whether she gives you stock or the cash? Let's take a look at her options.

1. Bessie can sell her shares of stock, pay the taxes, and give you the cash that is left over. If she is in the 15-percent capital gains tax bracket, she'll owe $1350 on her $9000 gain, and you'll get a check for $8650.

2. She can gift you the shares of stock. In this case, Bessie's cost basis transfers to you. It's as if you made the original investment. If you're also in the 15-percent capital gains bracket and you sell the shares as soon as you receive them, you'll pay the same tax bill—$1350—and have $8650 left over. If you're in

the 5-percent capital gains bracket, you'll pay $450 in taxes and pocket $9550. You could also just hang on to the stock and pay taxes when you sell.

3. Bessie can leave the stock in her will to you, so you inherit the shares at her death. In this case, the stock would get "stepped-up basis," which means the cost basis would be the price of the shares on the date of death (or six months later if the executor chooses). Your only tax bill would be on the gain you realize between the date of death and the day you sell your shares. If the stock was worth $10,000 when Bessie died and you sold your shares for $10,000, you would owe no taxes.

To Itemize or Not to Itemize

We have finished with the items on the first page of a tax return, such as wages, business income, capital gains, and contributions to IRAs. Now it's time for page two, which starts off with deductions.

There are two ways to claim your deductions: you can either take the standard deduction of $9500 for married couples or $4750 each if you file separately, or you can itemize your deductions by listing them on Schedule A of your return. You choose the method that gives you the biggest deduction because you want to subtract as much as possible from your taxable income. Be careful if you file separately because if one spouse itemizes, the other has to as well. The standard deduction is indexed to inflation, so it climbs a little each year.

"We don't own a house, so I thought we weren't eligible to itemize," said Cathy.

"You can use whichever method you prefer," I said. "But you may not benefit from itemizing. Let's add up your deductions.

"The first category is out-of-pocket medical expenses. Very few people benefit from this break because you can only deduct expenses above 7.5 percent of your adjusted gross income. In your case, you'd have to incur almost $4000 in out-of-pocket medical expenses before you could start deducting."

"Not even close," said Mike. "I pay for health insurance at work, but the money comes out of my paycheck before taxes, so I can't deduct it anyway."

"That's right," I agreed. "Next, you can deduct state, local, and property taxes you paid during the year. Mike had $2000 withheld from his paycheck for state and local taxes, and Cathy made estimated payments of $400 to the state. You don't pay real estate or personal property taxes.

"Interest is the next category. You can deduct interest paid on a home mortgage or home equity line of credit for both your main residence and a vacation home. That's not your situation yet.

"Charitable contributions are next."

"Those we have," said Cathy. "I added up all the checks we wrote to charitable organizations, and we donated $216 this year."

"Great job of record keeping," I said. "Did you donate any used clothing or household items? You can deduct the fair market value—usually what you'd get at a thrift shop—for items you donate to charity."

"I dropped off a few bags of my old clothes and a couple of boxes of pots and pans and towels to a local homeless shelter," said Cathy. "But I didn't keep track of it. When we buy a house, we'll probably sort through all our stuff and give away a lot more."

"Make sure you keep track of everything you donate," I said. "I think you'll be surprised at the size of your deduction when you add it all up. You can get guidelines on how much to deduct for common items from the Salvation Army and other charities. You can also buy a book called *It's Deductible* (*www.ItsDeductible.com*) that lists fair market values for all kinds of things—from sweatshirts to ironing boards to computers.

"You can also get a deduction for using your car for charitable activities, as well as for any out-of-pocket expenses. You can't take a deduction for the time you spent, though.

"A deduction can be taken for a large casualty loss like a tree falling on your car. Your insurance should cover these losses, so it's rare to be eligible for the tax deduction.

"The last category is a catch-all called miscellaneous deductions. You can generally only deduct expenses in this category that exceed 2 percent of your adjusted gross income—in your case about $1000.

"Employment-related expenses like uniforms, dues, job-hunting expenses, and business expenses that are not reimbursed by your employer are included in this group. Mike, if you took a computer course that was not paid for by your company, you might be eligible to deduct the cost. Only half the cost of business meals is deductible—the IRS figures you would have eaten anyway.

"Other deductible miscellaneous expenses include tax preparation fees, the cost of a safe deposit box rental, and investment-related expenses such as subscriptions to personal finance magazines, fees paid for investment and tax advice, and the cost of personal finance software."

"I'm not sure we'd get over the 2-percent threshold," said Mike. "It would be nice to have a few more deductions, but I guess I should be glad my employer pays my business expenses."

"I agree," I said. "A deduction is nice, but full reimbursement is better. There are a couple of miscellaneous deductions that are not subject to the 2-percent rule. For example, you can deduct your gambling losses, but only to offset any gambling winnings. Hang on to all those losing lottery tickets just in case you hit it big."

"Not us," said Cathy, grinning. "We don't gamble; we invest."

"Good answer," I said. "Let's add up all your deductions: $2400 for taxes, $216 for charitable contributions, plus we'll estimate another $300 for the stuff Cathy gave to the homeless shelter for a total of $2916. You're much better off taking the standard deduction of $9500. Typically, couples don't itemize until they buy a house and can deduct mortgage interest and property taxes."

The Cost of Tying the Knot

"I keep hearing about the marriage tax penalty," said Mike. "Is that a myth?"

"Until recently, if both spouses worked, they paid an average of $1,400 more taxes per year than two single people. Congress has recently taken steps to alleviate the hit," I said.

"I know how we can avoid any marriage penalty," said Cathy. "We can just file separately."

"The IRS is one step ahead of you," I said. "You can choose to file separately, but that won't necessarily help. Your deductions and exemptions generally get cut in half when you file separately, and several tax breaks are only available if you file a joint return. For example, you can't contribute to Roth IRAs or deduct student loan interest or qualify for dependent care credits if you file separately. Most couples don't save money by filing separately."

"If we lose benefits when we file separately," asked Mike, "why would we ever do it?"

"In some circumstances, the benefits of filing separately outweigh the tax breaks you lose," I said. "For example, if one spouse has significant out-of-pocket medical expenses, job-hunting costs, or unreimbursed business expenses, filing separately might make sense.

"To add to the uncertainty, some state income tax systems favor those who file separately. In Ohio, for example, some couples who both work can save hundreds of dollars by filing separately. You should ask your tax preparer to calculate your return both ways to make sure you choose the best method. You can do it yourself with good tax software."

Getting a Head Start

"The last item on my list involves tax planning. It's a good idea to do a quick trial run of your taxes sometime in September or October to make sure you're having the right amount of taxes withheld from your paycheck or, in your case Cathy, that you're paying the correct amount of estimated taxes," I said.

"We've always just held our breath and hoped for the best," said Mike. "Cathy had a loss last year, so we did okay, but I have a feeling we're going to get some bad news when we see this year's return."

"You can take the no-action path," I said, " but you're better off making adjustments as you go along. You can avoid penalties and manage your cash flow better."

Couples and Taxes

- Your marital status on the last day of the year determines how you file your taxes. If you are married on December 31, you must file married filing jointly or married filing separately for that year. (There is an exception—if you have been living apart for the last six months of the year, you may be eligible to file single or head of household. Be careful—this rule is strictly enforced.)

- Always pay attention to the tax return when you sign it. If you don't understand something, ask your tax preparer or other professional for help. The IRS allows some protection for innocent spouses who sign a tax return that turns out to be fraudulent, but the general rule is you are responsible for making sure the return you sign is accurate. If you have any doubts, ask before you sign.

"Penalties?" asked Cathy. "If we pay what we owe on April 15, we won't owe any penalties, will we?"

"I'm afraid it's not that simple," I said.

If you owe too much at tax time, you'll pay a penalty for having too little withheld from your paycheck or for making insufficient—or late—estimated tax payments. Even if you owe at tax time, you can avoid penalties if you follow some rules, called safe harbors. If the total of your withholdings and estimated taxes for the current year is equal to or greater than last year's tax liability and you pay your estimated taxes on time, you generally won't owe any penalties.

In Mike's and Cathy's case, if their tax liability last year was $5000 and Mike has $3000 withheld from his paychecks this year, and Cathy makes estimated payments of $500 a quarter, they won't owe a penalty even if they have to pay more taxes on April 15. They will have paid taxes—through withholding and estimated tax payments—equal to their liability last year.

If you think your income—and taxes—will be significantly lower than last year, you can use a different safe harbor test. If your withholding plus estimated taxes are equal to 90 percent of your current tax liability, you generally won't owe a penalty.

If you miscalculate and find out late in the year that you're likely to flunk both safe harbor tests, the best fix is to increase the taxes withheld from your paycheck. Withholding is considered to be spread out throughout the year even if it's bunched up at the end of the year. Making an estimated tax payment may not get you off the hook, because those must generally be made at regular intervals.

When you do tax planning, you're aiming for the "sweet spot." If you underpay your taxes during the year, you might owe a penalty on April 15; if you overpay, you're giving Uncle Sam an interest-free loan until you file your return and claim the excess.

Adjust your withholding by filling out a new W-4 at work. If you want less taxes withheld, increase the number of exemptions. If you want more taken out each paycheck, either decrease the number of exemptions or request that an additional amount be withheld—there's a space for that request on the W-4.

A rough rule of thumb is, if you file jointly and you're paid every two weeks, your employer will withhold an extra $50 per paycheck for every exemption you drop. To get a more precise answer, fill out the worksheet on the IRS Web site (*www.irs.gov*) or use the paycheck estimating tool at *www.paycheckcity.com*.

If you work with a professional tax preparer, ask if you can buy an hour or two of time in the fall to review your current year's tax situation. By doing it before the end of the year, you'll have time to make adjustments.

Big Refund? Big Mistake

What a great feeling. You finished entering all your information in your tax program and you peek at the bottom line—a $2600 refund. You can replace those old skis, go to Bermuda for a long weekend, even pay off some credit card debt. It's a gift from the IRS!

Hardly. When you get a refund on your tax return, it means you paid too much in income taxes throughout the year, either by having too much withheld from your paycheck or by overpaying your quarterly estimated taxes. The IRS is simply returning your own money—without interest. I'm sure the government appreciates the interest-free loan you made, but it's not smart for your own financial picture.

I know—it's like forced savings and that can't be all bad. But there are much better ways to save. If you just received a $2600 tax refund, you lost about $60 in interest. By submitting a new W-4 to your payroll office, you could get $100 more in your paycheck every two weeks rather than waiting for a windfall in April. Here are some ideas for using the extra money instead of lending it to Uncle Sam.

1. Use the money to pay off existing credit card debt faster. Remember, every time you pay off credit card debt it's like paying yourself the interest rate on the card.

2. Arrange to have $100 a month funneled directly into your emergency account so you have an extra cushion. This is a good move if your job seems a bit shaky or your home or car may need some repairs soon.

3. Start or add to a fund for a future purchase—a house, a new car, a vacation. If you'll need the money in less than a year, a money market fund is a good choice.

4. Set up automatic contributions to a Roth IRA. If you contribute $2600 each year for 10 years and leave the money in for 20 years, you'll have a $175,000 tax-free nest egg.

Tax Pro versus Do-it-Yourself Software

Tax software has become more powerful and more available every year, and yet more than half of Americans turn over their tax information to a CPA or other tax preparer rather than tackle the job themselves. If you have a fairly simple return—wage or salary income, some interest and dividends—you can probably do your own taxes. Even if you itemize deductions, tax software can guide you through your return. However, there are circumstances when a tax pro's fee can be an excellent investment:

- You are self-employed or own a small business.
- You have rental property. The depreciation schedules alone can be daunting.
- You trade stocks or stock mutual funds often.
- You own shares in a limited partnership or participate in a business partnership, or receive money from a trust or estate. In all these circumstances, you'll receive a K-1 form, which can be difficult to decipher.
- You are not reimbursed for employee business expenses at work.
- You had a significant transaction or event last year that will have an impact on your taxes such as converting an IRA to a Roth IRA or getting married or divorced.

If you decide to go it alone and prepare your own taxes, you can purchase tax software such as TurboTax or TaxCut. Mutual fund companies like Fidelity, Vanguard, and T. Rowe Price often offer discounts on tax software to their customers. Check out their Web sites for details. You may also be eligible for free electronic filing. Check the IRS Web site (*www.irs.gov*) for eligibility rules.

Some taxpayers have their taxes prepared professionally every three years and do it themselves in between. If the tax preparer uncovers a mistake you've been making, you'll still have time to amend your return.

Whether you do your own taxes or work with a tax preparer, I recommend electronically filing your return if you're getting money back. You'll get your refund much more quickly—usually within 10 to 14 days of filing. And, whatever you do, skip the rapid refund loans. The interest charges are outrageous.

What Cathy and Mike Have Learned

1. You don't need to be a CPA, but a little tax knowledge can go a long way. Many everyday decisions have tax consequences.

2. We have a progressive tax system in the United States, so the higher your income, the higher your tax bracket. Not all your income is taxed at your tax bracket—just the last chunk.

3. Self-employed people get hit especially hard on taxes because they have to pay both sides of payroll taxes.

4. Be careful not to overpay taxes when cashing in mutual funds or stocks with reinvested dividends or capital gains.

5. Plan for taxes by estimating income during the year and adjusting withholding or estimated taxes as appropriate.

Recommendations for Mike and Cathy

1. Keep careful track of income and expenses in your business. (Cathy).

2. Track the cost basis of investments (or make sure your mutual fund or brokerage company is doing it for you).

3. Talk to your tax preparer about amending last year's tax return to include Cathy's educational expenses.

4. Calculate your taxes filing jointly or separately to see which results in the lower tax bill.

5. Monitor your withholding and estimated taxes to make sure you're on track.

Your Homework

1. Figure out your own tax bracket.

2. Review the last few years of tax returns to see if you forgot any deductions or credits and need to amend. If you filed jointly, you cannot amend to file separately, though.

3. Don't forget tax benefits associated with education like the Lifetime Learning Credit and the deduction for student loan interest.

4. If you tend to get a big refund, adjust your withholding to reduce

the refund and funnel the extra money directly into a savings or investment account.

Resources

1. *www.irs.gov* for tax forms, instructions, publications and worksheets.

2. *www.vanguard.com* for information on keeping track of basis and other tax issues associated with investing.

3. If you are self-employed, check out IRS Publication 334, "Tax Guide for Small Business."

4. Annual income tax guides, especially those published by J.K. Lasser and Ernst & Young for an overview of the rules.

Estate Planning:
Get Specific

Chances are, the first time you opened this book you didn't flip right to this chapter. Of all my meetings with clients, estate planning is the one most likely to be approached with apprehension. It's not hard to understand why. Even though they are often referred to as the two sure things in life, who wants to talk about death and taxes?

Estate planning does not have to be quite so dreary. First of all, most couples can ignore estate taxes. Unless you are an unusually wealthy young couple with a net worth in the multi-million-dollar range, estate taxes are not an issue under current law. And although estate planning is about what happens after you die, it's also about what happens while you're alive. Finally, a well thought-out estate plan that clearly expresses your wishes will save your loved ones worry and expense. So it's not just about death and taxes; it's about love and values as well.

I encourage you to sit down with your partner and talk about what you want your estate plan to accomplish. Get specific. If you were to die, would you want your partner to be able to continue living in your house? Who would take care of your children? How would you like your possessions divided? Are there any charitable organizations you would like to include? Then make an appointment with a competent estate-planning attorney who can translate your wishes into the proper legal documents. You will feel so good when you have set up your plan—it's like giving a gift to your partner and the next generation. Mike and Cathy are eager to check it off their financial planning list.

"The fact that you two are about to become parents has certainly changed the focus of this meeting," I said. "In fact, if a couple has children, I bump the estate planning meeting up to much earlier in the planning process. In your case, the timing worked out well.

"Let's go ahead and set the agenda for today's meeting. What questions do you have and what subjects do you want to make sure we cover today?"

"Estate planning isn't something we've given a lot of thought to," said Mike. "We didn't even think we needed wills, but now with the baby coming, I guess it's different."

"My big concern," said Cathy, "is making sure we have things set up so in case something happened to Mike and me, our child would be taken care of. I'd also like to make sure Mike wouldn't be left with a mountain of paperwork if something happened to me. It's kind of spooky talking about these things, but I guess we have to do it."

"It is a little strange," I agreed, "but I think you'll feel a great sense of accomplishment when you sign the documents. Cathy outlined the big picture quite well. We'll talk about the key estate-planning documents you'll need and the pros and cons of trusts. We'll also discuss ways to leave property to heirs, and wrap up with some things to think about when naming beneficiaries and titling your assets. How does that sound?"

"It sounds like we have a lot to cover," said Mike. "I thought estate planning just meant getting a will, but it's clearly more than that."

The Four Documents You'll Need

I advise every couple to get a will. Lawyers are fond of saying nobody dies without a will—if you haven't written your own, the state will write one for you. That means the state will decide how your property gets divided up, and each state has its own laws about who gets what if a resident dies without a will. The problem is, you and the state might not agree, and dying intestate—the term for dying without a will—may involve extra time and expense for your heirs.

If you have children, it's crucial to have a will. Parents prefer to name the guardians for their children—the people who would raise their children in the parents' absence—rather than leave that decision to the state.

"That's for sure," said Cathy. "I love our families, but that doesn't mean they'd all be good choices to be stand-in parents. As much fun as your younger brother and sister-in-law are, Mike, can you imagine them acting as guardians for our children? They'd let the kids stay up as late at they wanted and skip class to go camping."

"They're probably not the best choices," agreed Mike. "So we definitely need a will."

There are four estate-planning documents couples need. A will, a durable power of attorney, a living will, and a durable power of attorney for health care. Let's start with the last two.

A living will is sometimes called a medical directive. It expresses your wishes regarding medical treatment you will receive if you are terminally ill. The durable power of attorney for health care appoints someone to make medical decisions for you if you're unable to do so. You might be unconscious, for example, and not be able to give your approval for a needed operation.

An attorney can draft these documents for you. The state bar association or a local hospital may have kits available with fill-in-the-blank documents you can complete and sign.

The next document you'll need is a durable power of attorney. The purpose is to name someone to make financial decisions for you if you're mentally or physically unable to do so yourself. The person you name can pay bills, move investments around, or make other decisions, depending on how the document is drafted. A durable power of attorney can give broad powers to the person named, so it's important to choose someone you really trust. Typically, you'll name your spouse or partner. You should also name a successor to step in if the person you named first dies or is unable to make decisions on your behalf. It's set up as a "durable" power to ensure that the authority will not be withdrawn if you become incapacitated. Otherwise, a financial institution might question its validity if the person who signed it was no longer of sound mind and body.

Another form is called a springing power of attorney. It requires a physician's certification to take effect. You can discuss both with your attorney, but durable powers of attorney are more common and less fuss.

The will is the most common estate-planning document. Your will is simply the document that expresses your wishes about what will happen to your possessions and who should care for your children after your death. It does not need to be complicated, but there are a few decisions you should make before you sit down with an attorney.

You'll need to name an executor—someone who will serve as your personal representative after your death. He or she makes sure the provisions of your will are carried out. Ideally, you should choose someone who knows you well, is organized—because there's a lot of paperwork involved—and who knows something about finances. Above all, your executor should be someone you trust.

"My mother was the executor for my great grandma, and it was a lot of work," said Cathy. "She hired an attorney to help her through all the legal and tax stuff, but she spent hours and hours making sure everybody got what they were supposed to get. I don't think she realized what she was getting into."

"Being an executor is a big responsibility and can involve a fair amount of work," I agreed. "You will probably choose each other as executor, but you should also each name a successor executor."

"Can we name the same people who are the successors for our powers of attorney?" asked Mike.

"You can," I said. "Attorneys often recommend your successor executor be someone about your own age who lives in the same state. If you name someone from out of state, the court might appoint an instate co-executor, which can be costly and cumbersome."

"So maybe my sister who lives here in town is a better choice than my mom," said Cathy.

"The next decision is whom you want to name as your heirs," I said. "Again, the logical first choice is each other. But what if Mike died before you did, Cathy, or vice versa?"

"Well, then we would want our child to inherit everything," said Cathy.

"It's a little trickier with children," I said, "because minors cannot inherit directly. Your attorney will probably recommend you set up a trust for your child, either in the will or outside the will. We'll talk about the advantages and disadvantages of those arrangements in a bit, but for the moment, let's assume you set up the trust inside the will— that's called a testamentary trust.

"You also need to name a guardian for your child—the person or persons who will raise your children in your absence—and a trustee who will administer the money for the benefit of the child. The trustee invests the money and makes distributions in accordance with the provisions of the trust. When the child becomes an adult—or later, if the trust requires it—the trustee will distribute the remaining funds. Many couples name the same person to be both guardian of the child and trustee of the funds, but you can name two different people if you wish."

"I can see how you might want to name different people," said Cathy. "My sister is terrific with kids but she's not a money genius. On the other hand, your older brother knows a lot about investments, Mike, but he's single and I don't think parenting is exactly up his alley."

"You're right," said Mike. "I think I'd go with your sister to be both guardian and trustee. We're not money geniuses either, but we do okay."

"Unless their financial situation is complex, most people choose the same person to fulfill both roles," I said. "Then again, some people go the opposite direction and name a bank or trust company to handle the money because they prefer the objectivity of an institutional trustee. The downside is the cost involved—an institution will typically charge one to three percent of the money annually for its services. Plus, an institution will be less flexible administering the trust. I agree—it's not an easy choice. "

"You said the child gets the money when he or she becomes an adult or later," said Mike. "What did you mean?"

"You can decide when the child will get the money in the trust," I said. "If you have built up a big nest egg or have a house that's worth a lot of money, you may not want the child to get a huge windfall when he or she turns 18. You may wish to have the money doled out, say one-third every five years after the child becomes an adult. You can also specify that, until the funds are completely distributed, the trustee will have the discretion to pay out amounts from the trust to cover educational costs, or a down payment on a house or wedding expenses for the child. You have quite a bit of latitude, but the attorney will rein you in if you try to get too controlling."

"Do you mean we couldn't say our daughter would only get her inheritance if she went to medical school?" asked Cathy.

"Or married someone as handsome as her father," added Mike.

"It sounds like you two get the picture," I said.

"This is all so far away," said Mike. "I like the idea of spreading out the inheritance so our child wouldn't get a big check at age 18. I know what I would have done with a lot of money at that age and it would have involved wheels, not mutual funds. How specific do we need to be?"

"You can make it pretty simple," I said, "and that's probably a smart choice for now. You can discuss different scenarios with your attorney. That's another advantage of working with someone with estate-planning experience who has seen lots of wills and trusts."

"So we need to name executors, guardians, trustees, and think about the terms of the trust," said Cathy. "What else?"

"You may wish to include charitable bequests in your will," I said, "or mention items you would like to leave to other people besides to each other and your child."

"I have a ring my aunt gave me for graduation that I would like my niece to have someday," said Cathy.

"If you think of other special things you'd like to leave to friends or relatives, you might want to make a separate list that is referred to in the will," I said. "Then you can change the list without changing the will. Of course you can change your will any time you like. You can just change part of it by adding a codicil or you can scrap it and start all over. I encourage you to review your will every few years and certainly after a big event like a new baby or a move to a different state. Once you die, the will becomes set in stone—'irrevocable' in legal terms."

Trusts

A trust is a legal contract that allows a trustee to manage property for the benefit of one or more beneficiaries. The grantor sets up the trust and, if it's a living or revocable trust, the grantor is often the trustee— the person who controls the trust—as well.

That's the legalese. I prefer to think of a living trust as a basket. If you set up the basket, you're called the grantor, and if you name yourself trustee, you also manage the basket. When you die, the beneficiaries of the trust get the property in the basket, or another trustee takes over management of the basket until the property is distributed. You can put as much or as little as you like in the basket, and you can take out anything any time you like. You control the property in your basket, and if you become disabled, the person you named as successor trustee can take over for you.

When you put property in the trust, you retitle it in the name of the trust, but the income is still reported under your Social Security number. You can put your checking or savings account or mutual fund accounts—even your house—in your trust. Retirement plans like your 401(k) plan or IRA are already in a form of trust, so those stay outside the trust basket.

Some people set up a trust to avoid probate—the court-supervised process that oversees the distribution of property after death. The probate court makes sure the property is transferred according to the terms of the will, or if there is no will, according to the laws of the state. In some cases probate can be a costly and drawn-out process. Property inside a trust does not go through probate, thus saving time and expense. Also, probate is a public process, so by avoiding probate a trust preserves the privacy of the individual who died and the heirs.

Many people think they'll automatically save taxes by setting up a living trust, but that's not the case. While you're living, the income from the property in the trust is taxed to you just the same as if it were outside the trust basket. In order to save estate taxes, specialized trusts must be set up. Couples with substantial assets often establish trusts—called A/B or credit shelter trusts—with specific provisions designed to avoid or minimize estate taxes, but that's beyond what most young couples need.

There is one other reason parents with young children might consider setting up a living trust. If you add trust language to your will, the trust isn't set up until you die. The money you designated for your trust will go through probate first. The probate court will continue to supervise the trust—typically by requiring periodic reports from the trustee on how the money is being invested and distributed. If you set up a living trust—that's a trust outside your will—the court doesn't get involved because the trust doesn't go through probate.

Some couples like the idea of having the court oversee the administration of the trust, and others think it's a nuisance and added burden. If you're confident that you have chosen a competent and caring trustee, you may not see much value in having the court looking over him or her.

Talk over the merits of setting up a separate trust with your attorney. You'll pay more to set up a living trust than simply to add trust language to your will—typically several hundreds of dollars more—but you may decide a trust fits your plan.

Naming Your Heirs

Although naming a beneficiary in your will is one way to determine who inherits your property at your death, the will usually doesn't control all—or most—of your assets. You have already chosen beneficiaries for your retirement plans and life insurance policies, and those designations override any language you have in your will about who will inherit your property.

If you named your favorite Uncle Felix as the beneficiary of your IRA and then specified in your will that you wanted all your worldly possessions to go to your beloved partner, your Uncle Felix would still get your IRA. That's why it's so important to update the beneficiary designations on all your retirement plans, insurance policies, annuities, and employee benefits like stock option plans when you get married or become a couple.

Many states allow you to designate beneficiaries on nonretirement bank accounts or investment accounts. These are called payable on death—POD—or transfer on death—TOD—accounts. You may even arrange to have your house go directly to a beneficiary at your death. Any asset with a named beneficiary goes directly to that person without going through probate.

Some couples decide to set up their accounts so just about everything will go directly to named beneficiaries, skipping probate. If you plan to do this, make sure you keep track of all of your beneficiaries. If you decide to name your children the beneficiaries of your bank accounts or your house, you may need to change the forms each time a new child is born. Remember, the person whose name is on the beneficiary form inherits the property no matter what you specify in your will.

The next way to pass property along to your heirs is through joint ownership. If you own property with another person as joint tenants with right of survivorship (abbreviated as JTWROS), if one of you dies, the surviving owner automatically gets the account, skipping probate.

You can also own property with another person or persons as tenants in common. This is different from joint tenancy because you can own unequal shares. If you die, the surviving owners do not automatically get your share—you specify in your will who inherits your piece.

If you have children from a previous marriage, for example, and you bought a house with your new partner, you might want your children to inherit your share of the house if something happened to you. Owning the house with your partner as tenants in common allows you to set things up that way.

Some states, like California, have community property laws that govern how assets acquired during marriage are handled. If you move to one of those states, you'll need to check how your assets are titled and sit down with an attorney to review your estate plan. That's part of the challenge of estate planning—the laws vary from state to state.

Naming Beneficiaries

"It seems like it's pretty important who we name as our beneficiaries," said Mike.

"That's right," I agreed. "Let's review a few do's and don'ts. First, it's usually advantageous to name a specific individual or individuals, or in some cases a trust, as beneficiary. If you leave the form blank or just name your estate, the assets will go through probate, and there may be undesirable tax consequences.

"Second, you can name primary and secondary or contingent beneficiaries. The secondary beneficiaries only inherit if you and all the primary beneficiaries are dead. A couple will typically name each other as primary beneficiary and the children or a trust for the benefit of the children as the secondary beneficiary."

"So I name Mike and Mike names me as primary beneficiary," said Cathy. "Our children would be our secondary beneficiaries, unless we decide to set up a living trust."

"That's right, except you'll have to add special language if the child is a minor because a minor can't inherit money directly," I said. "Attorneys usually recommend language like 'Jane Doe, Custodian for the benefit of Michael Stanford, Jr.'"

Gifts

We've talked about how property gets distributed to your heirs at death, but you can gift property while you're alive, of course. You might not be in a position to do much gifting for awhile, but you might receive money, and you should know a couple of rules. Under current law, any person can gift up to $11,000 per year to any other person free of gift or income taxes. In general, you won't owe income taxes on a gift, no matter how generous it is. However, if the donor gives you more than $11,000 each in a year, he or she may owe taxes on the gift.

A married couple can gift up to $22,000 to an individual, even if all the money comes out of one account. That means your parents could gift you and your partner $22,000 each, every year without incurring gift tax. If medical or education expenses are paid directly to a hospital, doctor, or school on your behalf, the payments are exempt from gift taxes, no matter how big the amount.

Your Taxable Estate

"As long as we're talking about taxes, what about estate taxes?" asked Mike. "They always seem to be in the news, and we haven't talked about them yet."

"You're right, we haven't," I said. "Estate tax laws have been changed several times in the past few years, so anything I say today might not be valid later. As things stand now, however, your estate would not be subject to federal taxes."

"I wouldn't think so," said Mike. "Our total net worth is less than $40,000."

"But your taxable estate is higher than that," I said. "What is the death benefit amount on the term insurance you purchased?"

"$500,000," said Mike. "Why?"

"That amount gets counted as well, so your taxable estate is over half a million dollars," I said. "Still not in the taxable range, but a lot higher than you thought."

"When my great grandma died, she left a small life insurance policy to my mom, and I remember my mom saying at least she didn't have to pay taxes on that," said Cathy.

"We're talking about two different kinds of taxes," I said. "Life insurance proceeds are not subject to federal income taxes. However, the proceeds are pulled into the taxable estate for determining estate taxes."

"Taxes upon taxes. Where does it end?" asked Mike.

"There are some big exemptions to the federal estate tax," I said. "First, there is an unlimited marital deduction, which means you can leave as much as you like to your spouse without triggering the federal estate tax. Unmarried partners don't get that tax break. Second, anything you leave to charity is exempt from estate tax."

"So if I left everything to Mike, there would be no estate taxes due," said Cathy. "What if Mike weren't around and I left everything to our children?"

"There's no unlimited children deduction, so if your estate were big enough, you'd trigger estate taxes. That's why couples with several million dollars worth of assets need to structure their estates carefully."

"One last tip before we end our meeting. If you inherit an IRA or a retirement plan, I recommend you speak to a financial planner or estate attorney. There are special rules about how you take money out of inherited retirement plans, and the penalties are stiff if you ignore them."

What Cathy and Mike Learned

1. They should talk about their estate plan together and hire a competent estate planning attorney to implement the plan.

2. They need four basic estate-planning documents, and they might want to set up a trust as well.

3. They probably don't need to worry about federal estate taxes because their taxable estate is less than $1 million.

Recommendations for Cathy and Mike

1. Talk over different scenarios regarding your property and your loved ones.

2. Decide whom you want to name as successor executors, successors to your power of attorney, and guardian and trustee for your child.

3. Sit down with a competent estate-planning attorney to discuss your estate.

4. Review pros and cons of living trusts.

5. Sign your documents and review them every few years or when a significant event occurs, such as the birth of a child or a move to a different state.

Your Homework

1. Sit down with your partner and develop your own scenarios.

2. Interview estate-planning attorneys and choose an experienced attorney you feel comfortable with.

3. Speak to your family about your plans and especially to anyone you name as executor, trustee, or guardian.

4. Sign your documents and review them regularly.

Resources

1. Barney, Colleen and Collins, Victoria. *Best Intentions*. Dearborn Trade Publishing, 2002.

2. Berry, Dawn Bradley. *The Estate Planning Sourcebook*. Lowell House, 1999.

3. *www.nolo.com*—Wills and Estate Planning topics.

Note: Although there are several kits and software available for do-it-yourself wills and trusts, I recommend that you work with a competent, experienced estate-planning attorney instead. You can use the checklists in the kits to think through the decisions you'll have to make prior to consulting an attorney, but you're taking a risk if you rely on a kit rather than the advice of an expert to put together your estate plan. I'm a do-it-yourselfer for a lot of things, but not for legal documents. Interview a few attorneys and ask them about their experience and their fees. In most areas, an attorney will prepare a basic will for less than $200.

CHAPTER 13

Before You Get Married

I f you are planning to get married, this chapter is for you. In addition to making up the guest list and shopping for a dress or tux, I encourage you to think about the financial side of marriage and talk over some money matters with your partner. It may not sound romantic, but it's a smart thing to do.

Prenuptial Agreements

Speaking of romantic, what could be less amorous than a prenuptial agreement? Sometimes called an antenuptial or premarital agreement, this document describes how your worldly goods will be divvied up in case the marriage ends in divorce or one of you dies.

Why would you sign such a thing, or ask your future spouse to sign one? Couples prepare prenuptial agreements simply because they don't want the law to dictate who gets what if the marriage ends. A properly executed prenuptial agreement can safeguard assets, protect loved ones, keep a business in the family, or streamline divorce proceedings.

Some prenuptial agreements even cover details of your married life together such as how child care will be handled and who will pay the mortgage. However, attorneys often caution against getting too specific and encourage couples to talk things over rather than detailing their requirements for day-to-day living in a legal agreement. There must be a foundation of trust for you to function as a couple.

Who Needs One?

Most couples don't need a prenuptial agreement, but for some it makes sense. If your situation matches one of the following, I suggest you consult an attorney and discuss whether you and your partner might benefit from one.

- You have children from a previous marriage. In most states, a surviving spouse has the right to inherit one-third to one-half of the estate. A prenuptial agreement can override the law and make sure your property goes to your children.

- You own a business or are involved in a family company. If you divorce, a prenuptial agreement can prevent a small or closely held business from being split up or controlled by your former spouse.

- You each have significant assets or one of you has considerably more than the other. Young couples don't usually start out with big nest eggs, but you might have received a large inheritance or are the beneficiary of a trust fund. A prenuptial agreement can specify that premarital property will be kept separate in case of divorce and will go to the heirs you name in case of death. Some agreements stipulate the amount of spousal support that will be paid if you divorce. Be careful, though—you may escape paying alimony, but you cannot sign away your responsibility to provide support for your children.

- You are concerned about being saddled with your spouse's debt. I'll talk about personal debt such as credit card balances later in this chapter, but you might want to consider protecting yourself against business liabilities that your partner has racked up.

- Finally, you might be giving up a career or lucrative job to get married. A prenuptial agreement can spell out how you will be compensated for your sacrifice if the marriage fails.

Are They Always Valid?

In general, there are four essential ingredients for a valid prenuptial agreement:

1. It must be in writing and be executed before the marriage.

2. Neither party can be pressured into signing. If your spouse-to-be springs the document on you as the guests are being seated, chances are the court will throw out the agreement.

3. The agreement must be fair and based on full disclosure of assets and liabilities by both sides. You should understand the financial information provided by your future spouse. If you don't, ask before you sign. You might want to have a professional appraisal performed on hard-to-value assets like a small business.

4. Each party should have the benefit of independent counsel. This is *not* a do-it-yourself document, and one lawyer cannot fairly represent you both. I also recommend hiring an attorney who specializes in family or divorce law. Your cousin Ernie, the corporate counsel, is not a good choice, even if he will review the document for free.

Are They Worth It?

Prenuptial agreements are expensive to prepare because each one is tailored to the couple's particular situation. Lawyers' fees of $800 to $3000 are common. Probably more distressing is the emotional toll these agreements can take on a couple, just as they are preparing for a joyous event. As one attorney described it, prenuptial agreements go to the very core of trust. You might see such an agreement as a sign that your spouse-to-be doesn't love you enough to share, while he or she might assume that because you love each other, the agreement shouldn't be an obstacle.

If you decide to go forward with a prenuptial agreement, make sure you start talking to each other and to your attorneys well in advance of the wedding date. You'll have a better chance of agreeing if you each approach the subject in a calm, caring way.

If you decide to skip the prenuptial, there are other steps you can take to protect your assets. A good estate plan can accomplish many of the same goals. And, when all is said and done, a written document is no substitute for honest, open communication with your spouse.

Marrying into Debt

Although we often think of marriage as a social covenant, we should remember that it is a financial contract as well. In addition to sharing a home and life together, you might be concerned that you will also share your new spouse's credit card debt or less-than-stellar credit rating. In these days of mounting consumer debt and millions of personal bankruptcies, it's a real concern. I encourage you each to read the chapter on credit and debt for general guidance, but there are a few things you should do before you get married.

First, I recommend that you each get an up-to-date credit report and make a copy for your partner. You can obtain an instant credit score, credit history, and tips on improving your score from *www.myfico.com* for under $20. It's worth the investment.

Second, it's best to maintain separate credit cards and keep loans, such as car financing, in separate names. That way, your credit score won't be damaged if your spouse has been careless about paying back debt on time. However, a problem can arise if you apply for a loan together, such as a mortgage. You might not qualify for the going interest rate—or you may even be denied a loan—if one of you has a low credit score. You may end having to qualify for a loan on your own, which may significantly limit the amount you're able to borrow.

Goals and Dreams

By the time they set the wedding date, most couples have had lots of conversations about what kind of life they hope to have together. Going through the goal-setting exercise outlined in Chapter 3 can help you crystallize those dreams and share them with each other. It's easy to get caught up in all the preparations for the big day. Take time out to focus on the big life ahead, as well.

My, Your, and Our Money

Conversations about checkbooks and budgets might seem like something that can wait until you're back from your honeymoon. Maybe they can, but preparing a general spending plan now can smooth things later. If you tend not to track your spending, now is the perfect time to start recording your expenses—in Quicken®, on a spreadsheet, or even in a notebook.

Once you each have a baseline on how you spend your money, it will be easier to figure out a combined budget. As the saying goes, two can live more cheaply together than apart, and you will probably realize some savings in areas such as rent, utilities, and groceries. However, added expenses crop up such as saving for a house or children or helping a partner pay off student loans or other debt. There is also a tendency for couples to feel like they have "settled down" when they make a commitment to each other, and their focus shifts to some long-range plans such as building a nest egg and an emergency fund. As one young couple explained it to me, "As singles we thought about how we would spend our weekends, where we'd go out to eat, and which vacation spots were hot. Now we feel like grown-ups, and although we still have fun, we're getting more serious about our money."

Holding the Line on Wedding Costs

I would be neglecting my professional responsibility as a financial planner if I didn't caution you about the dangers of overspending on your wedding. More couples are contributing to or even paying the full cost of their weddings. And many couples find they are struggling with the bills for months or years after they are married. You'll have enough to deal with as newlyweds; you don't need the pressure of a huge credit card balance as well.

Although wedding expenses vary widely, an average wedding can easily cost $20,000 or more. If you put half the cost on a credit card and paid $200 a month at 15 percent, it would take you six-and-a-half years to pay off your wedding.

Alternatively, you may have already saved $10,000 or received that much in gifts. If you were to use that money toward the down payment of a house instead, you might be able to get into a house faster, buy a bigger house, or avoid paying private mortgage insurance. If you and your spouse socked that money away in Roth IRAs, by the time you celebrated your silver anniversary you could have accumulated an $80,000 tax-free nest egg.

Nest eggs and down payments may not seem very romantic, but starting your life together on a solid financial footing will be better for your future than having a blowout party. Every dollar you can save on your wedding is another dollar toward your financial security.

Resources

1. For more information on prenuptial agreements, visit *www.nolo. com* and search for "prenuptial."

2. For wedding planning and budget tips, check out *www.usabride. com* and *www.theknot.com*.

CHAPTER 14

Special Issues for Unmarried Couples

The basic principles of money management and financial planning apply to married and unmarried couples alike. Setting goals, investing wisely, and putting money away for your financial independence are smart moves no matter what your marital status. In some areas of financial planning, however, the rules are different for unmarried couples.

This chapter is not a comprehensive guide for couples who have chosen not to get married or for whom marriage is not an option. It is more of a checklist of issues and strategies that unmarried couples can fold into their financial plans.

The first step is to talk openly with your partner about the decisions that will shape your life together, such as buying a house, paying bills, planning vacations, and parenting. Some couples decide to write contracts that spell out who owns what and how expenses will be shared. If you like the idea of writing a living-together contract with your partner, it's wise to get help from an attorney who specializes in working with unmarried couples.

Even if you choose to forego a formal contract, don't skip other documents such as wills and durable powers of attorney. Married couples who neglect to plan can often rely on existing laws to get the job done. They can inherit from each other and make many decisions on each other's behalf without written documents. Unmarried couples, however, do not enjoy the same protection and can end up with unintended consequences if they fail to act.

So talk and dream and plan with your partner and then find out what you'll need to do to make your plans happen. Here are some ideas to get you started.

Employee Benefits

The good news for unmarried couples is that more and more companies and government entities are extending health insurance, parental leave, and other employee benefits to domestic partners. According to Nolo Press, the definition of domestic partner and the types of benefits offered vary by employer. Benefits might be available to all unmarried couples or only to same-sex couples. Some employers require couples to register as domestic partners in order to be eligible for benefits. The Nolo Web site (*www.nolo.com*) has information on how to locate employers who offer benefits to domestic partners and how to work with your employer to extend domestic partnership benefits.

Taxes

Do married or unmarried couples fare better under our tax laws? It depends. The marriage tax penalty has been eased but not erased. If your incomes are roughly equal you'll probably pay lower taxes if you're not married.

If you're not married, you might be eligible for other tax breaks and, with some planning, you might be able to reduce your tax bill even more. Here are some ideas:

- If your incomes are unequal, you can save taxes by shifting deductions to the taxpayer in the higher bracket. The higher-earning partner can write the checks for the mortgage, property taxes, and charitable donations and claim the deductions. If you are in the 15-percent tax bracket and your partner is in the 25-percent bracket, together you'll save $500 a year on $10,000 of mortgage interest if your partner takes the deduction instead of splitting it with you.

- Some income thresholds are the same for single and married taxpayers, making it easier for singles to qualify for the tax break. Taxpayers are eligible to convert traditional IRAs to Roth IRAs if their Adjusted Gross Income (AGI) is under $100,000, and the limit's the same for singles and couples. Married taxpayers who file separately are not eligible to convert IRAs.

Likewise, itemized deductions are reduced for both single and married taxpayers whose AGI is greater than $139,500. (This penalty is due to start phasing out in 2006.)

- It's easier for two single taxpayers to meet the eligibility requirements for contributions to Roth and deductible IRAs than it is for couples. Eligibility for Roth IRA contributions starts to phase out at $95,000 for single taxpayers and $150,000 for married couples who file jointly. Married taxpayers who file separately are not eligible to make Roth IRA contributions at all, although they can hang on to Roth IRAs they set up in previous years.

- The child tax credit starts to phase out at $75,000 of income for a single taxpayer and $110,000 for a married couple filing jointly. A single person earning $70,000 qualifies for the child tax credit, but married taxpayers filing jointly who earn $70,000 each—a total of $140,000 of income—don't qualify.

- The hurdle for qualifying for the earned income limit is lower for two single taxpayers than for a married couple, although some relief for married taxpayers is being phased in.

The news isn't all good for single taxpayers, though. As you might guess, you'll miss out on spousal IRAs if you're single. If you're married, you can fully fund an IRA even if you don't have earned income, as long as your spouse has a paycheck and makes less than $150,000. If you're single, you have to earn your own paycheck to qualify for an IRA.

Gifting

Married couples can make unlimited gifts back and forth to each other with no tax consequences. Single individuals can only gift $11,000 each year to another individual without triggering a gift tax or dipping into their $1 million lifetime exclusion. If you're not married and you add your partner's name to the deed of your house, you may be gifting half the value of the house and get stuck with a gift tax. It's best to consult an estate-planning attorney before making large gifts to your partner.

Owning a House Together

If you and your partner wish to own a house together, you have a few choices about how to title it. If you own the house as Joint Tenants with Rights of Survivorship (JTWROS) and one partner dies, the house automatically goes to the surviving owner without going through probate. A JTWROS title trumps a will, so even if you name someone else in your will to inherit your share of the house, the surviving owner gets the house. This method of titling property can only be used if you each own equal shares.

If you don't split ownership 50-50 or if you want to name a different beneficiary for your portion of the house, titling the house as Tenants in Common is a better choice. If one of the owners dies, his or her share will go to whomever is named in the will.

In addition to deciding how to title the house, you and your partner should discuss other aspects of joint ownership such as who is responsible for maintenance and repairs, and what will happen to the house if you break up. You can incorporate these decisions into a living-together contract or draft a separate contract just to cover house responsibilities.

Estate Planning

If you and your partner are not married, estate planning should be at the top of your financial planning list. In this area, the law favors married couples. A surviving spouse can usually inherit property (or split it with the children) even in the absence of a will. Medical professionals are more likely to allow a husband or wife to make medical decisions for a spouse even without a valid durable power of attorney for health care. If you're not married, you'll need legal documents to back up your wishes, or your partner could be shut out of inheriting your property or participating in health decisions on your behalf.

Your estate plan should include the same four documents married couples need: a will, a durable power of attorney for finances, a living will (or medical directive), and a durable power of attorney for health care. Property with a designated beneficiary, like retirement plans and insurance policies, and property titled with rights of survivorship will be distributed directly to the beneficiary or surviving owner. However, any other property you own will be distributed according to the terms of your will. If you are not married and you die without a will, this property will go to your children or, if you don't have children, to your parents or your siblings.

Let's say you own a house, a car, an IRA, a brokerage account, a savings account, and some personal property. You can name your partner the beneficiary of your IRA and you can either own the house together as joint tenants with right of survivorship or, in many states, you can arrange for the house to be transferred on death (TOD) to a beneficiary. These steps will ensure that your partner gets your IRA and house even if you don't have a will. You can usually designate a beneficiary for the brokerage account (again, a TOD designation) and for your savings account (known as Payable on Death or POD designations). If you set up POD and TOD accounts, the only property your will would control are your car and personal possessions like furniture, clothes, and jewelry.

That doesn't mean you can dispense with the will. You may forget to name beneficiaries as you accumulate accounts, or you may wish to specify how your personal possessions get distributed. In your will you name an executor to make sure your wishes are carried out and you designate a guardian for your minor children. In the absence of a will, the courts are likely to skip over your partner and name a relative to be executor or guardian to your children. If that's not what you had in mind, you need a will.

In addition to the four documents named above, many unmarried couples set up living trusts in order to keep their estates private and facilitate transfer of property. Assets in a trust skip probate—a public, court-supervised process—and are transferred directly to the beneficiaries. Trusts have other advantages: They are less frequently contested than wills, and it's easier for a successor or co-trustee to step in and manage the assets in a trust than to invoke a power of attorney.

Your marital status dictates how your estate is taxed. Due to the unlimited marital deduction, even if you're a multibillionaire, your spouse can inherit your estate tax free. If you're not married, however, there's a $1 million cap (in 2003) on the amount you can leave tax free to your heirs. The tax-free limit for state inheritance taxes is usually lower, but the rates are lower, too. Few young couples have accumulated a net worth over a million dollars, but life insurance policies count in that total, so you may be closer than you think.

Finally, the rules for inheriting retirement plans or IRAs depend on marital status. Spouses can roll over inherited retirement accounts into their own accounts and hold the money there until retirement. Nonspouses have to start drawing money out and paying taxes from inherited accounts immediately.

Taking Charge

Although this chapter seems to focus a lot on death and taxes, the main lesson is simply not to leave things to chance. Unmarried couples do not have a marriage contract to define their responsibilities and privileges so they have to figure out their own. Talking to your partner about how you'll share your lives and face decisions and plan for the future isn't a burden—it's the foundation of a good relationship between two people who care about each other.

Resources

Curry, Hayden, Denis Clifford and Frederick Hertz. *A Legal Guide for Lesbian and Gay Couples*, 11th Edition. Nolo Press. 2002.

Berkery, Peter M., and Gregory A. Diggins. J. K. Lasser's *Gay Finances in a Straight World*. John Wiley & Sons. 1998.

www.nolo.com

www.unmarried.org

CHAPTER 15

Getting Help: How to Choose and Work with a Financial Advisor

I wrote this book as a guide for couples who want to learn how to manage their finances on their own. Even if you're the most dedicated do-it-yourselfers, however, there might be times when you'd like a professional opinion on how you're doing or need help getting started on a financial plan. Despite the array of personal finance books, Web sites, and software available, sometimes it makes sense to consult a financial advisor. Before you pick up the phone, though, here are a few things to consider.

First, I recommend that you sit down with your partner and go through the goal-setting exercises in Chapter 3. Then talk about what you expect to accomplish with a financial planner. Where could you use some help? Which pieces of your financial picture are unclear or troublesome? Assume you've hired an advisor and it's a year later. What changes would you like to see in your finances at that time? Your expectations will determine the services you look for and the kind of relationship you develop with your advisor.

Working with a Planner

There are plenty of good reasons to get professional help with your money. You might want advice on an important financial decision, like how to finance a new house or how to invest a 401(k) rollover. Or you might be preparing for a personal event that will change your financial picture, like marriage or a new baby.

Some couples feel they are doing a pretty good job with their finances but would like to get a reality check or a second opinion on how well they're doing. Other couples feel they just can't seem to get on track and would like to work with a financial advisor to help them map out a plan. You can even hire a financial coach who will check in with you regularly and steer you back on course if you stray from the plan.

A not-so-good reason for a young couple to hire an advisor is because they have no interest in learning some basic money rules and would prefer to hand over responsibility for their finances to someone else. This approach doesn't work very well in any area of your lives. Although you rely on your physician for good medical advice, you don't call every time you catch a cold or need to decide between the steamed veggies or the chili-cheese fries.

How you work with an advisor will depend on your degree of comfort with managing your personal finances as well as the time you're willing to devote to the process. The more you're willing to learn and pitch in, the better you'll do and, in general, the less you'll pay.

Compare working with a financial advisor to hiring an interior designer. Let's say you just bought a new house and you want to furnish it. You could ask a full-service interior designer to prepare a plan for every room in the house, choose all the furniture, and arrange to have the walls painted and papered. You'd have a fully decorated house in a few months and, as long as you and your decorator communicated well, you'd probably be happy with the results. Of course, you'd have a big bill to pay as well.

For some couples, it might make sense to approach financial planning this way. You can hire a financial advisor to do a complete plan, rearrange your investments, set up meetings with attorneys and insurance agents, prepare your taxes, and even enter your information in a personal finance program like Quicken®.

On the other hand, you might have already accumulated some furniture and knick-knacks, but they don't seem to hang together well. You might hire a designer to prepare a decorating scheme and help you with some of the big decisions like choosing a new sofa, but you take it from there. You might call the designer every year or two to review the plan, update some accessories, or help with a special project like a nursery.

You can work with a financial planner in the same way. Your advisor might put together a comprehensive blueprint for your finances and give you specific guidance on rearranging your investments and setting up a spending plan. It's up to you to carry out the remaining recommendations, like getting a new will, shopping for term insurance, or refinancing your house.

Finally, you might decide you just want to hire a decorator to walk through your house and give you some pointers on rearranging the furniture or changing the color scheme. Similarly, some planners will work on a project basis or hourly fee to give you an overview of your financial situation and offer some specific advice on one or two areas. You're on your own for implementing the recommendations. For some couples, this is all they need; for others it's a good way to test the waters before signing up for a comprehensive plan.

What to Look for in a Financial Advisor

Finding a good financial advisor is not easy, but if you're willing to do some homework and interview a few candidates, you can locate one. I wish I could say that every person who claims to be a financial advisor is competent and ethical, but I'm afraid that's not the case. The truth is many so-called "financial advisors" are not advisors at all but salespeople for whom financial planning is just a sales pitch in disguise. Their goal is to convince you to buy their products—expensive annuities, loaded mutual funds, or permanent insurance.

With that caution, let me reassure you there are many wise, trustworthy advisors who will put your interests first and make a lasting, positive influence on your life. You just have to do a little research to find them.

How do you go about choosing a good advisor? Unlike physicians, financial advisors are not closely regulated. In general, financial advisors must register with either the Securities and Exchange Commission (SEC) or with the state(s) in which they do business. Registration is not a good indication of competency, although some states require a minimal level of proficiency.

A benefit of the registration process is the requirement that advisors complete Parts I and II of a long form called an ADV. The ADV contains information on the advisor's background, investment philosophy, fee structure, as well as disciplinary information. You can look up Part I for any registered advisor at *www.sec.gov.* Advisors must provide clients with a copy of Part II. Insurance agents, brokers, attorneys, and accountants are exempt from registering if financial planning is only incidental to their work. You want to work with a professional financial advisor, not someone who does this on the side, so always ask for Part II of the ADV form when interviewing advisors. If your request is refused, move on.

Imagine you are meeting with your ideal financial advisor. What would that person be like? If you think about other professionals you have worked with, like your physician or attorney, you can probably come up with several characteristics you would look for. Here are my recommendations:

1. Objectivity. The best way to ensure that your advisor is working for you is to hire a fee-only advisor—someone who charges a fee for advice and doesn't sell any products or receive any commissions. It might seem strange to care so much about how your advisor is paid, but I believe there is an inherent conflict of interest if an advisor is paid for selling products rather than for giving objective advice.

2. Competence. Obviously, your advisor should be knowledgeable and up to date. Advice based on inaccurate or obsolete information can sink a plan. An advisor's credentials can be an indication of competence. There's a confusing array of designations and certifications in the financial planning field, but I recommend looking for a Certified Financial Planner™ (CFP®) certificant. Planners who have earned the CFP® designation have passed comprehensive exams and must comply with continuing education requirements.

The ChFC (Chartered Financial Consultant) designation is similar, with more emphasis on insurance. A CPA/PFS is a Certified Public Accountant who has taken extra courses in personal finance. If your concerns are mainly tax-related, this might be a good choice, but I prefer the broader based CFP® designation.

You might find an excellent planner who has not earned any of these designations. If that's the case, make sure he or she has education and experience in the field—preferably a master's degree or law degree plus at least five years of experience as a financial planner.

3. Comprehensive Advice. One of the challenges to figuring out your financial plan is making sure all the pieces pull in the same direction—toward your financial security. If you're considering selling an investment, you want to understand the tax consequences. When you have the choice of paying down a debt or adding to your nest egg, you want to make sure your advisor can explain the impact

on your cash flow, tax bill, and progress towards your goals. The best way to get the full picture is to work with a comprehensive advisor.

Brokers, insurance agents, and tax preparers only see a slice of your financial picture. Stockbrokers get paid when you buy and sell investments; they don't get paid for general financial advice. Although they might occasionally crunch numbers on saving for retirement or college, the emphasis will always be on buying investments or other financial products.

A knowledgeable, trustworthy insurance agent can help you secure your safety net. But don't look for comprehensive advice from an insurance agent. It's a little like taking your car to an auto mechanic who only does transmission work. It doesn't matter if your car really needs a brake job or new tires or just an oil change—the recommended fix will only involve the transmission. If you consult an insurance agent for your financial planning, the recommendations will involve insurance products, even though there are often much better solutions.

4. Customized Advice. Some large national firms will offer to prepare a financial plan for you for a few hundred dollars. You fill out a long questionnaire; they feed your answers into a software program or send them off to the home office. Then they present you with a leatherette binder with color charts and graphs and lots of numbers. Although the information can be an interesting snapshot of your financial picture, there's a good chance the binder will end up on a bookcase or in a drawer, forgotten. It's as if I went to a nutritionist who told me I was 20 pounds overweight and then sent me on my way. Without understanding how I got to be overweight or helping me decide which steps I should take to change my lifestyle—plus some encouragement along the way, I'd probably just slip back into my old habits. So look for an advisor who prepares a plan that's specific to your situation, with clear steps on how to implement the recommendations and measure your progress.

5. Financial Education. Your relationship with your advisor should be a learning experience. That means your advisor should be able to explain your financial choices in plain English and answer your questions in terms you understand. You should walk away from each meeting feeling more confident and more informed. I don't mean you should feel like you've sat through a financial planning lecture, but you should be thinking "Now I see how that works" or "I finally understand that" or simply "Aha." When you're interviewing an advisor, you

might want to ask a question like "How do I tell a load mutual fund from a no-load fund?" or "Can you explain the difference between term and permanent life insurance?" If the answer seems to go on forever or you're puzzled by the response, you probably need to keep looking.

6. Professionalism. You should expect your advisor to be honest, courteous, and responsive. You'll be sharing personal information, so your advisor should be discrete and keep your information confidential.

That's a long list but a reasonable one. You might have to interview a few planners before you find the right one, but the search is well worth the effort. After all, it's your financial security that's at stake.

How Financial Advisors Are Paid

When you go into Wal-Mart and pick up a bottle of shampoo, it's easy to figure out how much it costs—just look at the price tag. It's not that easy when shopping for financial advisors.

Although you shouldn't pick an advisor solely on cost, you should know how much you're paying for advice. And the way your advisor is paid will influence the kind of advice you get.

In general, financial advisors are paid in three different ways: (1) by a fee paid by the client; (2) by commissions on the products clients purchase; or (3) by a combination of fees and commissions.

Fee-only advisors are paid by you—the client—and they work only for you, not for banks or brokerage firms or mutual funds companies or insurance companies. Because their compensation doesn't depend on selling you an insurance policy or an annuity or steering you toward a particular mutual fund, fee-only advisors offer objective advice based on your particular circumstances. They typically recommend no-load mutual funds for your investments, although some might suggest individual stocks and bonds as well.

Fee-only planners might charge by the hour, by a flat fee for a particular project or retainer, or by a percentage of the investments they manage for you. Your fee will depend on the type of agreement you have with your planner and how much work the planner expects to do for you. Hourly rates can range between $100 and $250; flat fees can be as little as a few hundred dollars for a general overview or specific project or as much as several thousand dollars for a complicated, comprehensive plan, implementation, and ongoing advice. Planners who base their fees on the assets they manage for you often charge 1 percent of your investments annually, although the percentage might be less for larger portfolios.

The second way advisors are paid is by commissions from products you purchase. Most stockbrokers and insurance agents are paid this way. If you consult an advisor at a bank, you pay a commission on the mutual fund or annuity you purchase.

The last—and most common—way advisors are paid is by a combination of fees and commissions. The planner might charge a flat fee for a financial plan that includes recommendations on retirement and college planning as well as investments and insurance. When you buy the products the planner has suggested, he or she gets a cut. Be careful— "fee-based" advisors can charge commissions as well as fees and are not the same as "fee-only" advisors who don't sell any products or earn any commissions. Many of the large, well-known companies employ fee-plus-commission advisors. The cost of working with one of these advisors might seem small until you add up all the commissions you pay on the products your advisor recommends.

Does it matter how your planner is paid? You bet it does. Commissioned planners only get paid if you buy a product from them, but you might not need what they are selling. If you're looking for advice on choosing funds in your 401(k) or figuring out how much house you can afford, a stockbroker or insurance agent might not be helpful because they don't get paid for giving advice—and they're probably not trained to look beyond their niche.

If you're looking for advice on choosing mutual funds, a commissioned planner will only get paid if you buy one of the products he or she sells. How would you feel about a medical diagnosis if your doctor got a percentage of every medicine prescribed? Or if your physician got a bigger commission by prescribing Antibiotic A over Antibiotic B?

Commission planners who work for a mutual fund company or bank often earn more when they sell particular products. Some investment companies sponsor special awards and trips for employees who sell large quantities of certain products. It makes you wonder if your advisor is touting Fund ABC because it's right for you or because there's a trip to Paris hanging in the balance.

If you work with a commissioned planner, before you buy or invest, ask exactly how much you would pay in commissions and other charges for the products you've been recommended. You'll typically pay about 5.75 percent up front or 1 percent per year of any money you invest in commissioned or load mutual funds. If you buy a life insurance policy, as much as 100 percent of your first-year premium can go to your agent. Commissions on annuities run between 8 or 9 percent of your initial investment plus 1.25 percent of the value annually.

Let's say you plan to roll $20,000 from a 401(k) plan at a previous employer into an IRA. If you work with a planner who sells load or commissioned mutual funds, about $1150 will be scooped off your investments immediately, if you invest in A shares, or about $200 a year for the next 6 to 8 years, if you invest in B shares. That's a steep price if all you're getting is some help filling out a form and recommendations for mutual funds off a list of funds the planner sells.

So what's the bottom line? There are smart and ethical people who charge commissions, but I believe it is difficult to reconcile your interest in obtaining objective, competent advice and the commissioned planner's interest in selling you products—often those with hefty loads. Don't be fooled by statements like, "You don't pay me; my company pays me." The dollars coming out of your investment might go to the planner's company before they are funneled into the planner's pocket, but you're still paying a commission. We all get compensated for our work. Find out how much you will pay—either directly to the advisor or indirectly off your investments—before you hire an advisor.

I recommend that you look for a comprehensive, competent fee-only advisor who works with clients like you and with whom you feel comfortable. The best advisor for you is someone who you trust is putting your interests first, is giving you good advice, and cares about your specific circumstances and goals.

Locating a Financial Advisor

You might feel comfortable asking friends or family members for the name of a good advisor just as you would ask them for a referral to a doctor or lawyer. However, I recommend that you also gather some names on your own and interview at least two planners before you decide. Professional organizations are good places to start your search.

The National Association of Personal Financial Advisors (NAPFA) is the association of financial advisors who have met the highest standards in the industry. All NAPFA-Registered Financial Advisors charge on a fee-only basis exclusively, fully disclose all fees and any conflicts of interest, and sign a fiduciary oath that affirms their commitment to putting the client's interests first. They must be either a CFP® certificant, a ChFC, a CPA/PFS, or have equivalent background and experience, plus they have to show that they can provide competent advice by submitting a written comprehensive financial plan for approval. You can get a list of NAPFA-Registered Financial Advisors in your area as well as a set of questions you can use when interviewing planners by calling 1-888-FEE-ONLY or visiting *www.napfa.org*.

Members of the Alliance of Cambridge Advisors are fee-only planners who charge flat fees and typically work with middle-income individuals and couples. Cambridge Advisors are also NAPFA members and they take a comprehensive approach to planning. Visit their Web site at *www.cambridge advisors.com* to find a Cambridge Advisor in your area.

The Garrett Financial Network is a group of fee-only planners who charge on an hourly basis and who also work with middle-income clients. Their Web site is *www.garrettfinancialnetwork.com*.

The Financial Planning Association (FPA) (*www.fpanet.org*) is the largest association of financial planners. Most members either charge commissions or a combination of fees and commissions, although many fee-only planners are also members. The FPA has endorsed the CFP® mark but not all FPA members are CFP® certificants.

Sample Questions to Ask before Hiring a Financial Advisor

1. How do you get paid—by fees exclusively, by commission or by a combination of fees and commissions?

2. What are your credentials and background? How long have you been a financial advisor?

3. May I have a copy of your ADV-Part II?

4. What kind of clients do you work with?

5. Will you be able to give me advice on all aspects of my finances?

6. Do you prepare taxes for your clients?

For a more complete set of questions, *visit www.napfa.org*.

	NAPFA-Registered Financial Advisor	CFP®	CPA/PFS	ChFC	CFA®	CLU
Explanation	Advisor who meets all membership requirements of NAPFA	Certified Financial Planner	Certified Public Accountant with Personal Financial Specialist	Chartered Financial Consultant	Chartered Financial Analyst	Chartered Life Underwriter
Type of Advisor	Comprehensive, fee-only financial advisors	Financial planners; may charge fees, commissions, or a combination	CPA specializing in personal finance	Financial planners; may charge fees, commissions, or a combination	Investment analysts; most work with institutions like pension or mutual funds	Insurance specialists and agents
Requirements	CFP™, ChFC, CP/PFS, or equivalent; submit sample financial plan; offer comprehensive planning; charge on fee-only basis exclusively; sign fiduciary oath; meet continuing education requirements	Complete coursework; pass comprehensive exam; meet experience, ethics, and continuing education requirements	CPA plus pass comprehensive exam; meet experience, ethics, continuing education requirements	Complete course work; pass exams; meet experience, ethics, and continuing education requirements	Pass three levels of exams; meet experience and ethics requirements.	Complete course work; pass exams; meet experience, ethics and continuing education requirements
Web site	www.napfa.org	www.cfpboard.org	www.cpapfs.org	www.amercoll.edu	www.aimr.com	www.amercoll.edu

Figure 15-1 Deciphering the Credentials of Financial Advisors

You Can Take It from Here

I f you and your partner have started to develop your own financial plan, congratulations—you're on your way. You might have already figured out where you are now and where you want to go, and started sketching out a financial road map. Defining your goals is like setting out mile markers along the road—get a will by next month, set up automatic contributions to a Roth IRA in six weeks, pay off at least one credit card before the end of the year. As you travel down the road and take control of your money, you'll gain confidence. Nothing but smooth sailing ahead, right? Well, not necessarily.

Even the most carefully thought-out plan needs to be reviewed and tweaked from time to time. Life is unpredictable, and occasionally you'll need to pull out the guidebooks again, take a detour, or revise your map. Cathy and Mike had to adjust their spending plan and rethink their house-buying strategy when they found out they were expecting a child. Remember—financial planning is not a product you can put on a bookshelf; it's a process.

The best way to track your progress is to set up a series of regular reviews. There are several advantages to scheduling financial planning sessions with your partner rather than just promising each other you'll look at your money situation from time to time.

First, we're all busy, and anything that doesn't get on the calendar isn't likely to get done, whether it's an oil change for the car or a review of your financial plan. Second, you can dispel a lot of the uneasiness people feel about their money if you have a good sense of whether you're on track or not. The number-one question clients ask me is "How are we doing?" Scheduled checkups will help you answer that question.

You're also more likely to be successful at managing your money and reaching your goals if you monitor your progress. Your investments will fare better if you track your performance against benchmarks and make adjustments from time to time. Buy-and-hold is a great strategy; buy-and-abandon isn't. Studies have shown that rebalancing an investment portfolio periodically tends to increase the average rate of return. That's not a license to try to time the market—just to realign your investments when they get out of whack with your blueprint. Likewise, if you review your insurance policies every few years and get new quotes, you'll probably pay less for the same coverage over time. Monitoring your spending will help you catch leakages before they wreck your progress.

Finally, it's easier to strike a balance between obsessing over your money and neglecting it if you set aside specific times to look at your finances with your partner. You'll work better as a team, as well.

Ready to mark your calendar? Here are some guidelines for setting up your review sessions.

Monthly

Cash flow is the element in your plan that is always in flux so it needs more regular attention. If you have set up your spending plan on software like Quicken® or on your own spreadsheet, update the information monthly from your check register, credit card statements, pay stubs, and mortgage statements and reconcile your bank accounts. If you also track your investments on personal finance software, enter information from any new statements.

Even if you haven't set up a formal tracking system, you can get a good idea of how you did during the past month by tallying up all your expenses in some discretionary categories like eating out, entertainment, clothes, gifts, and vacations. A paper-and-pencil system won't give you the ability to generate reports and charts, but it's a start. No matter which system you use, I suggest you and your partner take turns with the data entry task, so you'll each see the details of how your cash flows. If only one of you regularly does that chore, it's too easy for the person who enters the data to become the enforcer of the spending plan. That's a job you should share.

Once you've updated your records, set aside an hour together to see how you're doing. Compare your actual spending with your plan to detect any problem categories. Don't use this time for finger pointing or recriminations. If it becomes a painful experience, one or both of you will just scratch it off the calendar. Overspending in a couple of categories a few times during the year won't derail your future. You might find that you were overly optimistic about your ability to stick to the spending plan in certain areas and you'll need to adjust your plan. Or maybe an unforeseen expense has depleted your emergency fund and you need to start rebuilding it. Maybe you need to increase your "no questions asked" accounts. Just remember to reward yourselves for your successes and talk about ways to fix the problems.

Quarterly

If you are tracking your investments on a personal finance program, gather your retirement account and other investment statements and update your information quarterly. Review performance, if you like, but I don't recommend making changes based on just one quarter's worth of data.

Semiannually (Spring and Fall)

Twice a year should be adequate for reviewing your investments—you might even find that once a year is sufficient. First, look at the overall performance of your portfolio. There are a few ways you can calculate this. If you have all your mutual funds with one fund family or one brokerage, you might be able to use tools on the company's Web site. Alternatively, you can enter your investment data in a personal finance program and select performance reports. You can get a rough estimate of how well your investments have done by getting performance data on each of your mutual funds from annual reports or your funds' Web sites or from Morningstar data, either on their Web site or at your library. Then weigh the fund's performance by the percentage you hold. For example, if you had 75 percent of your money invested in large company stock funds and 25 percent in small company stock funds, you might compare the performance of your portfolio to one invested 75 percent in the S&P 500 index (the index of the 500 largest companies in the United States) and 25 percent in the Russell 2000 (a small-company stock index). Morningstar provides performance data of relevant benchmarks for each mutual fund; the annual report of each of your funds will contain this information as well.

In your 75-25 portfolio, if the S&P 500 Index gained 8 percent and the Russell 2000 gained 4 percent, you would expect your investments to have risen by 7 percent (8 percent times 75 percent and 4 percent times 25 percent). If they did better, you're lucky. If your investments performed more poorly than expected, make sure you are using the correct benchmark.

The next step involves looking at the funds individually. You have to know when to hold or when to fold your mutual funds, and the trick is to make consistent comparisons. If you have invested in a small company fund, it doesn't matter that the S&P 500 or the Dow Jones average had a record year. Those are measures of large-company performance, and a small-company fund invests in completely different companies. It's like comparing your grade on a history test to the grades fellow students got on an English test.

Look at how your fund performed compared to its benchmark and to its peers—other funds that invest in the same slice of the stock or bond market. Again, Morningstar provides this information for each mutual fund. If your fund has underperformed its peers by 25 percent or more for six months, I suggest you put it on the "watch" list and do some more research. Look for red flags like a change in manager or investment mandate. A hike in the fund's operating expenses can damage performance. Check the performance of funds on your watch list again at the next semiannual review, and if there hasn't been any improvement, start looking for replacements. I usually wait at least a year before switching out of a poorly performing fund especially if I'm aware of an anomaly that I don't expect will affect future performance. One of my favorite mutual funds had an uncharacteristically bad year after the attacks on the World Trade Center because it held a higher percentage of airline stocks than its peers. I still had confidence in the managers so I held on, and the fund's performance has improved significantly since its low point.

Of course, if you hold index funds, you can skip these steps because, by definition, your funds will not underperform the market—they *are* the market. An S&P 500 Index fund will do just what the S&P 500 Index does (minus a deduction for operating expenses).

The final step is the most important of all—figuring out if your investments are still divvied up the way you set them up. Mike decided he wanted his investments split 75 percent in stocks and 25 percent in bonds. If stocks had surged over the past several months and bonds had slumped, 80 percent of his current portfolio might now be in stocks and only 20 percent in bonds—a considerably riskier portfolio than he had intended. He would be smart to rebalance—either shifting 5 percent out of stocks into bonds or realigning his 401(k) contributions so more new money goes into bonds than stocks.

I recommend doing the rebalancing in a 401(k) plan or IRA to avoid the possible tax consequences of selling investments. I also prefer rebalancing with new money rather than selling existing investments. Some advisors recommend rebalancing when the gap between actual and planned percentages is more than 3 percent; I prefer scheduling reviews every 6 to 12 months and only making changes if the gap is 5 percent or more.

You should also look at how your investments are divided in other categories as well. Even if you are still at your benchmark of 75 percent stocks and 25 percent bonds, you might have a significantly larger percentage than intended in large company stocks if they have had a good year. You'll need to add more money to your small company stock funds to stay in balance. This kind of balancing can usually be done just once a year.

Rebalancing investments is not an exact science, so don't worry if your percentages don't always match up. But don't let things get too far out of whack. By rebalancing, you're following the classic investment rule of buying low and selling high. You're selling investments that have performed well (or not adding to them), and you're buying the poor performers. Even though the buy–low/sell–high rule has become something of a mantra, it's often hard to implement because investors hate to let go of a good thing and put their hard-earned dollars in a "dog." As long as your "dog" is performing poorly because that slice of the market is doing badly rather than because your fund is out of step with its peers, buying more of it to rebalance your investments is the smart thing to do. In 1998 and 1999, even a top-notch small-cap value stock fund looked like a loser compared to funds that invested in large companies. However, if you neglected to add some money back into your small-cap value fund when it was low, you would have missed the boom in this sector during the next three years when these funds left the blue-chip funds in the dust.

Annual Tax Planning

Autumn is a perfect time to do a dry run on your tax return to make sure you won't get hit with a big bill in April. You should also check to see if the government is hanging on to too much of your money. Use last year's tax return and recent pay stubs as your guide. Personal finance and tax preparation software packages have tools for estimating your taxes. Some Web sites like *www.smartmoney.com* have tax planning worksheets, and the IRS site (*www.irs.gov*) has tools for estimating how many exemptions you should claim to have the right amount of taxes withheld. You can try a paper-and-pencil estimate, but I find it's too cumbersome to try different scenarios if I have to erase a bunch of numbers each time.

You can increase your exemptions if you think you're due a big refund or ask your employer to withhold more taxes if you think you'll owe more than $1000 at tax time. If you're paying estimated taxes, you can adjust your quarterly payments. Just remember the rule on penalties—as long as you pay quarterly taxes or have money withheld equal to your tax liability for the previous year, you won't owe a penalty even if you have to write a big check at tax time. If you think you might owe in April but are having enough withheld to avoid a penalty, you might want to sock an extra amount into a savings account rather than pay it out to the government before April.

In addition to checking if you're on track with taxes, make sure you're properly funding your retirement accounts. Check your pay stub to see if the right amount is being funneled into your 401(k) plan; check your investment statements to make sure you aren't over- or underfunding your IRAs.

Your annual tax review is a good time to remember to bundle up all those used clothes you've been meaning to give to charities and to send any cash donations you've intended to make. I also recommend weeding out the losers in your taxable portfolio (investments outside of retirement plans) so you can take a tax loss on that year's return.

Annually (January or February)

When the holiday excitement has subsided, I recommend setting aside a few hours with your partner to review the big picture. Some of my clients call this "Dollar Day." Here's a list of typical agenda items:

- Review your short- and long-term goals. If your lives have gone through significant changes during the year, you might wish to have another goal-setting session. Adjust your goal milestones as appropriate.

- Update your personal balance sheet and compare it to last year's version to highlight improvements and weaknesses. Which assets gained value and which lost? Have you paid off debt or acquired more? Is it good or bad debt? Calculate the ratios described in Chapter 2.

- Talk to each other about what has worked and what hasn't worked over the past year. Were your goals too optimistic or too timid? How are the mechanics of money management working? Perhaps one partner still feels the burden of making the cash flow work and you need to divvy up responsibilities. One of you might be encouraged by your progress and one might be impatient that you didn't accomplish more. Remember—you're trying to move several goals ahead simultaneously, and you won't see consistent progress in every goal every year.

- Every few years, get quotes on your insurance policies to see if you can save any money. Make sure your coverage is up to date. Review your wills and other estate-planning documents. Of course, if there's been a significant event in your life like the birth of a child, don't wait for your annual review to update your wills and insurance coverage.

Your annual money roundup should be something you look forward to, not dread. Set up the time in advance, hold it in a nice setting—your own living room can do just fine. Be open with each other. If you're really worried about your finances, tell your partner, and figure out solutions together. But don't just focus on the problems; remember to congratulate yourselves on your successes as well. Finish up by rewarding yourself with a nice dinner out—your spending plan can stand it.

Checking in with Cathy and Mike

It's been almost a year since our last meeting, and Cathy and Mike and I have arranged to get together to review their progress.

"It's been quite a year," said Cathy. "Emily is nine months old. I finished my MBA, and Mike's applying to a Master's in Information Technology program."

"You two have been busy," I said. "How's your job, Mike?"

"It's fine," said Mike. "I decided I won't be able to advance as quickly as I had hoped without some extra education. Because the company will pay the tuition, I figured it was a good time to start a master's degree."

"What about your business, Cathy? Has it been a good year?"

"Business has been good, but I had to rearrange my child care situation," said Cathy. "I was sharing a babysitter, but that didn't work out very well. My friend needed the babysitter full time and, besides, it was very expensive to have someone come to our home. Last month I started taking Emily to a babysitter who takes care of an 18-month-old child as well. Emily seems to enjoy the company, and our expenses are a lot lower. I'm glad I had a babysitter in my home the first few months, but I'm happy with this arrangement now. I never imagined how stressful it would be to figure out child care."

"It sounds like you've done a good job," I said. "How is the process of drawing up your wills and powers of attorney going?"

"Signed, sealed, and delivered," said Mike. "A few weeks after Emily was born, we met with the attorney and she drew up all the documents for us. Check that one off our list. We decided not to set up a trust for now, although we might change our minds later."

"You've got the most important documents in place," I said. "Congratulations."

"We also got more life insurance," said Cathy. "We went with term life insurance as you suggested. I feel better knowing our safety net is more secure. And the premiums haven't put a big dent in our spending plan."

"Speaking of spending plan," I said, "any surprises on that front?"

"Well," said Mike, "it turns out babies are very small but very expensive. We went over budget outfitting the nursery, so we haven't made as much progress paying down our credit cards as we hoped. But we haven't increased the amount we owe either."

"After the changes you've experienced in the last year, holding the line is an accomplishment," I said.

"Mike has kept up his contributions to his 401(k), though, and I started a SEP-IRA," said Cathy. "We decided not to convert my IRA to a Roth IRA; instead we put some extra money into our house fund. I have also researched programs for first-time home buyers and I think we'll qualify for one that only requires a 5-percent down payment."

"Cathy and I worked out a plan to have $8000 in our house fund by this time next year so we should be able to buy a $160,000 house," said Mike. "Both sets of parents have agreed to chip in on the closing costs instead of buying birthday and Christmas gifts for us."

"I'm hoping to move up that deadline by a few months," said Cathy, "so I'm watching our spending plan like a hawk. We set up our plan on the computer and have done a pretty good job of updating it each month."

"We haven't paid too much attention to our investments lately," said Mike. "I check the quarterly statements when they arrive, and we plan to sit down soon and see how we've done this year. We both feel pretty comfortable with our asset allocations and our choices of funds. I don't mind letting things ride for a few months."

"It's hard to fit it all in," I said. "Has it helped to put your money checkups on the calendar?"

"Definitely," said Cathy. "In fact, I've set up a business Dollar Day to go over my business income and expenses, client list, and outstanding projects. Sometimes I get so involved in the business, I forget to step back and look at the big picture."

"I think you two have done very well," I said. "It sounds like you already have some goals for the coming year, with the house topping the list."

"That's the number-one priority," agreed Mike. "I'd like to get back on track paying off the credit cards. I know I've been guilty of overspending in the past, but now I'm less comfortable having debt hanging over my head."

"I still like the idea of converting my IRA to a Roth IRA," said Cathy. "Maybe we can do that next year. We haven't set up a college fund for Emily, yet, either, but my parents are already contributing to a 529 plan for her. I don't feel too bad about putting that goal on hold for a while."

"What about taxes?" I asked. "Any surprises?"

"Emily's arrival certainly helped with our tax situation," said Mike. "I'm guilty of one blooper—I forgot to sign up for the dependent care program at work when she was born, so we'll have to claim the tax credit this year instead. I'll make sure to sign up during open enrollment next month."

"You two have done a great job," I said. "Not only have you implemented many of the recommendations we discussed, you are also thinking ahead about what you need to do to accomplish your next goals. You seem a lot more confident about making financial decisions. It's been a pleasure meeting with you. I look forward to checking in with you from time to time and following your progress."

"I feel pretty good about where we are," said Cathy. "Mike and I have learned a lot during the past year. We know where we'd like to be in a few years and we have a much better sense of what we need to do to get there."

"I'd say we're more aware of how our decisions about money affect our life," said Mike. "We know more so we worry less. That's a really good feeling."

INDEX

ABOUT THE AUTHOR

Jill Gianola, CFP® is the founder of Gianola Financial Planning and is a NAPFA-Registered Financial Advisor. A popular columnist for leading Web site *iVillage.com*, she has been featured or quoted in *The New York Times, Fortune, Money, Kiplinger's Personal Finance,* and other national publications.